BUILDING MODEL LOCOMOTIVES

BUILDING MODEL LOCOMOTIVES

F. J. Roche
and Col. G. G. Templer

REVISED BY
S. W. Stevens-Stratten, F.R.S.A.

LONDON

IAN ALLAN

S.B.N. 7110 0049 2

Published in the United Kingdom by Ian Allan Ltd, Shepperton, Surrey and printed by Press at Coombelands Ltd, Addlestone, Weybridge, Surrey

Contents

Foreword

This book comprises a long series of articles on building model locomotives that appeared in *The Model Railway Constructor* from 1947 to 1951. The articles covered practically every facet of the subject and applied equally to all the smaller scales used by the model railway enthusiast, although the larger scales as used by the live steam enthusiast and the model engineer were not forgotten and many of the constructional details have proved to be of use—not to mention the dimensioned drawings.

These articles were, and are, regarded by many people as a standard reference work that has been unsurpassed for detail, written in a humourous and easily assimilated style. So much of what was written at that time is still valid today, and as the original issues of the magazine have long since been out of print, it is felt that there is a demand for the present volume to encompass, between two covers, all the articles including the drawings and discussions.

The articles were originally commenced by the late F. J. Roche, but in late 1950, after a period of ill health, he was joined by one of his greatest critics, Colonel G. G. Templer and thereafter the series continued as a joint effort. In order to present the full story, and where possible to illustrate two different methods of obtaining the finished article I have included the written discussions of both Colonel Templer and Michael Longridge as an Appendix, for I feel that their ideas are invaluable. This particularly applies to the chapters on wheel turning.

There have been several developments during the last 21 years since the manuscript was originally written, but I have tried not to alter the original text more than was absolutely necessary. I would not, for instance, recommend the use of Spirits of Salts for soldering, for I feel that the present day multi-cored solders have reached such a peak of perfection that there are few cases where this safe and non-corrosive flux/solder cannot be used. Likewise, the use of such adhesives as Araldite and similar twin-epoxy resins were not in everyday use at the time of the original writings, and it will be obvious to readers that these can be used with good effect in many instances during construction.

The use of plastics and polystyrene sheet are comparatively new in modelling techniques, but I feel that as the original articles are concerning metal-work, the omissions of such material is of no effect. It is seldom that the model constructor mixes the two media in building a locomotive.

Unfortunately, I have not been able to obtain the original illustrations, some showing Mr. Roche's own locomotives, that accompanied the articles, but have substituted a selection of photographs of scratch-built locomotives showing a varied range of fine models.

The format has been purposely designed with a wide margin to enable the reader to make notes in the appropriate places. This I hope, will be helpful when working from the book.

I trust that the reading of this book will spur many modellers to scratch build their own locomotives and I look forward to seeing their efforts on various layouts or on exhibition in the future.

S. W. STEVENS-STRATTEN, F.R.S.A.

Ewell,
September 1968

Designing the Locomotive

It is the intention in this book to take our miniature locomotive through the shops from the drawing board to the track as if it were a real one, hence this section is devoted to the drawing office where any mistakes made should be rectified before we start making any part of our machine. Mistakes after this stage only lead to disappointment and loss of enthusiasm. Many of us have locomotives lying about unfinished where our thrill in making has palled through making mistakes at the start. When you have read these contributions it is the author's earnest hope that these little memories once so vivid will at last find their way to their happy hunting ground, the railway track.

In fig. 1 will be found a locomotive that has no dimensions given on the drawing. How often has that happened when the engine we wish to make was found in a technical journal or a historical treatise on the locomotives of that particular designer? Well somewhere in the text will be found some dimensions—usually the diameter of the driving wheels. Sometimes the wheelbase may be given, but whatever dimension is given, take this as the basis of the scale for the drawing you have found.

In some cases we find that the driving wheels were 6 ft. 6 in. Well this is an easy one for us to start drawing—we get the dividers and place each leg on the rim of the wheel in the drawing and transfer it to the bottom of the drawing in the book (if it is yours !). If you have borrowed the book do it on a separate piece of paper. Step out this dimension twice with the dividers and you have at once two little marks measuring 13 ft.

Now divide this into 13 equal parts by trial and error, or calculation if you are mathematically minded. When you have done this take one of the thirteen divisions and sub-divide it into halves, then into quarters. If it is not too small sub-divide each quarter into three, you now have a scale of feet and inches. In the drawing in fig. 1 the driving wheels are 6 ft. This is very easy and all we have to do is to sub-divide the 6 ft. dimension into 6 equal parts and again sub-divide one of them into inches as before, and we have a scale of feet and inches for our little drawing in the book.

We now want to transfer this to our own drawing board and commence drawing the locomotive to the scale in which we are going to make it. First of all, presuming the scale is 7 mm. to the foot, we take our dividers again and stretch them to the maximum dimension we are likely to want. We will say for example 14 ft. Well, 14 multiplied by 7 equals 98 mm., make two pinpoints in the paper 98 mm. apart, and sub-divide it into 14 equal parts as before. Sub-divide one of them into inches as we did on the drawing in the book, and we should now have a scale of feet and inches for our model. We can now forget all about millimetres and fractions thereof, they are entirely irrelevant. All we have to do now is to measure off the drawing in the book any part of the locomotive we want to find the size of, say the height of the footplate. We find it is so many feet and inches. Measure off the same dimension on your scale and proceed to draw the loco line by line from the rail upwards.

When drawing a locomotive to scale always use the rails as your base line. If you use succeeding lines, such as the footplate, to measure the centre of the boiler, the centre line of the boiler to measure to the top of the chimney, etc., an error in either of these initial dimensions will make your engine too high. If, however, you use the rails as the base line you will check yourself every time as you go along. It seems quite easy, doesn't it? Yes, I can hear you saying, "But what about the width of the locomotive? " Very few drawings in technical journals give an end elevation—quite true. This is where we have to do a little research work, which if you are keen on your chosen locomotive, should add zest to the game. We know that almost from the earliest days of railways certain predetermined standards were laid down, such as the width of main frames, width of wheels, length of journals governing the length of crankpins and so governing the centre line of cylinders if they are outside and so on. Ah, I hear you saying, we have to build up our width. Yes, this is more or less so. A very near approximation is possible as the centre of buffers apart is standardised at 5 ft. 9 in. to 5 ft. 10 in. and in old engines with outside frames this dimension corresponded with the centre line of the outside frames, except of course on the old broad gauge. Even there the buffers were still 5 ft. 10 in. apart as long ago as 1837.

In old locomotives right up to the advent of outside piston valve cylinders of modern days the length of the buffer beam, usually of wood, faced sometimes with steel or iron, was usually 7 ft. to 7 ft. 6 in., depending on the period of construction of the prototype. Webb's engines on the LNWR had buffer beams of 7 ft. 6 in., also the Midland engines of the same period, namely, 1888-1900. Outside framed engines of the latter railway had buffer beams of 8 ft., which were long for those days. Well, having determined our width thus far, the footplate was practically the same width, perhaps overlapping about an inch or so. The distance of the splashers from the outside edge of the footplate is an easy one as they always fitted closely to the driving wheel. We know that the back to back distance of full-size driving wheels was 4 ft. $5\frac{5}{8}$ in. (see fig. 4), and the width of the wheel was $5\frac{3}{8}$ in. Our splashers only needed to clear these dimensions so we now know where these are located.

The remainder of the end elevation can be built up from the side elevation we have drawn. Photographs showing the front end of the locomotive we are drawing will probably be among those that have been collected prior to starting on the drawing as most photographs of old locomotives are nearly always studies of them hauling a train and taken from the trackside, thereby getting a near front view.

Of course those who have access to a technical library will find a general arrangement of all those old engines dating back many years in volumes of the *Engineer* of the year of their build. Early volumes of the *Railway Gazette* also are useful in this respect. If you live in a small town the local public library will get them for you. For those who live in London the Patent Office Library in Chancery Lane will provide all the information you require on the early, and those of Victorian periods.

In fig. 2 will be found another method of converting a drawing to the scale the modeller wishes to work in. In this case the wheelbase is shown, and it adds up to the prototype length of 23 ft. It is desired to convert this to 4 mm.

1 SCALING A DRAWING HAVING NO SCALE ATTACHED

CONVERT THIS TO 7MM SCALE

1ST METHOD

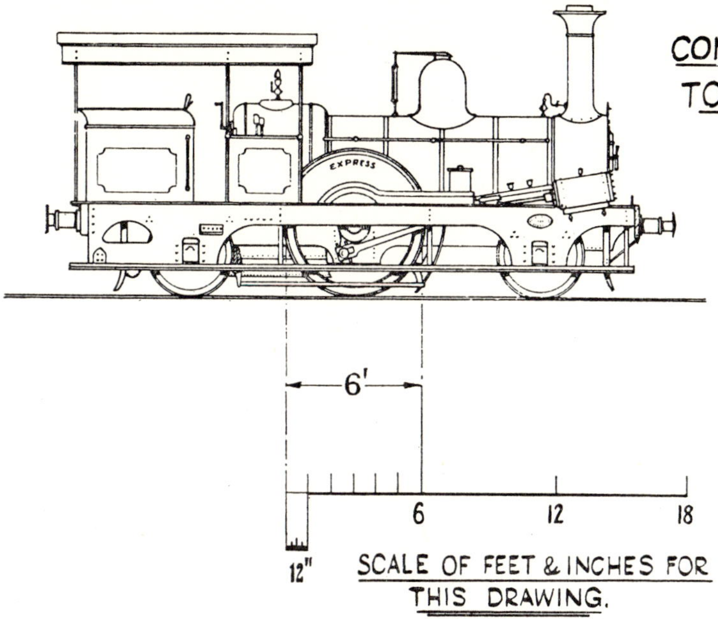

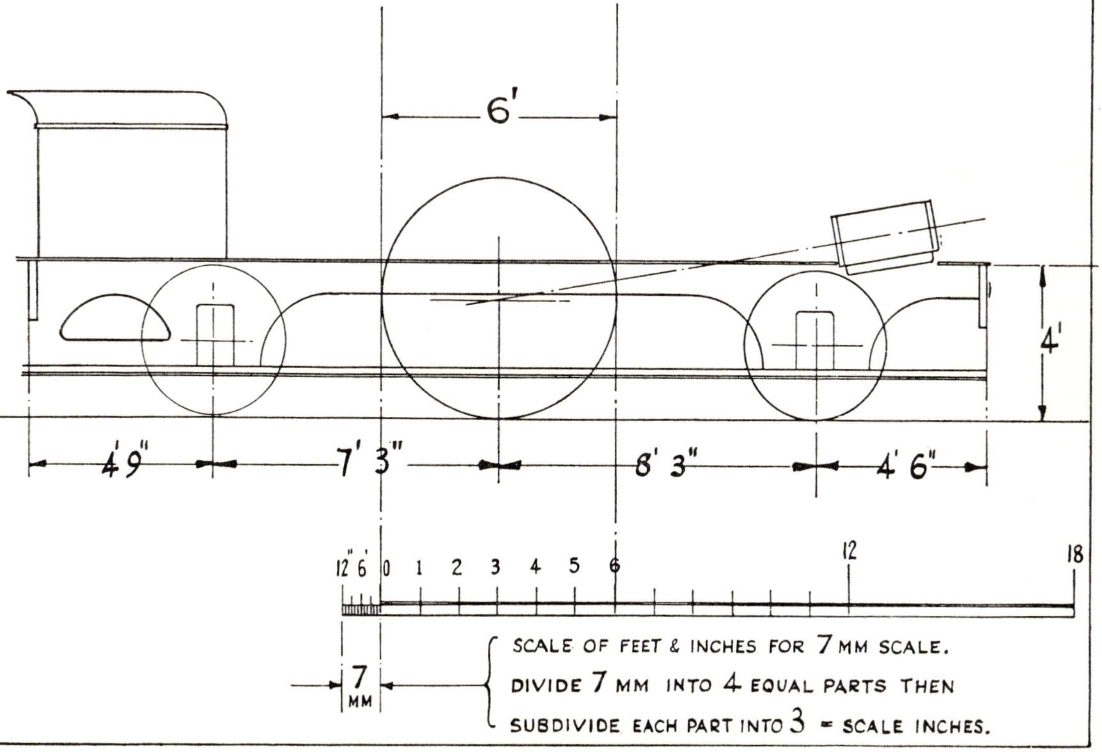

SCALING A DRAWING HAVING WHEELBASE SHOWN

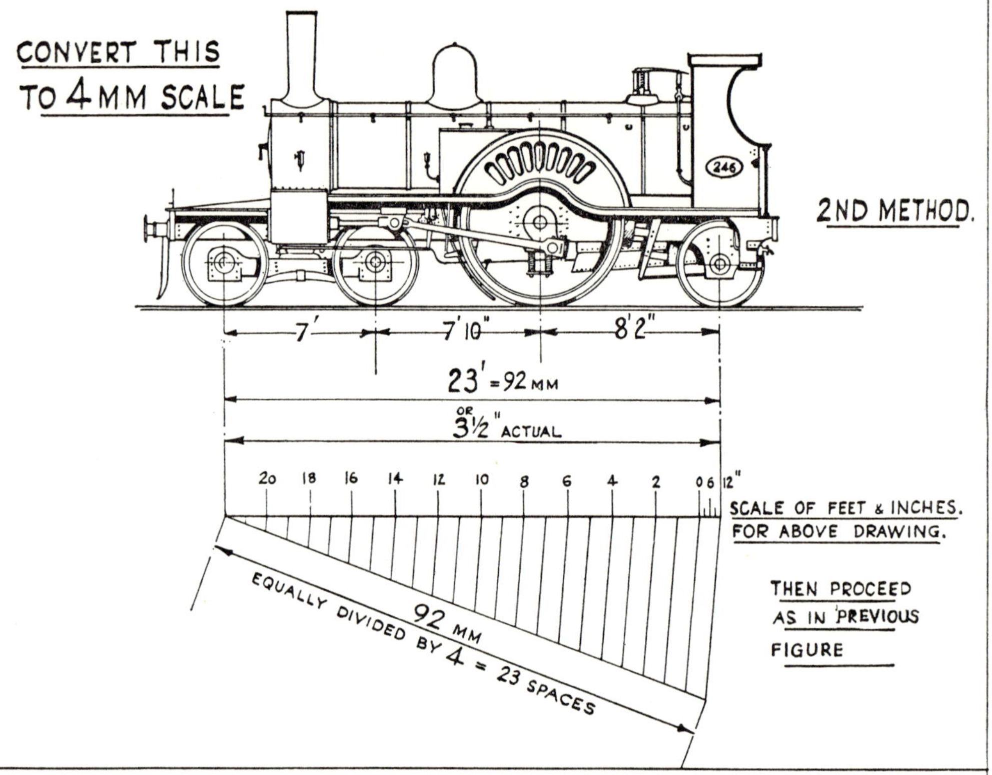

2

HOW TO DRAW AN ELLIPSE ~ FOR NUMBER PLATES ETC.

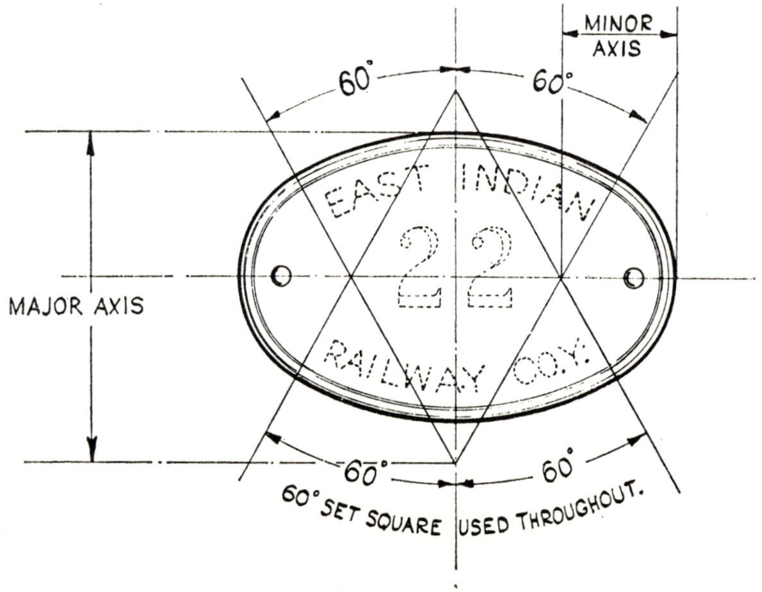

scale. Therefore 23 ft. equals 92 mm., or, if you like, $3\frac{1}{2}$ in. Procure a piece of card with which to make a scale ruler, and on its edge mark off $3\frac{1}{2}$ in. Then mark off a line 92 mm. long and mark off along it 23 spaces each 4 mm. apart. From these marks draw parallel lines to the edge of the piece of card as shown in the figure, sub-dividing them as before into feet and inches. We now have a scale for both drawings—that in the book and that for our model. This scheme is similar to the old school problem of dividing a line into a given number of equal parts.

It may happen sometimes that we have a drawing on which no even measurement is given. In order to construct a scale, somewhere or other we may find a measurement—for example we'll say 2 ft. $1\frac{1}{2}$ in. Well, the only thing to do here is to make this up to an even measurement by multiplication. Let us go back to school again and find the least common multiple, which in this case is 8. So 2 ft. $1\frac{1}{2}$ in. multiplied by 8 gives us 17 ft., so there we are. Now transfer the measurement of 2 ft. $1\frac{1}{2}$ in. to the bottom of the drawing in the book you have found it in, and step it out accurately 8 times by means of your dividers, and make a mark at each end. You know now that this represents 17 ft. All there is to do now is to sub-divide this into 17 equal parts, and one of them into inches as already described. There is your scale for the drawing in the book. We now proceed to make a drawing for our model, in whatever scale we want as previously set out, and as has been previously said, forget all about millimetres.

A good thing to remember is that the larger the scale the more accuracy it is possible to get in the model. A model in 10 mm. scale for instance should be as accurate as it is possible to get to the nearest $\frac{1}{8}$th of an inch. In the smaller scales, say $3\frac{1}{2}$ mm. to a foot, the nearest one can get with ordinary home methods of measurement is to the nearest inch on the prototype, when one remembers the thickness of material used in construction is a scale 3 in. All one can say of the smallest scales is that they are proportionally correct—even the paint adds another inch to the overall dimensions! That is why in the past wheel standards and scale have been coarsened. Even our modern BRMSB standards are suitably coarsened for this very reason. It is only just possible in 7 mm. scale for a workman who is familiar with precision tools to produce a model to the nearest $\frac{1}{4}$ in. of the prototype. This means working in $\frac{1}{10}$th of a thousandth of an inch and with vernier gauges and micrometers. Who wants to bother with this, especially if it is his daily bread so to speak, and it has undoubtedly been the case during the last five years for many of us. It is quite safe to say that there is no such thing as an accurate scale model of any locomotive under an exhibition glass case 1 in. scale model, so take heart and ignore the super critic, who doesn't built models anyhow in all probability!

Also in fig. 2 is a method of drawing an ellipse. A very simple method using a 60 deg. set square throughout, this can be used to draw an ellipse of very tiny proportions whereas other well-known methods are far too clumsy to draw to a small size. This is known among draughtsmen as the W-method, but it is more like two V's one upon the other, one being inverted, and where the lines cross is the centre line of the ellipse. The apex of the V's form the pivot of the major axis, and the crosses on the centre line form the pivot of the minor or small axis. If the minor and major axis are known it is quite simple to draw, and if they are not known just draw two or three ellipses until the desired size you require is reached. Nothing looks worse than an ellipse drawn freehand if you are not an artist. An artist can very often draw a true ellipse freehand, but we are not all artists ! This method of drawing an ellipse will be useful if it is desired to draw out a particular type of number plate to a large scale for sending to an engraver for reproduction in metal, to the desired scale you require. The fact that it is not a true ellipse will not be noticed when the tiny number plate is returned to you. This method of reproducing parts of a locomotive by engraving is quite a good way of getting over awkward little jobs. To quote an example—most of the old engines had chequer plate in the cab, and on the old broad gauge 8-footer it was all round the engine. To reproduce this is quite easy if a piece of paper is covered with lines crossing each other at 60 deg. fairly thick at about $\frac{3}{32}$nd inch spacing. If a whole sheet of foolscap is covered in this way, it can be sent to an engraver with a note as to the desired size you want it for the model and in due course back will come a lovely piece of chequer plating about 3 in. by 4 in. It will probably be in copper, unless you state it must be in brass, but it will be painted anyhow, so it does not matter what metal it is reproduced in.

Other examples can be quoted but enough has been said to show the possibilities of this method, particularly in the smaller scales. An outside frame bogie side plate suggests itself complete with all the rivets and horn-plates; it all depends upon your skill as a draughtsman how the finished plate will look.

In fig. 3 will be found the proportions of wheels. If you are not making your own patterns, this drawing will be found useful for you to draw your wheels for the patternmaker, all the revelant sizes of spokes and tyres being given. Very nearly all models are spoilt by too little attention being given to wheel proportions. We are usually quite content to turn up the castings as supplied without giving a thought to filing the spokes down to reasonable proportions.

Up to recent years we have always had to put up with only 8 spokes in bogie wheels. This has now been rectified by different methods of casting, and the correct number of spokes in any wheel, driving or trailing, can now be obtained, so there is really no excuse for bogie wheels looking like buttons with 7 holes in them ! In the case of driving and coupled wheels it is also possible to obtain the balance weights in the proper place instead of formerly when they were all cast opposite the crank pin. The drawing shows that this position is anywhere except where they ought to be ! More will be said about wheels when we deal with wheel turning.

Figure 3 shows full-size wheel and tyre dimensions with particular regard to flanges. It will be seen that bogie and trailing wheels have thicker flanges than driving wheels, and it will also show how near the BMRSB has got to scaling down full size dimensions. The purpose in studying this drawing is to show the importance of the radius between the flange and tread. If there is no radius here in the model there will be frequent derailments. A study of the old standards (fig. 4) will repay the reader when he sees the generous radius given to the flange for running on tinplate track which had a round head to the rail. It was almost impossible to derail these early

3

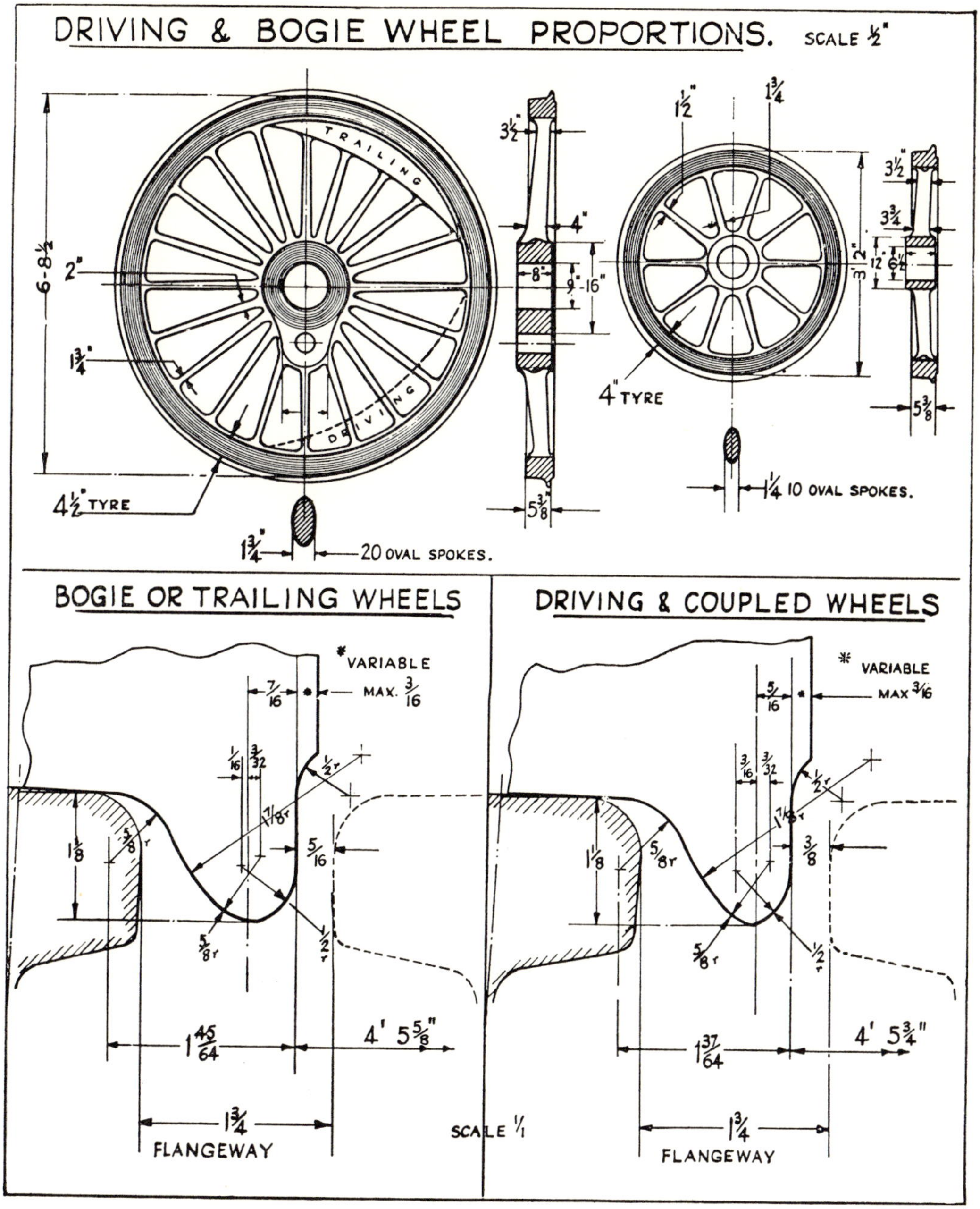

models at reasonable speeds, so we must reproduce these conditions nearer to scale with modern standards.

We know that model rail is usually drawn with a square head to facilitate the drawing in large quantities; while it is being laid it is only a matter of

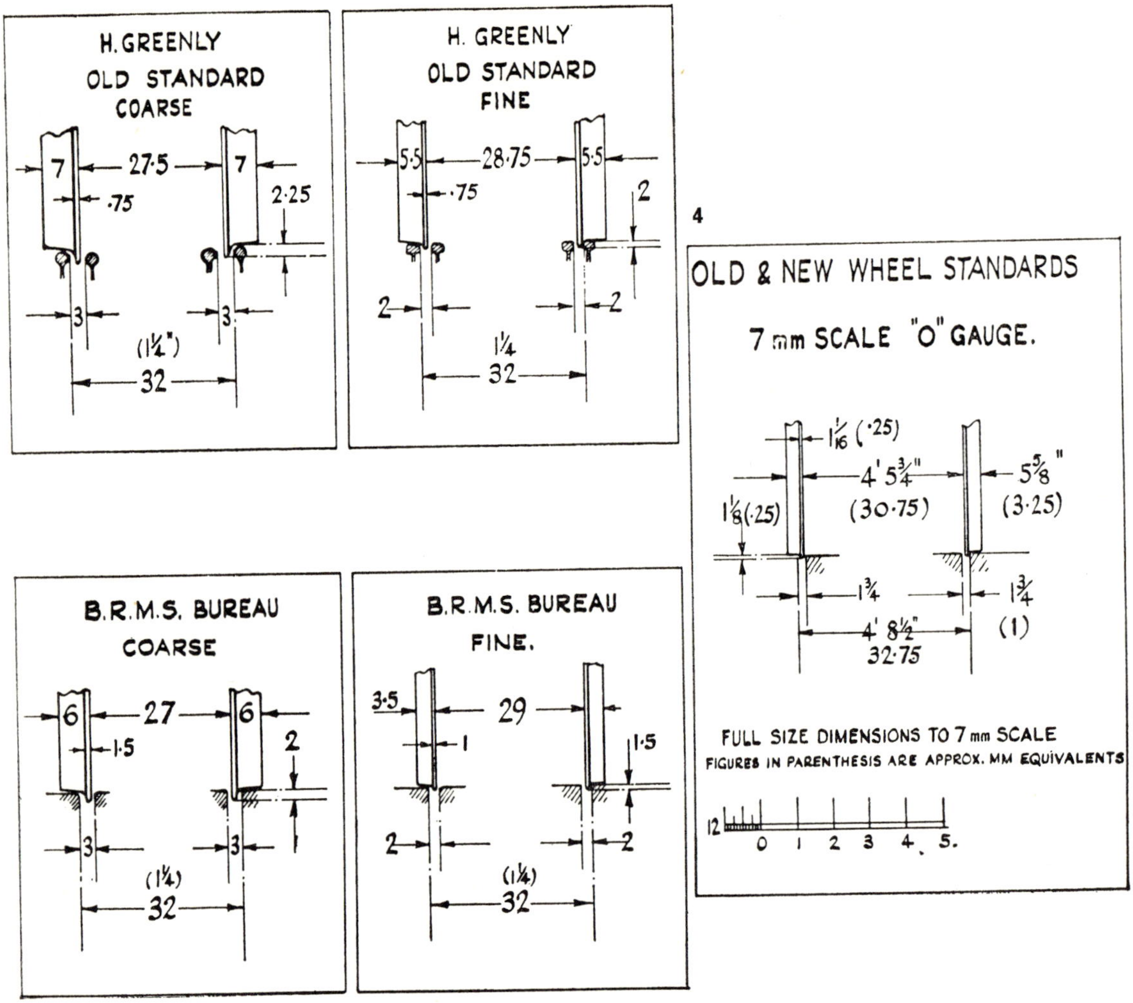

4

a minute or two to run a file along the running edge; coarse emery is quite as good. We have to clean the rail anyway for soldering, and a little time thus spent will amply repay the worker, and trouble-free running is assured. The drawing (fig. 4) also shows the importance of the flangeway. In modern standards this is nearer to scale than it used to be, so the back to back measurement of the wheels is very important. Too much stress cannot be laid on this fact. They must be 29 mm. back to back, just that and nothing more or nothing less. It is better to make a jig for this purpose to ensure that all the wheels on engine and tender are exactly 29 mm. and methods of fixing wheels to this dimension are important. These will be discussed later. The back to back measurement in the smaller scales of 4 mm. and 3½ mm. is even more important owing to the tiny flanges.

In figure 5 are given diagrams of free-lance engines. Very often it is the builder's intention to design a locomotive for himself. Using a prototype

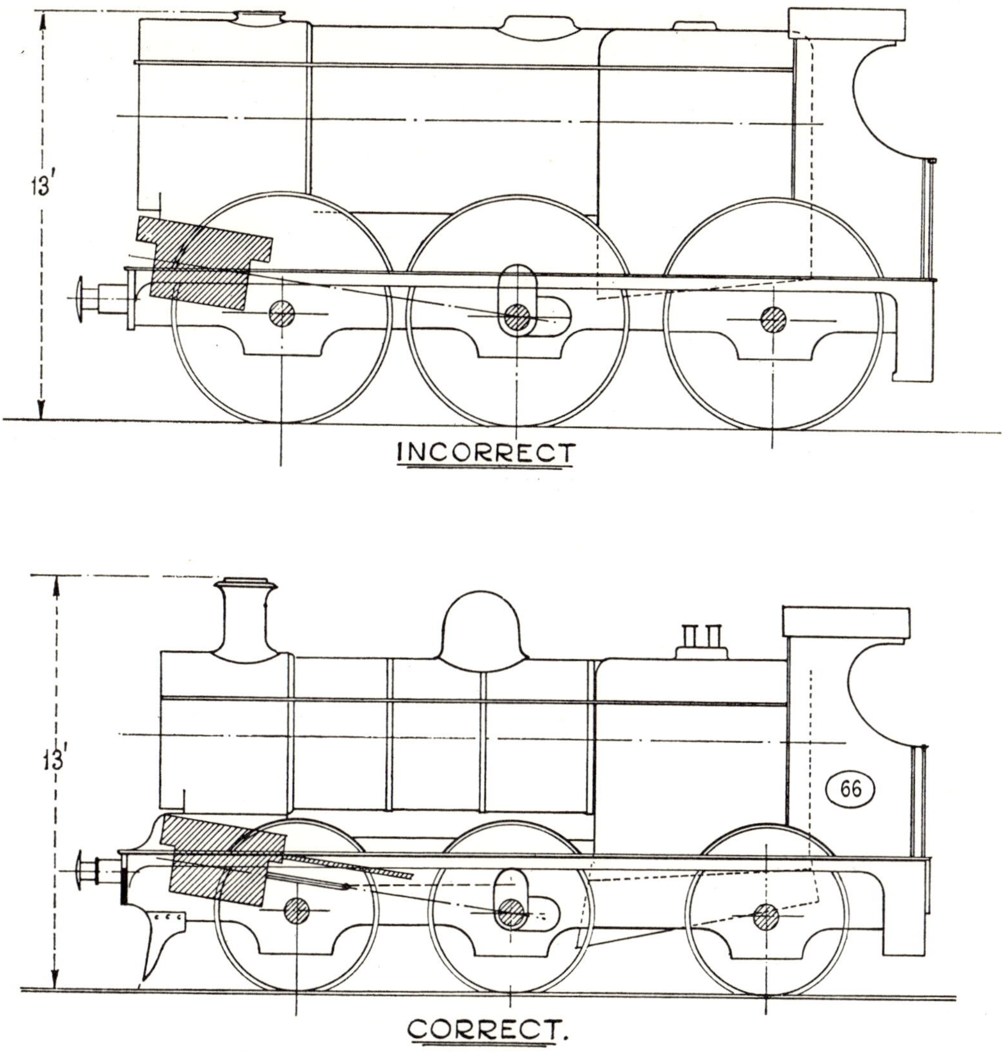

5 Scale interpretation

locomotive and shifting a chimney here, or taking a dome off there, or altering the cab is not in the author's opinion free-lance designing. This is only making a mess of a perfectly successful design, and if this sort of thing were reproduced in full size the engine would be a complete failure.

The origin of free lance is self-evident, and its journalistic meaning is also well-known. The term is very loosely applied to model locomotives. A disproportionate model sadly strayed from the builder's original intention, a locomotive that has been built round a mechanism found in the scrap box, and other efforts are all kindly described as free lance. Actually such fabrications are neither model nor free lance, and one would doubtless find a more accurate description from a model-making sergeant-major !

A free lance model locomotive is one that although not an exact copy of some existing engine conforms to actual practice or to possible practice both internally and externally. The enthusiast who ranges fancy free and does not, like so many, narrow his horizon to one company may, quite fairly, design and build his own locomotives to suit his preference in outline, wheel arrangement, etc., provided that he restrains his fancy within certain bounds. The design of engine should be governed by the class of traffic it will have to handle. He should regard himself as the superintendent of motive power for his railway, and he must have fundamental knowledge of boiler design, cylinder ratios, and general engineering practice before he can consider himself a free lance designer. If a live steam model is being built, the builder has to conform to orthodox practice if his model is to work. The fact that his model is to be electrically driven does not matter one iota; it must be capable of working, assuming it is a steam locomotive, which after all is what the designer is setting out to produce. The following pitfalls must be avoided at all costs. Coming to actual details, positioning of axles is quite important.

For instance the leading axles on a 0–6–0 goods engine should not occupy the space required for the cylinder block (see fig. 5). The wheels are too large, necessitating the cylinders being moved forward and the boiler raised to clear them and consequently the loading gauge would make the chimney look ridiculous. The lower shows a more reasonable design which conforms to accepted standards, and certainly looks more pleasing. The correct procedure is to follow full-size practice—namely, to lay out cylinders and valve gear, then the boiler, and the rest will follow naturally.

For instance, if a goods loco is planned draw three wheels of moderate size to scale (4 ft. 7 in. to 5 ft. 2 in.). If larger wheels are fitted the loco will come into the mixed traffic class with bogie or pony truck.

In considering layout, the centre line of the cylinders must pass through the centre of the driving axle. Cylinders often have to be inclined to get this result. Inclined cylinders position the bottom of the smokebox and the boiler. The diameter of driving wheels governs depth of frames, and the loading gauge determines the maximum permissible diameter of the boiler. Although inside cylinders are usually imagined in an electrically driven loco, it is necessary to lay them out correctly as very often the heads of the piston valves, and their tail rods usually protrude at the front of a modern loco, and one needs to know the inclination to achieve the correct angle to secure the latter to the front of the loco.

In designing a loco of your own, never be tempted to build it round the mechanism. Very often this is the very reason that one wants to design his own loco—their mechanism will not fit into any known English prototype ! This is responsible for many a model locomotive which "comes out where it should go in" figuratively speaking. Constructionally there are other points worth noting. When planning a 6-coupled model, it is always advisable to drive on the centre pair of wheels: a more balanced drive is obtained and daylight under the boiler is generally the result. It is quite easy to use a four-coupled mechanism, and add a pair of wheels on false frames at the front.

These remarks of course apply to the type of mechanism we are familiar with—horse-shoe magnet, three pole armature and side plates to hold the lot together drilled for wheels. This type of mechanism dates back to 1909, and has served us well, but the mechanism of the future will be entirely different. Modern methods in manufacturing aircraft instruments have produced small motors with enormous power and such tiny proportions that it will be possible to fit these into the smallest or the largest loco with ease, as they are circular, and can be fitted into the boiler. We shall have more to say on the subject of mechanisms later on, suffice it to say now that the methods of building a loco will have to be altered. The boiler will have to be made as a separate unit. Especially if it is a round-topped firebox type. This is as it should be, and is the author's favourite method of building a model; it is less like a can than the usual method.

Before leaving the subject of free lance designing there are one or two Don'ts to be noted. Never build a Wootten firebox over a driving wheel. This is an absolute impossibility with a normal design, as this type of firebox has a wide grate area and spreads over and above the frames. Only one actual loco in British practice has been so equipped, namely, the ex-GER *Decapod*, where the small 4 ft. diameter wheels made it possible. If a Wootten type of firebox is desired, an Atlantic or Pacific type is indicated. The ex-GNR and LNER Atlantics and Pacifics respectively are examples. Never design a 4-coupled loco with a wheelbase less than 8 ft. 6 in. Remember the firebox has to go in between these axles and leave room for the revolving cranks. This of course refers to express locos, and is the reason for 4–6–0 engines having a larger boiler to obtain depth of firebox, or conversely a small boiler high pitched, or alternatively, smaller driving wheels.

If the would-be designer of free lance model locomotives bears such considerations in mind at the drawing stage he will be assured of a realistic and pleasing result.

So many models bearing evidence of good workmanship and ingenuity in construction are completely spoiled by ignoring real practice, and it is realised that only the fringe of this subject has been touched upon, due to considerations of space. Fig. 6 shows what is virtually a free-lance design.

This drawing shows Sir Henry Fowler's Pacific, designed for the LMS. This engine was actually partly built at Crewe, it was to be a compound, and was the beginning of Midland practice on the combined railways. This fine engine was unfortunately never completed and, upon Sir Henry's retirement it was broken up, but parts of it were used in Sir William Stanier's Princess Royal class, notably the trailing truck frame. However, the genesis of the Royal Scots can be seen in the design. It is given a fictitious name in the drawing, the only disadvantages from a modelling point of view are the three drops in the footplating, but this should be no difficulty to the expert. This locomotive would make a fine model. It may be mentioned that another Pacific was designed for the LMS by Mr. George Hughes, it was a lengthened version of this standard 4-cylinder 4–6–0 for the Lancashire and Yorkshire Railway, and had inside framed trailing wheels. This engine was never commenced, although the drawings were completed. The drawing shown by fig. 1 is a locomotive built for the East Indian Railway by Stothert and Slaughter and Kitson's of Leeds, for local traffic in the Calcutta

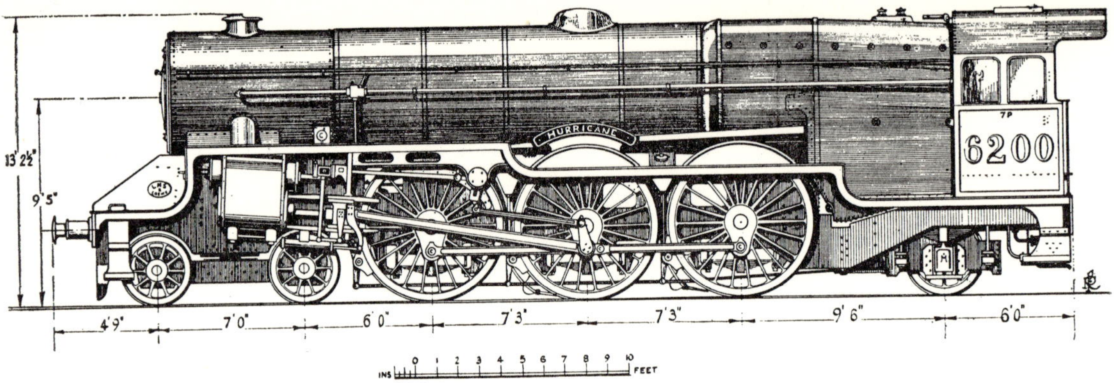

6 Sir Henry Fowler's 4-cylinder Compound "Pacific," 1930. L.M.S. 2 h.p. cylinders 16¾in. x 26in. and 2 l.p. cylinders 23⅝in. x 26in. B.P. 240lbs. sq. in.

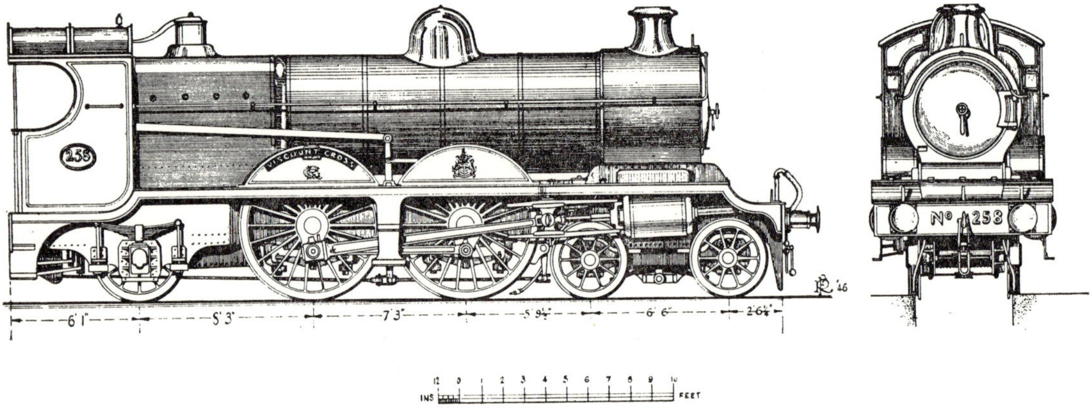

7 J. G. Robinson's 3-cylinder Compound Express loco. Great Central Railway, 1905. American projection.

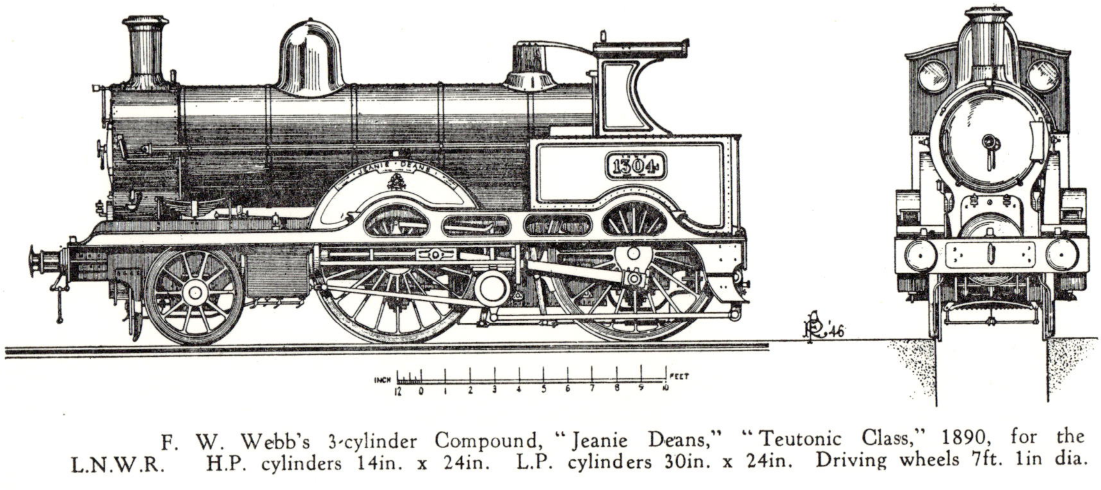

8 F. W. Webb's 3-cylinder Compound, "Jeanie Deans," "Teutonic Class," 1890, for the L.N.W.R. H.P. cylinders 14in. x 24in. L.P. cylinders 30in. x 24in. Driving wheels 7ft. 1in dia.

district. J. V. Gooch apparently had a hand in the design as it is similar to the Eastern-Counties (later GER) locomotives. This engine is preserved at Jamalpur EIR shops and kept in beautiful condition. It was used for troop trains during the Indian Mutiny, and worked between Howrah and Raneegunge, a suburb of Calcutta. The second drawing (fig. 2) is Massey Bromley's Single for the GER built in 1879 in its original condition. James Holden later modified them, particularly the framing at the front end. Before we leave the drawing office, a few remarks are offered regarding drawings for publication. Many of us have a little idea which we sometimes like to put on paper for the benefit of other enthusiasts, and send to the technical press. Do not try to draw the item to its actual size unless it is very large. Draw it at least four or five times full size. The publishers can always reduce it to the size you want it. Use pencil first, and draw *all* your curves with a compass first, and join them up with the straight lines. Never draw curves freehand; if your drawing has such small curves and arcs that your compasses will not get down to, then scrap it and draw it to a larger size. When the drawing is completed in pencil, ink it in, not with a mapping pen, but with proper draughtsman's pens. When the drawing is completed in ink, clean it with a soft rubber. Use proper Indian (black) ink, not household ink, this is useless for reproduction. Many articles sent to the Press are not published for the simple reason that the drawings illustrating it are incapable of reproduction, due to the simple rules mentioned not being adhered to. If the writer of the article cannot draw in perspective, then draw the elevation first, underneath this the plan, and, if necessary, at either end of the elevation draw the left hand view to the right, and the right hand view to the left of it respectively. This is known as English projection. If it is done the other way, i.e. the plan first, under this the elevation; and at either end the right hand view to the right and the left hand view to the left, this is known as American projection. Never mix the two, as your readers will not be able to read the drawing. It will be, to them, so much gibberish. To illustrate this refer to the drawing of the GCR Atlantic (fig. 7), this is American projection. The LNWR Compound is English projection (fig. 8). This should make the point clear. Hints on constructing these two locomotives will be given later on. Any treatise on draughtsmanship will be very useful to the amateur who aspires to draw items for publication to help their fellow enthusiasts. Some technical journals employ a draughtsman to redraw readers' sketches, and judging by some the author has seen he requires to be a thought reader ! If you cannot draw at all, it is better to employ a photograph to illustrate your point, providing the item is pictured in the most advantageous position to show all the details, it is usually all that is required. Finally, the drawings you use yourself, during the construction, cover them with a sheet of cellophane or celluloid, mounted in a frame. If it is a blue print, soldering fluid will cause it to be covered in white spots if it is left uncovered, and it will be unreadable.

Requisitioning of Stores

Having finished the drawings of our locomotive we now pass them out to the works for the requisitioning of stores, and the first items we will require are patterns for castings. In model work we usually only require wheel castings, unless we are building a locomotive in which nothing is obtainable from the trade. This is very often the case with an historical model—in fact in a model of this class we have to build almost everything ourselves and the following hints will be of assistance to those who like to accurately model a fine old loco of Victorian days.

The making of a pattern for a driving wheel is dependent on size of the wheel we require and whether we make it in metal or wood. From 10 mm. scale upwards patterns can quite comfortably be made in wood, but below this size it is better to make the pattern in metal; it will ensure a cleaner casting. It must be remembered that if we make the pattern exactly as we require our wheel—namely with the spokes open—only a large model wheel will have the correct number of spokes, which is usually 22 in an express engine wheel, 20 in a mixed traffic loco wheel and 17 or 18 below this. Bogie wheels have never less than 10 spokes, whilst tender and trailing wheels have 12 to 14 spokes. If we wish to make a pattern for a driving or bogie wheel in 7 mm. scale and below, do not make your pattern with open spokes, as owing to the homogenity of molten cast iron it will not flow into the tiny crevices required to get the correct number of spokes. This is the reason why very few O-gauge wheels have the correct number of spokes.

In fig. 9 is shown how to make a pattern with the proper draw on it. It will be obvious that if we make our wheel with oval spokes, as in the prototype, it will lock itself in the mould and the mould will have to be broken up round it and the casting probably rendered useless. The correct finish of the wheel is obtained by filing afterwards. In single-wheel locos do not make the balance weight or the pear shaped centre boss part of the casting. These can be added when the casting is obtained. In modern locos very few balance weights are crescent shaped. A much better effect can be obtained by adding these in their proper places yourself. When making patterns in wood use only a very hard wood, say beech or mahogony, and in the smaller sizes commence the pattern by the turning or filing of a circular piece of wood about 2 mm. thick for the base. If you make this too thick you will have a lot of metal to turn away when you receive the casting. Upon this make your pear shaped centre boss, with the sides slightly tapered, and glue it exactly in the centre. From this radiate the spokes evenly all round. To make the spokes obtain a piece of beech dowelling or satin walnut strip wood, and file it to a V shape. The length of this strip depends on the number of spokes we require. Cut each spoke separately and glue it in place with the sharp end of the V upwards. When this is finished you now have, for want of a better term, a rosette. Now obtain a piece of beech and turn a tyre complete with its flange about 2 or 3 mm. larger in outside diameter than the size of wheel you require and the same amount wider on the tread than you require, according to whether we are working to the true scale or coarse standards. Glue the rosette into the centre of this, and you now have a wheel pattern with a solid back. This will cast quite easily, and with the correct number of spokes.

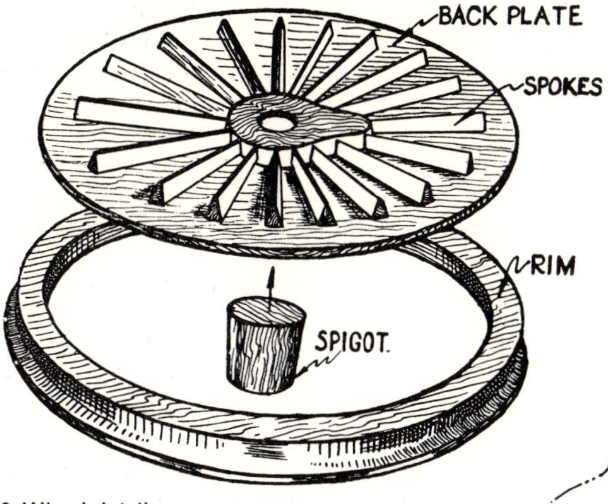

9 Wheel detail

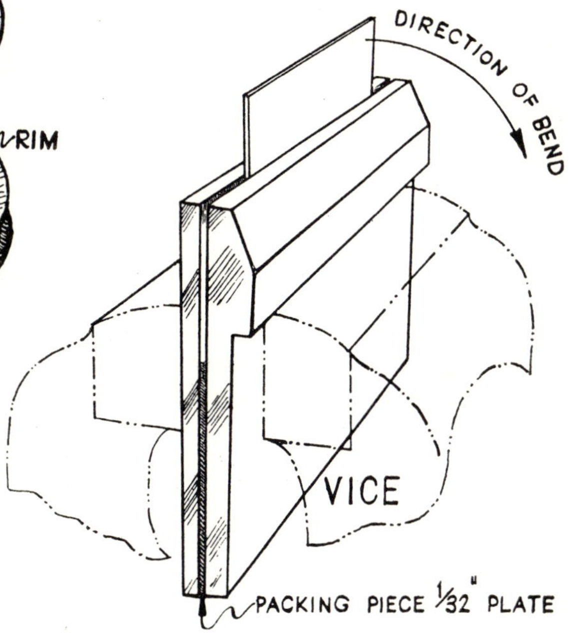

10 Bending jig

When we reach the turning stage all you have to do is to turn the wheel in the usual way, and completely finish the front, reverse in the chuck and turn off the surplus metal with a sharp tool until the spokes begin to show themselves. The intervening pieces of metal can be knocked out with a file. More will be said about wheel turning when we come to this subject. Before leaving the subject of patterns for wheels, some modellers prefer to have a spigot cast on the back of the wheel for holding the casting in the lathe chuck. If this is required a piece of dowelling can be glued to the back, exactly in the centre, just there and nowhere else. If this is not in the centre it is almost impossible to centre the wheel in an ordinary 3 jaw chuck. The author prefers to dispense with this spigot altogether as it is very seldom in the middle due to the contraction of the casting on cooling.

When you take your pattern to the foundry, impress upon them not to place the castings in a current of cold air, or throw them into water. If they do this they will become chilled and you will find it impossible to turn them. Small castings of this nature in cast iron must be cooled naturally. The knowledge that cast iron became glass hard on being rapidly cooled was very useful in the old days of 100 years ago; and was often used, until the advent of steel, for parts that were subject to a lot of hard wear. Wheels in OO gauge are usually made by what is known as the hot or sometimes cold pressing method, and as this method is only applicable to non-ferrous metals, iron or steel wheels are impossible (if they contain spokes) in these gauges. Hence recourse is made to plating, and deposition of white metals to obtain a steel-like finish, but they never look quite as nice as a nicely turned cast iron or steel wheel, and they unfortunately have the disadvantage of rolling the dirt from the track into their surface and impairing current collection. Bakelite and other plastic substances also have this disadvantage in a far greater degree, and with the modern trend of two rail track operation this problem seems at present to be incapable of solution except to use a very high voltage. Even then, if there is any sparking at the rail head, plastic wheels burn and are useless.

As we shall not be requiring cylinder castings for an electrically driven model, and as this subject is adequately dealt with by LBSC in the *Model Engineer* we will pass on to the next item we require, namely jigs and fixtures. In turning domes and chimneys it is very useful to make a little plate jig giving all the radii. and angles, and as the turning proceeds, offer this jig up to the work occasionally, until it passes over the fitting without showing any daylight. Your chimney or dome, or safety valve casing will thus be of the correct profile. It is much better than guessing, only an expert who has doubtless turned thousands of fittings can turn these by eye. Figs. 11 and 12 show some useful jigs for turning boiler fittings. These can be made

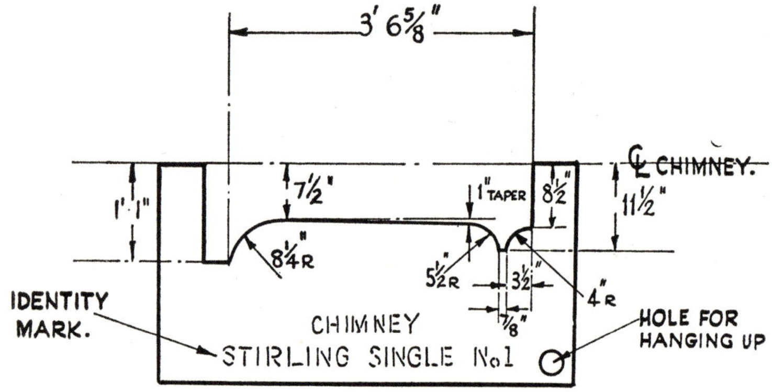

11 TEMPLATE FOR STIRLING CHIMNEY
FULL SIZE MEASUREMENTS SHOWN.
SCALE ¾″ = 1′

from a piece of scrap brass or tinplate, drilled with a little hole for hanging them on the tool rack, in case they are ever needed again. Sometimes different classes of engines all have the same type of boiler fitting—particularly when the prototype is one belonging to a railway where a large degree of standardisation has taken place, such as the GWR. These little jigs will be found useful and can be used again for a different class of engine. Fig. 10 shows another very useful device for bending metals. Several uses for this little jig can be found during construction—bending the tender side plates is one that comes easily to the mind. This should be made in mild steel, and as long as possible, if you are an O gauge modeller. One half this size (say 3 in.) will be found ample for OO gauge. To use it, place the metal to be bent into the slot up to marked line, place the jig in the vice, and tighten up. Then bend the piece of metal, and lightly tap with a small hammer all

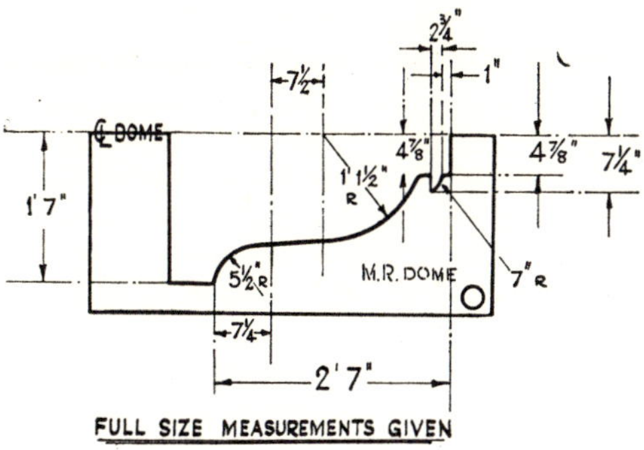

12 **Johnson's Midland Railway loco dome jig**

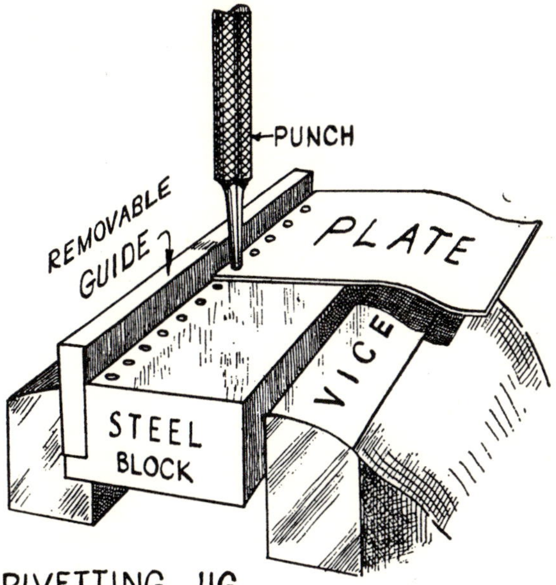

13 RIVETTING JIG.

along the top. The metal will be found to have a nice clean bend. A further refinement would be to harden the top edge of the jig if a lot of bending is to be done or one is building several locos at once.

Other jigs we will require are riveting sets for imitating rivets if no drilling machine is available. Methods of imitating rivets will be found in the chapter on tenders and tanks, but we will make the jig at this stage. In fig. 13 will be found all the necessary particulars for manufacturing a jig for imitating rivets. A punch will also be required. Make this from a piece of silver steel, and form the punch with a rounded point as shown. An old punch can be adapted by grinding if the modeller has a spare one in his possession. The block of steel containing the indentations must be made of carbon steel, and hardened after finishing. If you cannot do this yourself a toolmaker friend will harden it for you. It only needs to be heated to a dark straw colour and plunged into water, polishing with fine emery afterwards. It will then be found useful for imitating literally thousands of rivets without wear. The length of the jig is immaterial and at the discretion of the builder. One can make it large enough to take a whole tender side, but this is hardly necessary. A long line of indentations is all that is necessary, and makes the jig more universal, as several different combinations of rivetting can be indulged in. The method of using the jig will be discussed in the chapter dealing with rivetting.

The Tools

We now come to the subject of tools. In fig. 14 will be found a useful assortment of tools; A shows an electric power drill, this tool is very useful indeed, and virtually replaces the old fashioned hand brace. It is capable of a variety of uses—clamped in the vice it makes a useful little lathe for small turning by hand turning tools. The chuck is a precision chuck opened and closed by a key. A number of tools can be used with it besides the common twist drill. In G is shown a number of small grinding wheels of different shapes, also some die sinkers and mills. These can be used with the drill to grind or mill out awkward corners, such as the arch shaped openings in the main frame over the bogie wheels. Sometimes it is found that when the engine is erected it is necessary to grind out just a little more of the frame to get the mechanism in or perhaps sometimes we have not got quite enough out of the back of the splashers to enable the boiler to sit down nicely, these and other little jobs will suggest themselves to the reader. Die sinkers end mills are put up in a little wooden box as shown in J, and purchasable at all tool stores. Power drills are made by Messrs. Black & Decker, Wolf, and Bridges.

For use with small drills do not push the power drill through but let it drill through the metal by its own weight. A little practice is required at first, but once the operator gets used to it, he will never use a handbrace again.

B shows a set of small screwdrivers, variously known as pinion screwdrivers, watchmakers screwdrivers or simply turnscrews. These are very useful for tightening small screws of 10 BA and under. To use them, the first finger is placed in the cup at the top, and the second finger and thumb used to turn the screw, this gives absolute control over the tiny screws. They are usually made in the three sizes shown and supplied in a little polished wood box. C shows a pair of side cutting nippers for wire cutting up to 16 swg. Do not try to use them on wire larger than this as they will be strained. If it is desired to cut thicker wire a pair of toggle nippers can be used or a small saw, as shown in H. These saws are useful for small metal cutting; they are only 6 in. long, and take 6 in. metal cutting saws. With this type of hacksaw one can get more control when cutting thin plate. The larger type of hacksaw, adjustable, taking up to 12 in. blades will also be required for cutting steel plate. D shows a pin chuck for taking tiny drills with a spare collet attached for taking drills up to $\frac{1}{16}$ in. This can be put in the power drill or handbrace if the chuck of the latter is worn and will not take drills below $\frac{1}{16}$ in. E shows a Vernier caliper gauge, reading in inches and is constructed for use as inside, outside, and depth gauge. It is sometimes called a slide gauge. This tool will be found extremely useful for setting to any predetermined width, and using to check the width of, say, a footplate, all the way along from front to back. It need hardly be said that it is useful also for track laying, if set to gauge. This type of Vernier is quite cheap, but do not buy the more complicated type of Vernier gauge as used for checking items to .0001 in. or one-tenth of a thousandth of an inch. If anyone makes a model to these limits of a railway locomotive, even a steam locomotive, they deserve a gold medal, if it works without having hot boxes, or seized big ends.

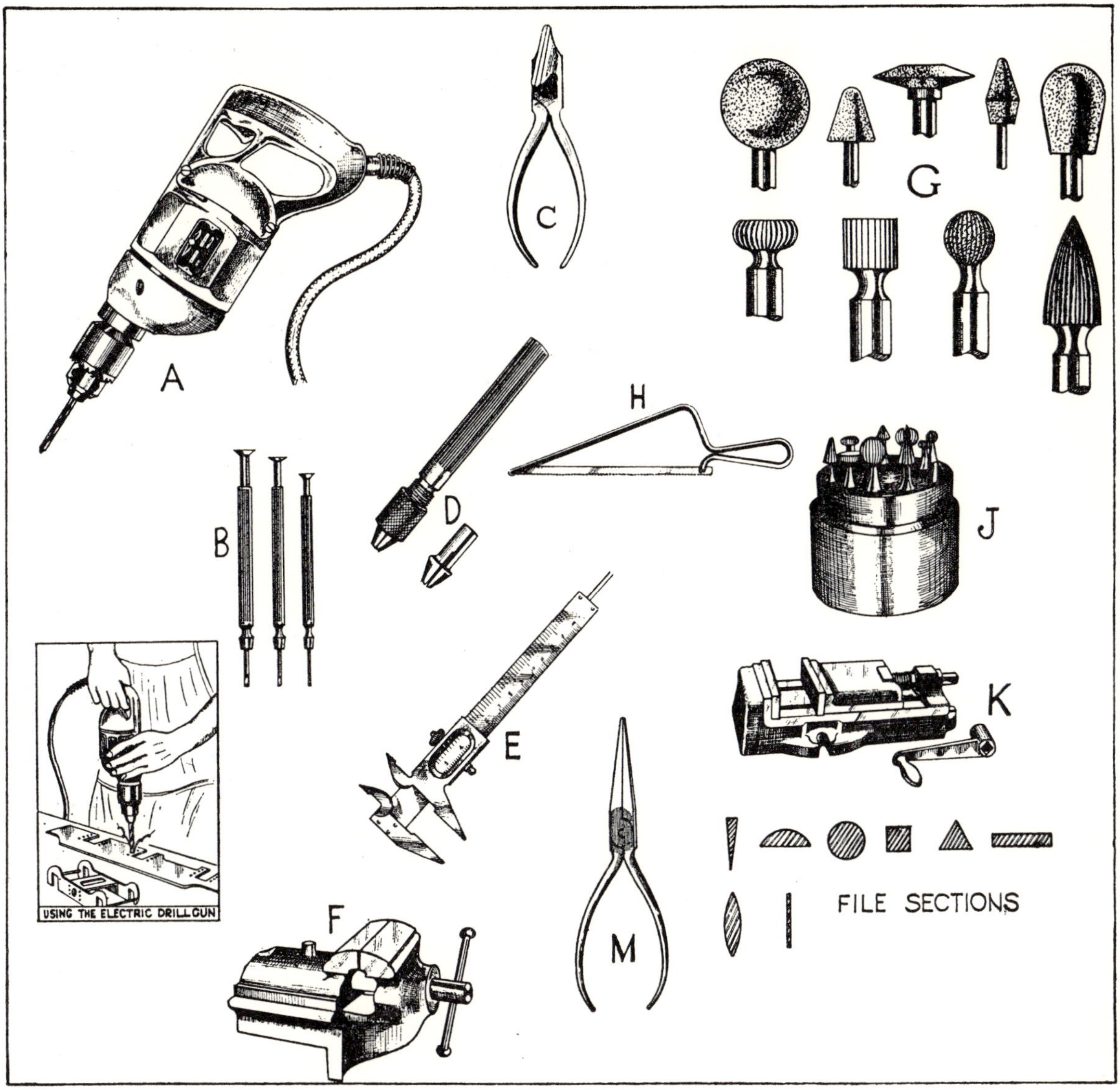

14 Tools: key to the letters is given in the text

One thousandth of an inch is quite sufficient for model work if the reader is inclined to work to precision limits, and for these folk a micrometer is necessary. Even if the reader does not work to such fine limits, a micrometer is a very useful tool, for turning; in the lathe it is almost essential for checking limits and fits when turning wheels, axles, bearings, etc. A useful size is known as a 1 in. scale.

M shows a pair of long nosed pliers. These are very useful, one or two pairs of these are necessary; other types of pliers are useful but not essential.

The representative selection of file sections is shown in this order: knife edge, half round, round, triangular (sometimes known as three corner), flat, fish belly and thin flat (or warding file). These shapes are universal in all sizes of files from Swiss or needle files to large 14 in. heavy duty files. The grades of files are fine, coarse, and bastard.

We now come to the subject of vices. A really good make of vice should be asked for and insisted upon, in view of the fact that there are very few really parallel vices of the common type, especially in the smaller sizes that a model maker requires. After very little wear, these vices begin to develop a rock in the front jaws, and when tightened up, one end is not touching its mate. To obviate this trouble the reader is recommended to purchase a precision vice as shown by F. This type differs from the common type in that the front jaw is stationary, and the rear jaw moves on parallel machined V slides, these vices are truly parallel and remain so throughout their life. Unfortunately these are only made in the small sizes up to $2\frac{3}{8}$ in. length of jaw. This is quite a useful size for all practical purposes up to the $\frac{1}{2}$ in. scale models, but above this the large version of the common vice such as a 6 in. will have to be obtained, but as a general rule these large vices are fairly parallel as their wearing surfaces are larger. Another useful type of precision vice is the type shown by K. This is known as a machine vice, and is made for use with a milling machine, or a drilling machine, but if the modeller has neither of these, there is no reason why the vice cannot be used. It can be screwed to the bench in the ordinary way by means of the cast lugs, and the removable handle made a fixture by pinning it on the shaft. This type of vice is perfectly safe to use when forcing wheels on axles, and similar jobs, requiring true parallelism.

Other tools we will require are the following: (these are not illustrated as they are fairly well known) 1, a pair of machinist's dividers. 2, a good quality engineers steel square made by Moore and Wright; these are guaranteed to be within .001 in. per foot in accuracy. They are made in three sizes: 2 in., 3 in. and 4 in. For those who have a lathe, a pair of spring bow calipers (outside), and ditto (inside) are necessary, these also are made in three sizes, 3 in., 4 in. and 5 in. A cheaper type relying on friction to keep them tight, and packed in a leather case are an efficient substitute. 3, a vee block is necessary for those who turn and fit their own wheels on axles. The vee block is useful for quartering the cranks. 4, toolmaker's clamps are useful for large models where two or three pieces of work may be clamped together for drilling. The main frames of a loco suggest an example. 5, a pair of tin snips; two kinds are needed, the curved type, for cutting circles of metal, and the straight type for cutting straight edges. 6, two or three hammers. One ball pein hammer with an 8 oz. head is useful for general work, and a small pein hammer with a 4 oz. head for small riveting. 7, a set of drills on a stand. According to the inclination of the modeller he may buy the Morse drills or the English $\frac{1}{4}$ in. to $\frac{1}{64}$ in. on a stand. The Morse drills range from No. 1 to No. 60, also supplied on a stand. Smaller drills than these down to No. 80 may be bought loose and kept in a small metal case, such as the girl friend's discarded lipstick case. 8, a handbrace, if the worker prefers this type of drilling machine. 9, taps and dies. These are governed by the size of model one is building. It will be obvious that if the model is a

15 SELF HEATING GAS SOLDERING BIT DRAWN APPROX. ½ SIZE

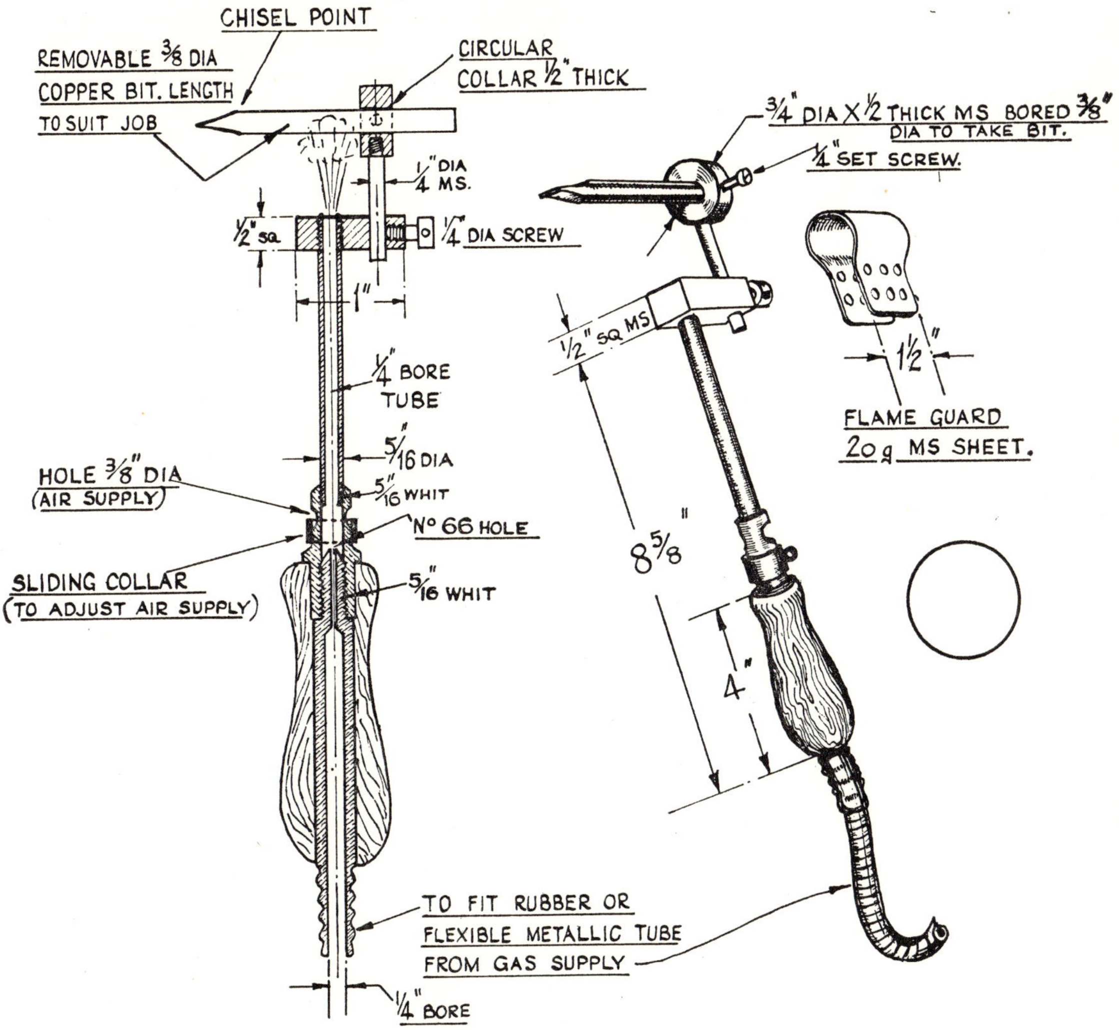

small one, a larger tap and die than 4 BA or ⅛ in. Whitworth will seldom be required. These are purchased complete in a box or loose, as one requires them. The author recommends the use of BA sizes in preference to Whitworth for small work. These are obtainable down to 16 BA.

For use with dies a die stock is needed, but if the reader buys the complete set, a die stock and tap wrench are included. 10, a set of box spanners will be found very useful. These are obtainable in sets from ⅛ in. to $\frac{7}{16}$ in. They will be found more useful than a pair of pliers for screwing nuts on bolts. Screwing a nut on a bolt by means of pliers is not recommended, as the nut has a habit of flying out of the pliers at the critical moment and getting lost among the works. This usually results in a lot of shaking and jerking of the model accompanied by railroad esperanto !

11, the all-important soldering iron. Here again the purchase of this is dependent on whether the modeller prefers an electric type, or gas type, or those one puts on a gas ring to heat up. The electric type is very handy as it never burns and the copper bit lasts much longer than the gas type. There is now on the market several quick heating electric irons which on operation of a trigger switch, heat up in 5 seconds. It is recommended when using an electric bit, that spirits of salts or bakers fluid be avoided, only paste flux is suitable for electric soldering bits. Fig. 15 shows a typical gas operated soldering bit suitable for home construction. These are very useful, and the gas can always be turned off or very low when the bit is not being used, or when soldering in awkward corners where the flame, if left on, might melt adjacent parts.

12, a set of centre punches will be required, and a scriber for marking out. Those who are watchmakers, know the latter as a scratcher for obvious reasons. Lastly, a most essential item of equipment—a 6 in. steel, preferably stainless steel, rule. A 12 in. rule might be obtained, but not essential. These rules should be obtained in a leather case for carrying in the pocket, and should be marked with metric, as well as English units. The good modeller always carries his rule with him, as sooner or later he will have to climb over a truck, or a wagon, or perhaps a locomotive (if the driver isn't looking) and measure up that little item that is not quite clear on the drawing !

The Materials

This more or less completes our list of essential items, of course it is not necessary that all these be purchased at once; it is quite usual to purchase them as one wants them, and, having purchased them, look after them, tools are expensive items in these days. The care of tools is second only to first class work, particularly measuring tools. Dropping a square on the concrete floor won't improve it ! Always keep the points of your scribers and dividers keen and when not in use push the points into an old bottle cork or a piece of soft wood. Verniers and rulers should be carried in the pocket, as, if they are non-stainless, the warmth of the body keeps them from going rusty, except in tropical climates, then, of course, the body is the last place one keeps them ! Perspiration is a wonderful rust producer ! In these conditions, only plenty of oil and grease will keep tools from going rusty, and once a tool has been cleaned and oiled never touch it with the fingers; wear gloves. These should be nice and oily too. Fingers are easier to wash than to get rust off a precious tool ! The author is not going to exhort his readers to keep their bench tidy and keep things in drawers, and trot out the old maxim: "A place for everything and everthing in its place," because he has been told that he is the untidiest beast unhung, and admits it ! He can always find things if his bench is in a muddle, but if it is tidied up he can never find anything ! It is all a matter of temperament. If a fellow is naturally tidy in all things he will keep a tidy bench, without being told, but if he is not—'nuff said. An untidy man can build just as good a model as a tidy one it has been found, and look at the time wasted tidying up, one can put another 10 minutes in on the model, and everything is ready for commencing the next evening!

Before we leave the subject of tools, a few words may be said about metal slitting saws, and the use of them. The fellow who has the gift of lightness of touch would make a success of cutting all his metalwork with a saw, but those who are rather inclined to be heavy handed should leave them alone and use the tin snips. If the latter tries to use a metal-cutting saw he will have a succession of broken saws, ending with shortness of temper and general disappointment. For those who can use them there is no better way of cutting metal, a nice clean cut is obtained almost up to the marked line, leaving very little to take off with a file, and several pieces can be tackled at once. A lot depends on the type of metal one is using whether one has any success with a metal saw. The type of brass sheet known as hard rolled is the best for use with a cutting saw. Ordinary sheet brass of the annealed variety is useless for cutting with this tool, as it is spongy and causes the saw to catch up and break.

While on the subject of metals for modelmaking, it may be said at this stage that there are three types of brass sheet; hard, half hard, and soft. The hard brass usually sold from a roll 6 in. wide, and has a definite grain in the longitudinal direction of the roll. While working with this brass always keep the grain in the long direction if it is desired to bend it. Bending against the grain will only break it.

This type of brass should be used where it is desired to have a large flat surface, such as the bottom of a tender or the tank sides. The type of brass known as half hard should be used for general work. The soft brass sheet is of little use, unless one wishes to make parts of brass that are normally made in copper.

Tinned steel plate or tinplate as it is commonly called is also a very useful medium for modelmaking. Its chief advantage is that being tinned it solders much better. Care should be taken during construction not to damage this tinning as it is really a rust preventative. If the tinning is scraped off, the metal underneath being a low grade steel very easily rusts, especially if spirits of salts is used as a flux. Another reason that tinplate is used is that it takes paint much better, and one also has the satisfaction that every material in the prototype is faithfully reproduced in the model; a good point to note for exhibition work. Real locomotives are not built of brass, nor nickel silver for that matter, which brings us to our third metal. This is very nice metal to work in, albeit a trifle more expensive. This also takes paint better than brass, is non-rusting, and is a good conductor of current, a great point in its favour for electric models. There were formerly two grades of this. One commonly called German silver had a larger percentage of brass in the alloy, and was therefore softer. The second grade is called nickel-silver and is a whiter metal altogether, and has a small percentage of bronze in it to toughen it, and in working it will be found to get quite hot if the drills, etc. are not quite keen enough or badly ground. There is also a material known as nickel-bronze that may be sold as nickel-silver. Beware of this as it is very tough indeed, and needs special high speed tools and plenty of lubrication to work it.

The above materials are all suitable for the superstructures of our locomotives. We will also want some steel for motion work. This can be obtained in sections such as round, square, and half round, from $\frac{1}{16}$ in. upwards. There is no excuse for making motion work of nickel-silver. Apart from the fact that it looks bad, it shows the mark of a lazy man who only *thinks* that nickel-silver is easier to work. This is entirely a myth. Mild steel is much easier to work; it polishes nicely and it is above all correct. The square section about $\frac{1}{8}$ in. square is ideal for motion work in gauge O as proper little forked-ends can be made from it for Walschaert's gear. The flat sections can be fluted for coupling rods etc. Most model-makers make their main frames from steel, so why jib at making the motion of steel? It is just one of those things that are done and no one knows why. Rust cannot be the reason as the motion is generally lubricated, and that in itself prevents rust. Another reason that steel should be used is that it can be case hardened if a lot of wear is anticipated, such as in a continuously working exhibition model. One cannot harden nickel-silver and the writer has seen an exhibition model after a fortnight of continuous running, fitted with nickel-silver motion. The rear coupled wheels could be turned half a revolution due to wear in the coupling rods, and the cross head was nearly falling out of the slide bars! An intensive session was indulged in behind those scenes the public never sees at exhibitions and the whole motion replaced with steel, ready for the opening next day! Needless to say no more trouble was experienced with that locomotive!

Finally, to round off our chapter on tools and materials we will want a selection of screws, nuts and washers. These can be obtained as small as 18 BA up to fig. 0 BA which is very nearly a $\frac{1}{4}$ in. diameter, while the 18 BA is roughly the diameter of a tiny lill pin, and the thread so fine that it almost cannot be seen with the naked eye! In constructing a model in the larger scales from gauge O upwards a good rule is to use the soldering bit as little as possible, except for large surfaces. Small parts should be screwed or riveted together. The model is a better engineering job and it has the advantage that if things go wrong it can be taken to pieces. Avoid as far as possible the use of cheese head slotted screws. If it is found necessary to use them due to their hexagon counterparts being unobtainable, then keep the head out of sight and the nut on the surface where it can be seen. Many excellent models have been spoilt by the use of cheese head screws, and points are lost in competition models by the use of them. The small screws can be used in gauge O where the cylinder covers show to the front such as in the GNR 8 ft. single, all the studs and nuts whereby the covers were screwed on can be seen. This was a feature on all the early locomotives and they looked very nice and engine like, whereas the largest size can be used for the bogie pin, screwing the mechanism in, and other places where heavy holding power is required. The use of locknuts is recommended, and these can be obtained as small as 8 BA, these are useful for securing the bogie on its pin and for securing the mechanism in. These are made by Simmonds Ltd., and have a fibre insert inside the nut which is the secret of its holding power; nothing is more annoying than to pick an engine off the track and find the bogie is left behind. A feverish hunt is made all over the layout for the missing nut, firstly to get the bogie back on the engine, and secondly, but most important, to retrieve it before it causes a short circuit, gets picked up into the motor, or derails the next train on the line! Simmonds' nuts, or any other make of lock nut will prevent all this.

A collection of washers is very useful for use as shims to take up wear, to retain springs in their places, and in small models to act as distance collars between the main frames and backs of the wheels to prevent the latter rubbing on the frames. Spring washers are sometimes useful instead of locknuts, and are often used where space would preclude the use of a locknut as these are necessarily longer than a normal nut.

We have requisitioned all our material and have all our tools. The shops are now ready to commence building our locomotive, so we can now sit down and wonder what we have forgotten, and how soon we shall want what we have forgotten, and having arrived at no satisfactory answer we will take our bread and cheese and bottle of beer, pipe and tobacco, into the workshop and commence at the noisiest, but most interesting part of the works, namely the boiler shop.

The Boiler Shop

The locomotive boiler from the earliest days has consisted of three parts,—the smokebox, the boiler, and the firebox. There are many who maintain that had George Stephenson never been born, the locomotive would be much the same as it is now, but the boiler would have been developed upon different lines. Timothy Hackworth was George Stephenson's great rival, but he did not use the multi-tubular boiler. This was attributed to a Frenchman, one Marc Seguin, although the latter gentleman's locomotive was not tried on the road until after Stephenson's *Rocket*, which was the first locomotive in this country to be fitted with this type of boiler.

Timothy Hackworth was the first inventor to contract the orifice of the blastpipe, although its use was known to Stephenson. These two important inventions materially contributed to the success of the *Rocket*. If the locomotive boiler had developed on the lines of Timothy Hackworth's Stockton and Darlington engines we would probably have our modern locomotives with the chimney at the rear like those used in America and Spain.

American engineers developed their locomotives entirely on their own. Although one or two locomotives were shipped from Stephenson's works to America, they had little or no influence upon American railroad practice. In fact, we ourselves copied American practice in the matter of bogies, taper boilers, and wheel arrangements. The 4–4–0, Atlantic, and Pacific types all came from America and their locomotive history is every bit as interesting as our own.

The development of the firebox itself is very interesting. First, it was just tacked on to the rear of the circular boiler barrel, and was several sizes smaller. It then went to the other extreme and became much larger than the boiler, resulting in the enormous haystack type of firebox common on the GWR in broad gauge days.

It then began to recede again and became just slightly larger than the boiler, and semi-circular as in the latter broad gauge and early narrow-gauge engines of William Dean. It then settled down and began to be a part of the

16 MAKING A CONED BOILER

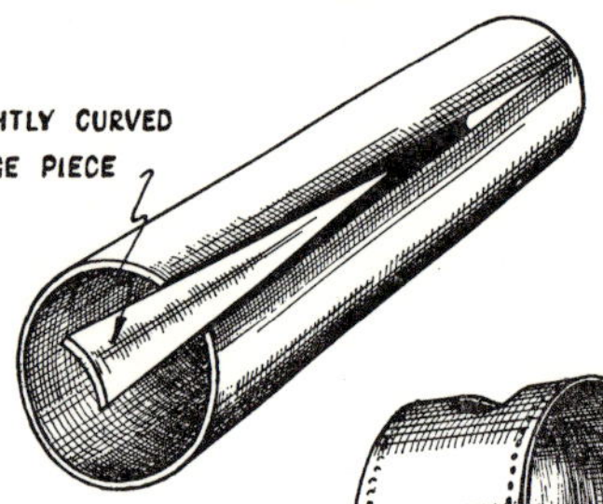

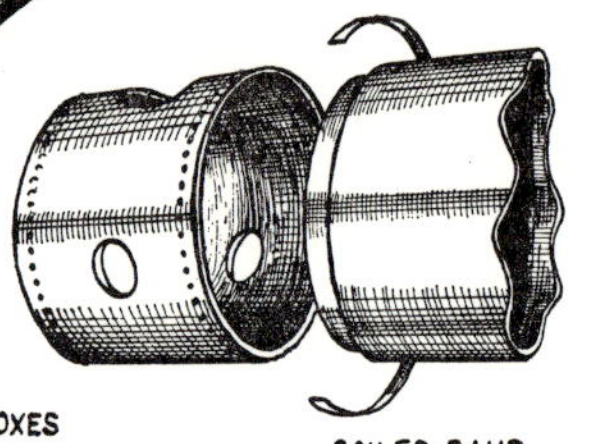

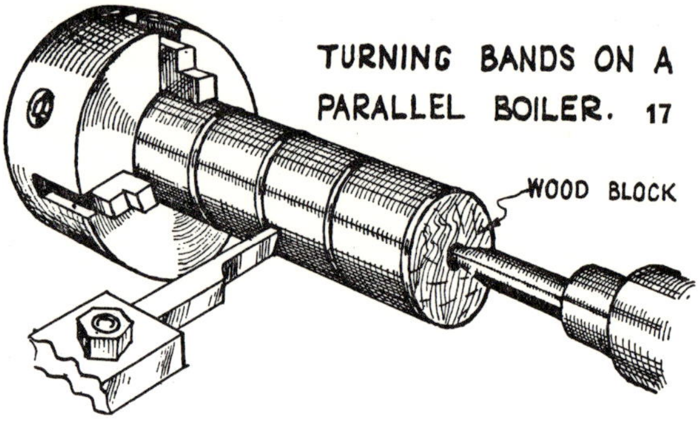

TURNING BANDS ON A PARALLEL BOILER. 17

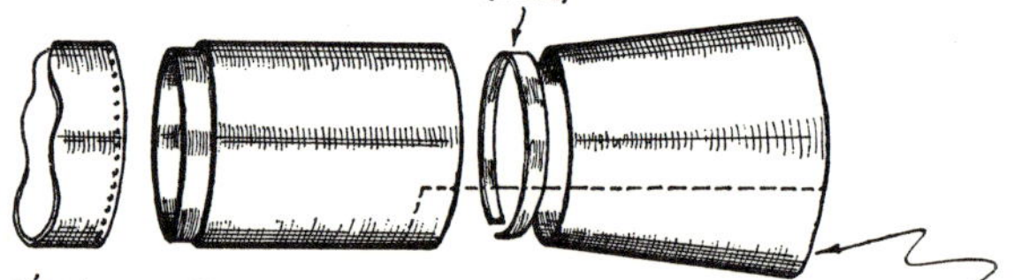

18 SEMI-TAPERED BOILERS

boiler resulting in the parallel type of boiler we know today. The Belpaire type of firebox is the invention of a Belgian engineer and bears his name, but one hears little of the mysterious Mr. Wootton who gives his name to the firebox as found on the LNER Pacifics. It was first fitted in this country to the late GNR Atlantic No. 251.

In modelling locomotive boilers, the parallel type of boiler can be turned in the lathe (fig. 17) from thick walled tube if the right diameter is obtainable. This method cannot be used for thin walled tube as the chuck will mark the same unless a piece of wood is inserted along the whole of its length. This may be alright for OO gauge but it is rather a big proposition in O gauge. The smokebox, if it is larger than the boiler can also be turned on the tube, in the same operation in which the boiler bands are turned, as shown in fig. 17.

Boilers can be made from sheet material by bending it around a round bar of steel or wood. The round bar must be slightly smaller that the diameter of the boiler required to allow for the thickness of material and to allow for the natural springiness of the metal. If this method is used a lap-joint should be made along the bottom, and the whole treated as tube for cutting out the motor aperture. Do not rely upon an edge joint as this will only break open again, unless of course boiler bands are soldered round it, but the writer does not recommend making boiler bands this way in gauge O and smaller as the metal for them cannot be obtained thin enough. When the painting stage is reached they are difficult to line out and it is much better to make them of parcel tape and line them out in the flat and stick them around the boiler in their appropriate places when the painting

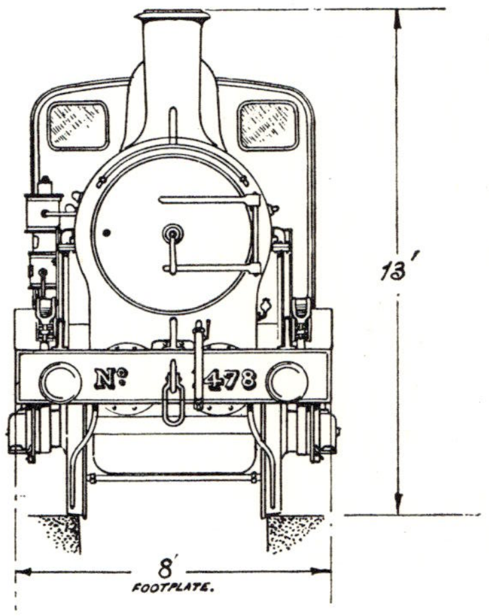

19 Frontal elevation of North Eastern Railway "Tennant" 2–4–0 of 1885

20 Side plan view of the "Tennant" locomotive, showing lining-out detail

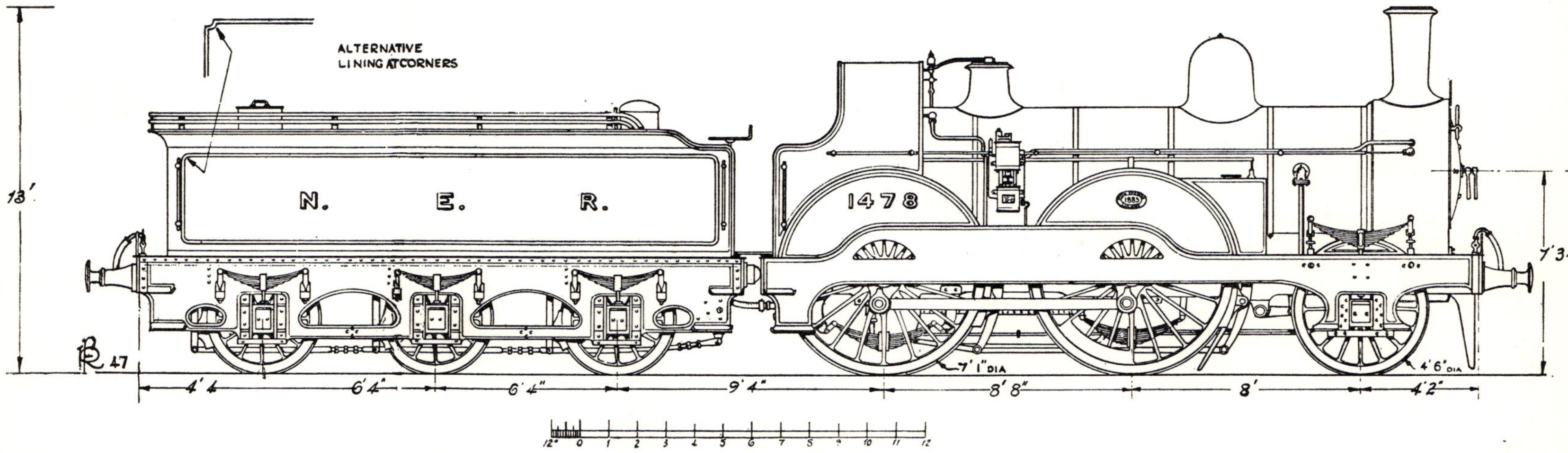

stage is reached. This will be discussed later. When turning the boiler in the lathe a piece of hardwood forced into each end is all that is required, the tube can then be supported in the back centre or the whole job turned between centres, including the smokebox if it is larger than the boiler. When all the work has been done on it, it can then be sawn at the break of the firebox, by a saw cut across the tube up to the centre line of the boiler. It is then cut from the rear of the tube with a pair of shears up to the saw cut and opened out to form the firebox. The depth of the firebox in an electrically driven model is unimportant, as it is rarely carried down below the footplate or running plate.

If the modeller has no lathe, the smokebox, if it is larger than the boiler, can be made from a separate piece of tube. Tube can be obtained in what are known as "telescopic" sizes, this means that one diameter is a sliding fit in another and they are obtainable from $\frac{3}{8}$ in. diameter up to 2 in. diameter. Do not make the mistake of buying tube that is thin because it is easier to solder. This is a mistake as it easily dents and is useless for screwing fittings into it at a later stage, such as handrail knobs, etc. It cannot be turned in the lathe and in models with a Belpaire type of firebox, and a separate smokebox the short length of tube required for the boiler will be found quite easy to solder; it has the added advantage that it is heavy and this is essential in electrically driven models.

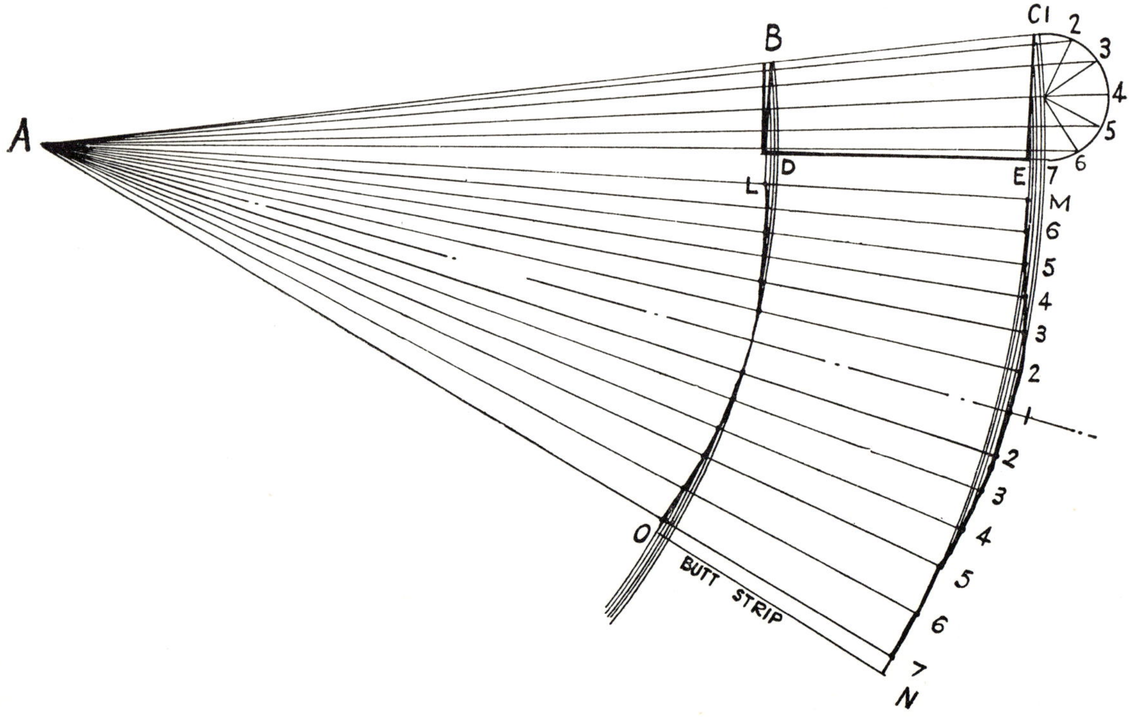

21 The development of a coned boiler.

Models which have a smokebox the same diameter as the boiler, should be made as shown in fig. 16. The smokebox really becomes a lid which is attached to the front of the boiler by means of a lip or ring soldered inside the boiler. A boiler band can be used to cover the joint or it can be filled with solder (if the fitting is not too good and filed up) and a paper band put on after painting as mentioned previously.

We come now to taper boilers. These require rather different treatment. Fig. 16 shows one method of making these. It is to split a tube along its length and to insert a wedge shaped piece along this cut which will give a tapered tube. The dimensions of the wedge shaped piece are obtained from the drawing of the loco being modelled by finding the inclination from the horizontal from the smokebox to the front of the firebox and multiplying this dimension by two. This wedge shaped piece is then soldered along the bottom of the boiler and if boiler bands are used these will hold it in place. If boiler bands are dispensed with, then it is advisable to solder a piece of metal behind the wedge piece, by holding it with a piece of wood inserted inside, and soldering the wedge from the outside. If plenty of flux is used the solder will run right through and hold it firmly, and it will not come apart when it is cut to take the motor.

Fig. 18 shows another method of making a semi-tapered boiler as fitted to GWR Bulldogs and some early American 4–4–0's. It is made in three pieces, the smokebox, the parallel part, and the tapered part. The joint ring is shown, and is soldered to the parallel part and then the tapered part is soldered to this. This type of boiler was known as the wagon-top boiler, and was the forerunner of the truly British type of boiler as developed by Mr. G. J. Churchward on the GWR. Another common method of making tapered boilers, where there are large splashers over the driving wheels, is to tip a parallel boiler forward. This is alright viewed from the side, but as one looks at a model from the top more than from the side, the discrepancy is at once apparent; there is no taper on the sides !

Another method for the same class of model is to make the tube entirely tapered top and bottom. The bottom is usually cut away to house the mechanism, so it is not seen. This results in a more satisfactory appearance from all angles. The best and the correct method is to develop the boiler from the flat as shown in fig. 21.

Taper boilers really form a section or frustum of a cone lying on its side. The development at each end on a flat plate will, therefore, be the arc described by the radius of a circle with an apex of the cone as a centre. A modification of this empirical rule is introduced by the fact that the bottom of the boiler is horizontal, therefore the maximum allowance will be on the bottom centre line of the barrel. This can be found by calculation on a drawing board of normal size. If a smaller drawing board is the only one available it can be worked out to some definite scale, or even on the kitchen table, if it is not a polished one ! The procedure is as follows: Draw figure B.C.D.E. from the drawing of the locomotive being modelled; this is the outline of the boiler. Now produce C.B. and D.E. to meet at a point A, then bisect the angle C.A.E. and draw line A.F. at H. by the line C.K. at right angles to A.F. With H. as centre and H.C. as radius draw a semicircle. Divide this into six equal parts and number them 1 to 7 and draw lines

2, 3, 4 and 5 and 6 at right angles to C.K. From A draw lines A2, 3, 4, 5, and 6.

With A as centre and AB and AC as radius scribe two arcs, and from 3 set off twelve equal parts, the sum of which is equal to the circumference of circle of radius H.C. and join the lines at point A.

If the boiler had formed a proper section of a true cone, the development L.M.N.O. would have filled all requirements, but unfortunately the cone is cut by an inclined plane at BD and CE and the relative distances between the base of the cone and the plane of intersection will require to be stopped off at the radius lines.

For all practical purposes it will be sufficiently accurate if the distances referred to are taken on the same plane, although it will be understood that the true lengths are obtained from the various points when transferred on to the base line AG. The relative distances are now marked off as shown on the development, by a small dot and these are linked up by a fair curve. It is advisable to allow an extra strip along the bottom for a lap-joint as shown in the figure. When the development is complete it may be cut out and struck on a sheet of brass or nickel silver and the metal cut to the pattern, it can then be rolled up and it will be found that it forms a perfect taper boiler, horizontal along the bottom and tapered on the top.

While still on the subject of the boiler itself, if the modeller is making an old timer, with a polished wood lagging on the boiler, obtain a piece of 1 mm. three-ply wood, and glue it to a piece of calico or old tracing cloth, the length of the piece being that of the length of the boiler, and the width being that of the circumference of the boiler. When the glue has dried, carefully scribe lines along its length, the distance apart being that of the prototype lagging, as if we were scribing the planks of a wagon. When this is done, polish with a ready mixed stain and polish obtainable at most oilmongers, to a mahogany shade. If the modeller is a carpenter by trade, then he will need no hints from me how to polish wood ! All that requires to be done now, is to wrap it round the boiler and secure with polished brass lagging bands secured with a nut and bolt underneath. The object of the calico will now be apparent. In curving it round the boiler the wood will break along the scribed lines, if they have been scribed deep enough, and a fine effect is obtained. It will look as though every piece of wood lagging is a separate piece. It need hardly be said that that is almost the last job on a historical model. If any part is left to be done after the lagging is on, it will, of course, be spoilt. The boiler fittings should be screwed on afterwards through the lagging. Wood lagged boilers were in use up to 1850.

The Firebox

The next job to be tackled is the firebox. The best and most engineer-like way of making a taper sided and taper topped box is to make a former of hardwood as follows: Mark off on the wood from the drawing of the loco. modelled the front elevation of the firebox, less the thickness of the metal being worked, the rear elevation of the firebox, again less the thickness of the metal being used. This process is shown in fig. 22. The wooden box is now cut down the middle and another piece, about ½ in. thick, inserted between them. The whole piece is now screwed together and then planed up with a small plane or chisel and spokeshave until the desired shape is formed, not forgetting the rounded corners at the front and the sloping back plate.

The metal-box can now be formed round this, and the metal should be of a fairly soft nature such as annealed brass or even copper. When the top has been formed, remove the former, take out the screws and replace the former inside. The waisted part can now be formed. When this is formed to the builder's satisfaction, the former can be removed by taking out the centre piece, when the remaining pieces of the former will fall out. Now screw the former together again, and form the front of the box. It is better to make this of copper. Do not bother at this stage to allow for the mechanism, as this portion can be cut from the front plate after the whole box has been soldered together. The back plate of the firebox is a straightforward job; just a flat plate, to which will be screwed the cab fittings. When all three pieces are formed they can be soldered together, not forgetting to place a strip of metal inside where the joint occurs at the front and sides. This is really the best method to make a modern firebox and it looks more realistic.

Another method is shown in fig. 23. This is to obtain a large piece of plate and mark off on it the side elevation of the firebox, from the drawing, the top elevation, also from the drawing, and adjoining this the other side of the box as shown in the figure. The metal plate can now be bent on the lines, and the firebox filed and cut to shape after bending. To make the front plate with the rounded top corners, a former is still recommended in O gauge, but in OO gauge it is usual to fill the top corners with solder, or little pieces of plate. This is hardly a satisfactory way as only an expert can get a nice, smoothly rounded top corner by scraping and filing. Great care must be taken to avoid digging into the metal with the scraper, as no amount of paint will cover up these scratches.

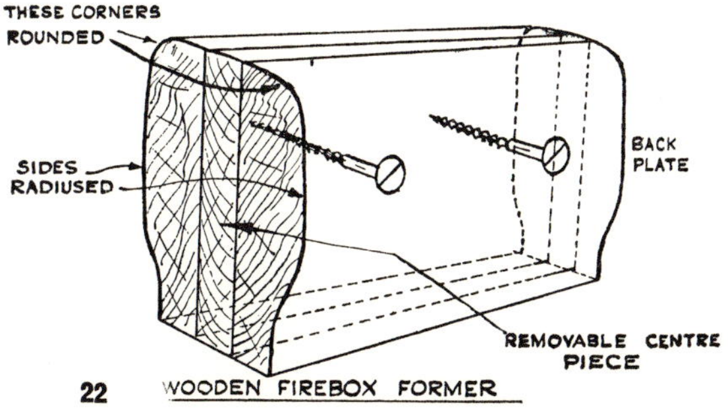

22 WOODEN FIREBOX FORMER

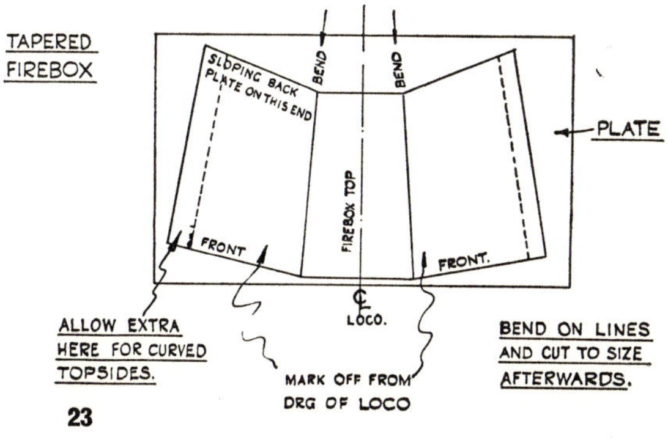

23

24

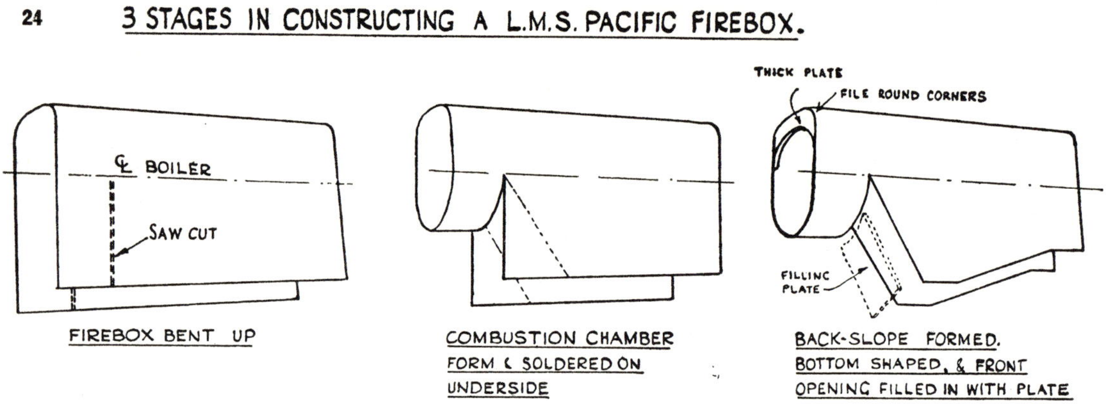

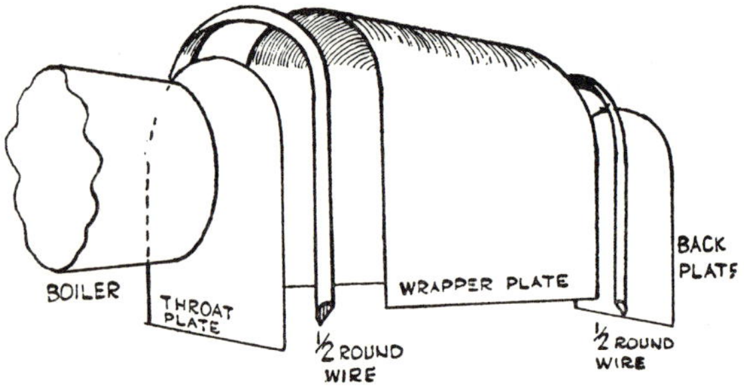

25 Semi-circular topped firebox

The *Royal Scots* of the LMS fitted with the original parallel boiler had the easiest firebox to model as the top front corners were fairly sharp, and in OO gauge it was quite sufficient just to bevel the metal. Another advantage of this boiler was that the firebox was not waisted in, and this goes for all ex-Midland and LMS locomotives of Fowler design. The ex-Great Central locos of Robinson's design also had this straight sided firebox.

Unfortunately nearly all LMS locomotives had the Great Western pattern firebox with very rounded corners, and to get a real workmanlike job it is really best to use a former for the firebox, or at least for the front of it.

Another difficult type to model is the LMS Princess Royal and Princess Coronation firebox. This is a combination of the Belpaire and Wootton type of firebox. A method of making this is shown in fig. 24. It is really treated as an elongated Belpaire in the initial stages. It is then split with a saw where the combustion chamber starts. This is marked off from the drawing. It is then bent up to a circular shape at the bottom, and soldered with a butt joint. The next process is to cut the part which is at an angle, or the hopper part of the box, and to cut and file a piece of plate to fill up the front, as shown in the figure. Now obtain a piece of thick plate and fill up the top corners and file to shape as described for the ordinary Belpaire.

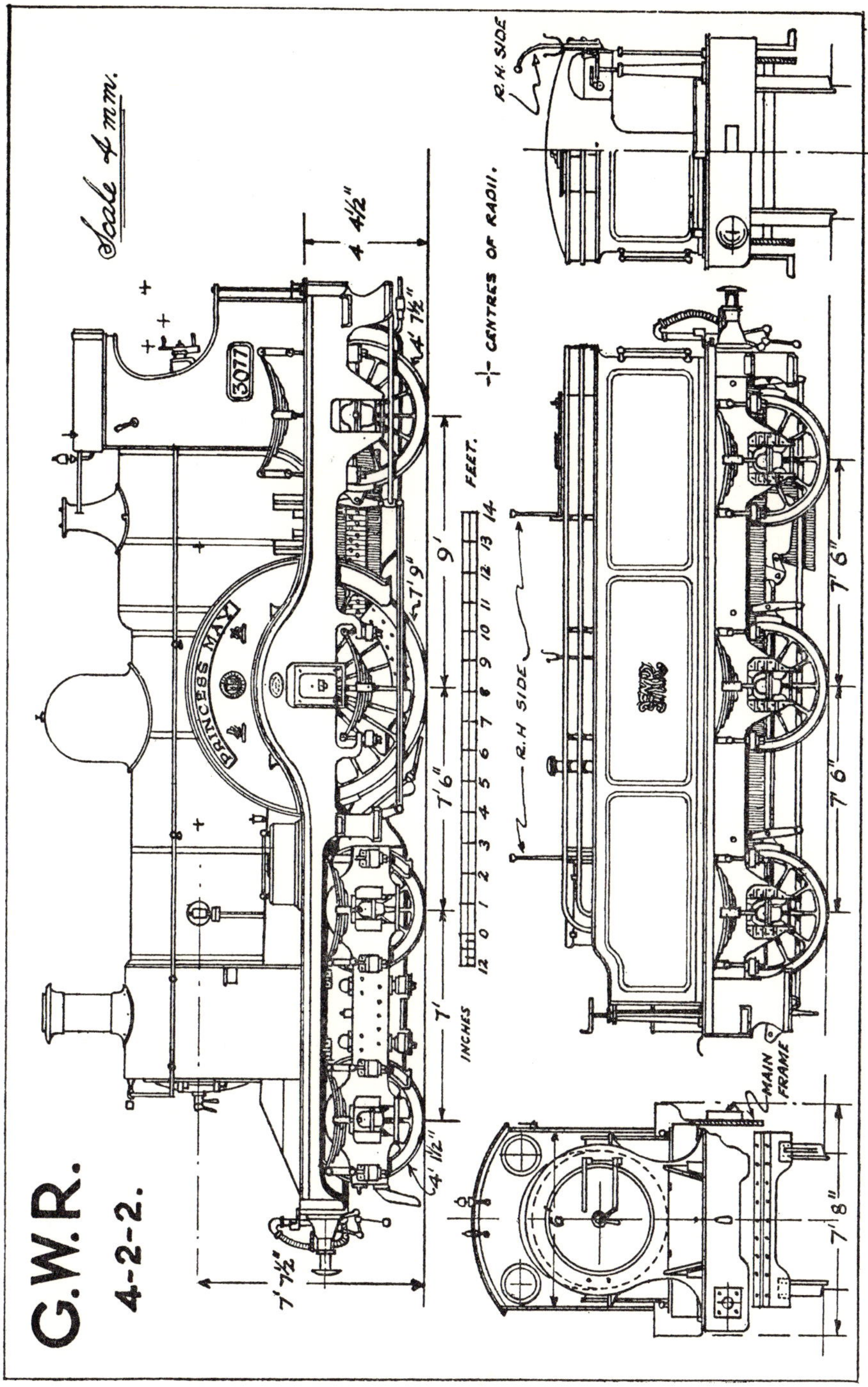

26 Great Western Railway 4-2-2 *Princess May*

The boiler is now soldered to the front and a bottom put in the box. It is now a unit, which can be cut away where the mechanism intrudes into it. The mechanism should not intrude very far into the firebox, as this is such

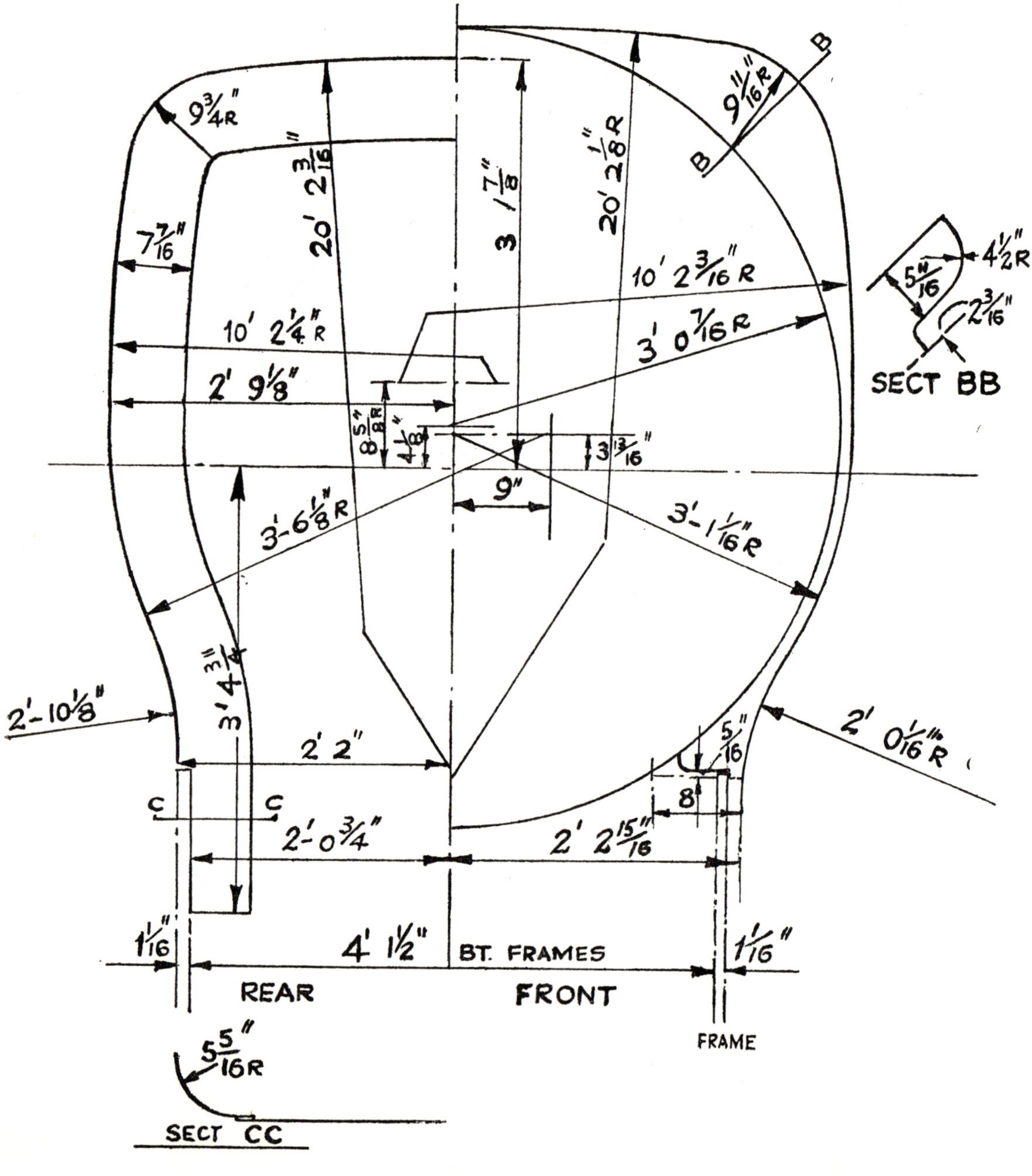

27 Firebox clothing and moulding for LMS 5P5F locomotives

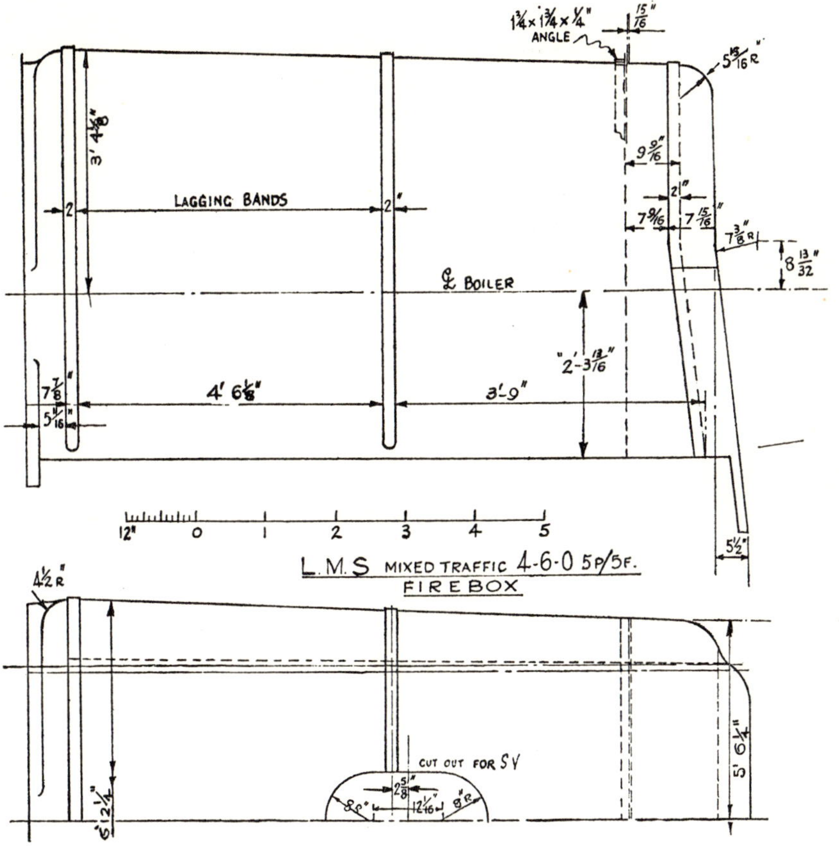

28 LMS mixed traffic 4–6–0 5P5F firebox: scale $\frac{3}{4}$":1'

a long engine, and the driving wheels are fairly well placed forward. The foregoing method is suitable for both O and OO gauges.

Those who make their boilers from tube and sheet can make their firebox from a parallel sheet of brass with a semi-circular top. The construction of such a firebox is shown in fig. 25. The half-round wire is polished, so be careful to get no solder on the outside; it should be soldered from the inside.

The throat plate is shown as a complete plate in the sketch, but it will be obvious that this will have to be cut away when the firebox and boiler are soldered together, in order to house the mechanism, as most of the firebox will be required for this; the boiler being rather small.

The drawings in figs. 27 and 28 give all the necessary radii and measurements for constructing an accurate representation of the LMS Stanier mixed traffic locomotive firebox.

These drawings are also useful for modellers of all GWR engines using this type of firebox, the builder making allowances for differences in length to suit the locomotive. The drawings closely approximate to the Castle type of firebox. Note that the top of the box is slightly arched and not flat as it is sometimes seen in models of modern LMS and GWR prototypes.

The Smokebox

The next item on our boiler is to make the smokebox. These are of two types—the all-circular type supported on a saddle, and the shaped or waisted type. Illustrated by fig. 29, a smokebox of the latter type is quite a revelation in the amount of detail that can be incorporated on the outside. This is a drawing of the ex-GER 4–4–0 locomotive *Claud Hamilton*, and shows the original condition of this handsome engine. The way to make this type of smokebox is to make a back and a front to the drawing less the thickness of the wrapper-plate. This wrapper-plate should be made the full length as shown on the drawing and the front and back soldered inside it. Do not attempt to make it the other way, *i.e.*, try to bend a piece of metal to correspond exactly with the front and back plates. It can be done, but unless the modeller is an expert sheet metal-worker and a careful fitter, it will be found quite a job to bend metal exactly where one wants it to bend.

When making the front plate, unless it is desired to make the door open, it can be made solid. The back may also be made solid and the boiler butt-soldered to it, and a ring of half-round brass put round the boiler at this end where it joins the smokebox. The boiler can also be forced into the smokebox in small models and a piece of plate put underneath and the whole soldered together. Do not forget to put a back in the smokebox, as nothing looks worse than a smokebox open at the back as is sometimes seen on models.

The all-circular type of smokebox calls for little comment as this is merely a piece of tube, a slide fit on the boiler as mentioned previously. It should be made of thick tube if the modeller has a lathe and the brass ornamental beading at the rear can be turned on it. If no lathe is available this beading can be filed on the back of a piece of tube of the same thickness as the boiler, by bevelling it, soldering it to the boiler and then getting another piece of tube, and sliding it on to this. Care must be taken to get the right thicknesses of tube otherwise the smokebox will be too large in diameter. Another reason that the front and back plates of a waisted smokebox should be soldered inside the wrapper, is, that often the wrapper-plates incorporate rivets, and this also applies to the circular smokebox, therefore, it is better to make the ornamental beading from a piece of tube and wrap the riveted wrapper round this, leaving sufficient of the tube inside to show the brass beading.

We have now discussed the firebox, boiler and smokebox. There now remains the detailing of these components. There are quite a lot of details on the firebox, if they are made properly. There are the washout plug covers, and the staybolt holes alongside each side of the firebox. Firstly, the washout plug covers; these are usually little domed excrescences covering them. Make sure they are the same both sides of the engine. Some locomotives had them staggered each side of the top, this was to make sure that the water used for washing out the boiler went inside the boiler and not out through the opposite plug, but the majority of locos have them opposite each other. There are several ways of making these. One is to make a little press tool, one half with a cupped shaped recess in it, and the other with bump on it. When these are made obtain a piece of very thin metal and press it between the two dies. It can be trimmed afterwards. Another way to make them in models of OO gauge is to form them with a hot soldering iron, by putting a small dab of flux where the little cover is to go and carefully touching it with the iron, and a little blob will form. Practice on a piece of spare metal at first and the knack of doing it will soon come. Yet another way is to solder a piece of brass plate about $\frac{1}{16}$ in. thick, and roughly the size of the plug, on to a piece of rod, and file it to shape in the vice; it can then be melted off, and soldered to the firebox. It will be already tinned from being on the rod, and should solder easily. To make these super detail a little hinge should be soldered one side and a little knob at the other (a pin head will do), as these covers are hinged on the prototype, and turn in a lateral plane to get at the plug underneath.

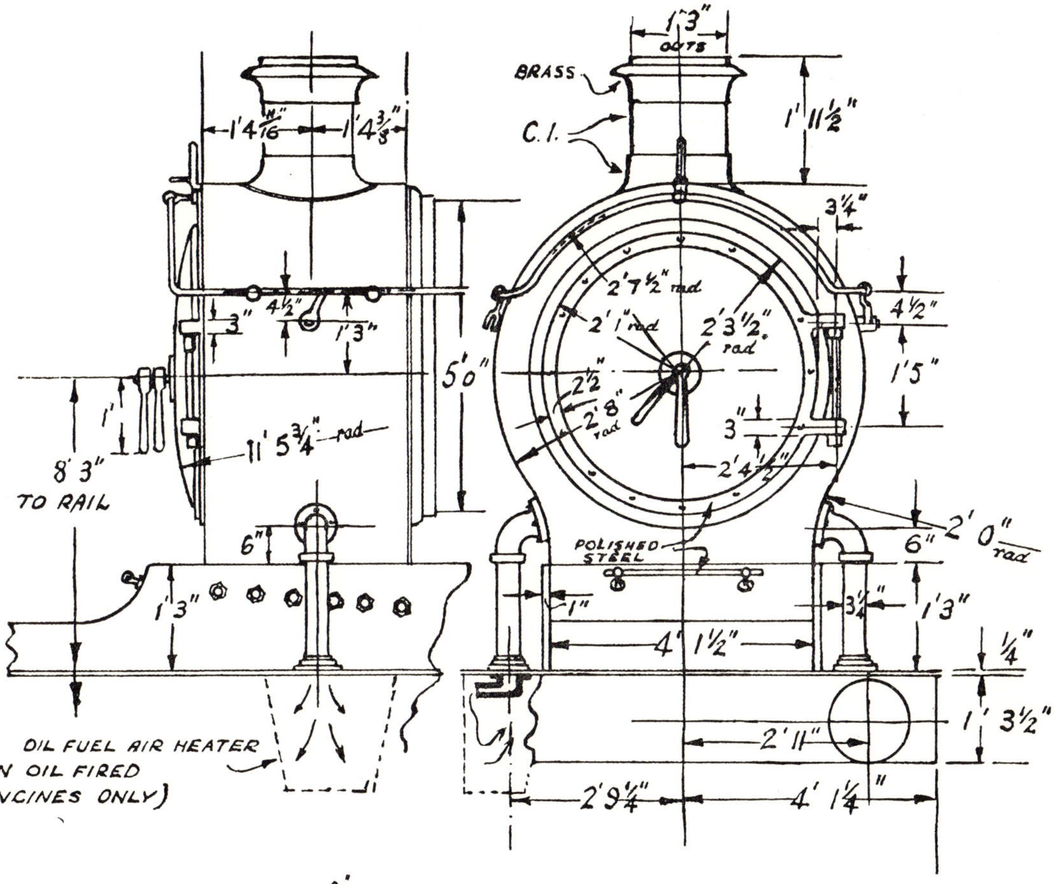

29 Great Eastern Railway 4-4-0 loco standard firebox

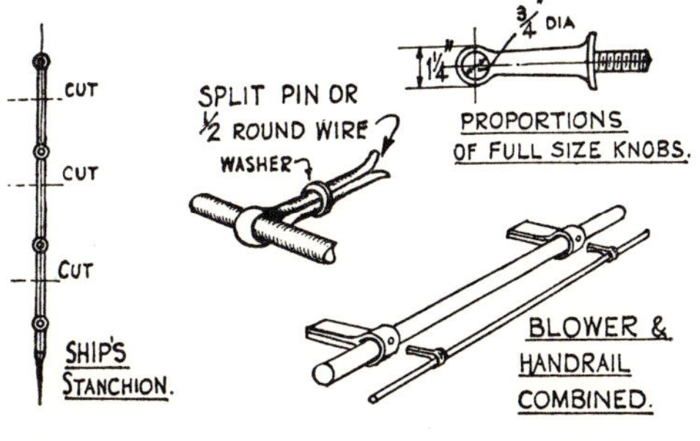

30 Handrail knobs

Next we come to the staybolt holes in the sides of the firebox. These should be made as follows. Drill them carefully with a small drill (say No. 60) and taking care to get them all in alignment nothing looks worse than these holes to be out of alignment. The drilling and marking out should be done with the former inside as there is a risk of denting the sides of the firebox, but if the punching is carefully done there should be no risk in this direction. When the holes have been drilled with the small drill, obtain a piece of plate to go behind these holes and tack this in position. Drill through again with the small drill into this plate. When this has been done remove the plate from behind, and open out the holes already drilled in the sides of the box with a drill that has been dulled, or needs sharpening. The reason for this will be apparent when drilling is started. A small burr will form round the hole, and this is just what we want, as there is a beading round these holes on a full sized engine.

Now we have the strip with the small holes in it to operate on. Insert in the holes a piece of square wire, or some 16 BA bolts, and solder them in. The piece of plate is now soldered behind the holes in the firebox, and we have a real super detail firebox. Is not this better than just a row of holes in the side of the firebox? Very often one can see through these to the other side, which is, of course, all wrong. When the painting stage is reached do not paint those holes over with the body colour, or the nuts will be gummed up. These are carefully picked out with black. Remember that it is a model of a steam loco that we are building and the firebox holes should be as accurate as any other part of the loco.

On GWR and some LMS locos there are two holes drilled in the top of the boiler near the firebox and also two on the top near the smokebox. On the real engines these holes are to ventilate the boiler clothing underneath.

The next item is handrail knobs. There is plenty of scope for improvement here, as there are far too many models with oversized handrail knobs. In OO gauge these can be made from half-round brass wire 1/64th wide, or they can be made from 1/32nd split pins. If this is unobtainable ordinary round wire can be used, and if the handrail is soldered in place, by touching each knob with the soldering iron, a little knob will be formed, do not use too much solder or the job will be spoilt. For O gauge, the writer's method of making handrail knobs is to turn them in the lathe, to the proper size, but it is realised that not everyone has a lathe. For these folk, there is the method of using ships handrail stanchions of the three ball, or four ball type. It will be apparent when these are purchased, that the top ball will make one handrail knob, but cutting it below the knob according to the length of knob required, and threading it 10 BA, and screwing it into the boiler, or if the boiler is too thin for this, it can be soldered on the back, inside the boiler. The half-round wire method can be used for O gauge, but it is correct to solder a washer along its length somewhere according to the length of knob required.

On a tapered boiler these handrail knobs are different lengths. Fig. 30 shows various methods of making handrail knobs. For the blower pipe, if this is outside the boiler the same methods can be used for the knobs of this as for the handrail, but larger in proportion. Some locos have the blower pipe and handrail combined such as the GWR and early LNWR engines. In this case the blower pipe is soldered in to its knobs and then it is drilled on top of each knob with a fine drill and smaller knobs inserted in this to take the handrail (see fig. 30).

The next item we have to make is the smokebox door. If it is desired to incorporate smokebox fittings, a hole will have to be cut in the front of our waisted type of smokebox. This is where our little end mills mentioned in the chapter on tools will come in handy. A ring of holes can be cut with a drill as close together as possible inside the marked line of the smokebox door. If the drill holes are close enough the piece can be almost knocked out. Now use the end mill to smooth off the jagged edges, and we will have a nice circular hole. If it is not desired to incorporate smokebox fittings, the door can be soldered direct to the front of the smokebox as mentioned earlier, or it can be screwed on. If the front plate is thick enough to take a tapped hole, the screw can be an imitation of the handwheel or handles on the front of the door.

The door itself can be made in several ways, but try to avoid using commercial ones if at all possible. It is a great temptation to use these but the writer has yet to see one that looks neat enough. They are spoilt by the handwheel, or handle on its front being cast on the door. This cannot be helped owing to die-making difficulties. If this type of door is used then file off the imitation fittings in front, and make these separately. One way of making the door oneself is to turn it from a brass blank of sufficient thickness to obtain the dishing effect. This can be obtained from the side elevation of the loco being modelled. Brass blanks can be obtained from most metal merchants, or model suppliers. For the circular smokebox, another brass blank will be required to form the ring which fits in the front of the circular

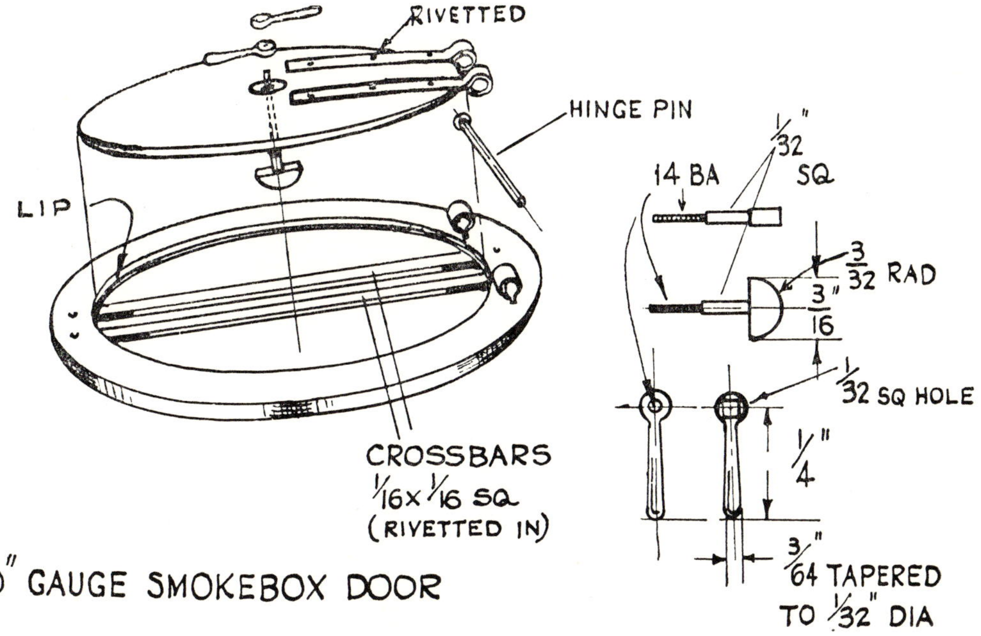

31 "O" GAUGE SMOKEBOX DOOR

smokebox. This ring should be turned with a lip inside for the door to seat on (see fig. 31). When both these are turned and finished they should be laid on the bench, the door dropped in place and the hinges, fashioned from strip metal, soldered to the door. Two hasps are made from the same strip and soldered underneath the straps on the circular ring. Insert a pin through the lot and the smokebox door is complete and will open if required.

For smokeboxes not desired to open, the door and ring can be turned from a larger disc of metal all in one piece and the hinges of course will be merely dummies. If no lathe is available, smokebox doors can be made from annealed brass sheet and formed on a soft block of wood with the ball end of a hammer. When it is sufficiently dished it can be filed all over the front to remove the hammer marks and then polished with sand, or emery paper. It can then be treated as a turned door for fitting the hinges. Another source of smokebox doors is the watchmaker's junk-box. The writer has seen several nice smokebox doors made from the backs of wrist-watches, providing they are not too domed. If they are chromium plated there may be difficulty in soldering the strips on the door unless the plating is scraped off.

When making an opening door it is advisable to rivet the hinges as well as soldering them on to the door as it makes a much stronger job. If the modeller has been a little careless and the door does not open quite far enough, someone else is sure to strain the hinges by opening the door too far. It is a good plan to incorporate the safety-chain found on full size locos to prevent the door hinges being strained when the heavy door swings back. On the GER loco door illustrated by fig. 29 it will be seen that it has a polished steel ring upon which is the hinge. The GCR 4–4–2 illustrated earlier also has this type of door. This should be made if possible of stainless steel sheet, or if not available, of nickel silver. Carefully mark out the ring and its hinge, leaving sufficient of the hinge part to bend up into a ring to fit over the pin. When this is finished the centre can be cut out by drilling and filing out or with a fret saw and the whole soldered to the door. It can be riveted as well if the door is to open. Another way to do this if the builder is at all worried whether he can cut the centre out without bending the ring, is to cut out the centre of the ring from the sheet, solder the door behind this hole and file up the outside, afterwards using the edge of the door as a guide. Be careful not to file the edge of the door, and don't file through the hinges! This type of door was found on nearly all early GWR locos with the addition of the hinges.

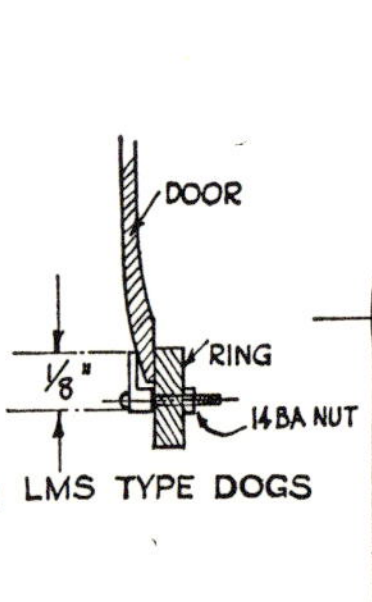

32 LMS TYPE DOGS

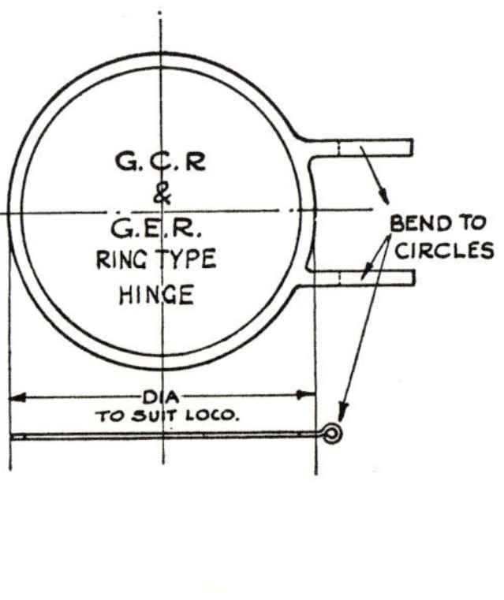

Boiler Fittings

Another source of smokebox doors for OO gauge is the wife's button box! Usually in this will be found some buttons covered with material. These are generally metal and consist of two parts—the domed top and a flat back upon which is incorporated the loop for sewing to the garment. Take out this loop and plate—it is only pushed in—and leave the domed shaped portion which will make quite a nice looking smokebox door.

Other types of this button, more domed than usual, will also make a nice water pick-up dome for a tender, but more of that anon.

Before leaving the subject, it is as well to mention that if the smokebox door has a lot of detail incorporated such as number plates, lamp brackets, etc. and is not intended to open, the fixing dogs, as on LMS earlier types of locomotives, should be put on before the door is fitted to the loco. It is much easier to juggle with the door alone than with the whole boiler.

The writer cannot ever recall a small electrically driven loco with an opening door having fixing dogs such as the LMS used, as every one of these has to be undone before the door will open and that is not very often, we should imagine, unless it is a steam model. Even then if the door opens the dogs are usually dummy and come away with the door! Of course, this is all wrong, but luckily the LMS dispensed with this type of fixing and returning to the purely British type of door with straps and hinges. The fixing dog method of closing the door is almost universal abroad, and, admittedly, it does ensure an airtight door! These dogs work on an inclined plate similar to a ship's watertight door, but on a locomotive the dishing of the door, for want of a better term, automatically provides the inclined plane and the farther they are pushed over the tighter the door becomes. These dogs are shown by fig. 32. While we are still on the smokebox we may as well deal with the inside fittings, as quite a lot of modellers these days like to put smokebox fittings in.

If the smokebox has been made as a separate unit, and before it is fitted to the boiler, obtain a piece of perforated zinc as sold for meat safes or ventilators. Cut this to a circle and solder inside the rear end of the smokebox; this will make a fine representation of the tube plate. Yes, we know the tubes do not go to the top of the boiler, but do not forget that the superheater header goes across the front of the tube plate at the top, so these holes will be covered up. Fig. 33 shows the inside of a GWR King smokebox. The Castle smokebox is exactly the same, and the LMS Princess Royal and other LMS 4-cylinder locos have the same type of fittings. The flanges shown on the pipes in the model can be made circular, as this is quite good pipe fitting practice, although the GWR and some other lines employ heart shaped flanges.

If a full set of fittings is going to be put in the model it is best to build all these up on the zinc plate before it is soldered to the smokebox, and when complete take great care to get them truly vertical with the chimney. The chimney should be fitted last of all and it should have a petticoat pipe.

Various types of boiler fittings dimensioned to full size dimensions will be illustrated in this series and from these can be prepared drawings to any scale the builder is working to. Great importance must be given to getting these right as if they are not, the whole character of the model is lost. It is fairly safe to assume, at least in the writer's experience, that only about five out of every ten models have the boiler fittings of this kind correct, and I think judges at exhibitions will bear me out in this.

It is simply because insufficient study has been given to the subject and probably from lack of drawings so it is hoped that those given will com-

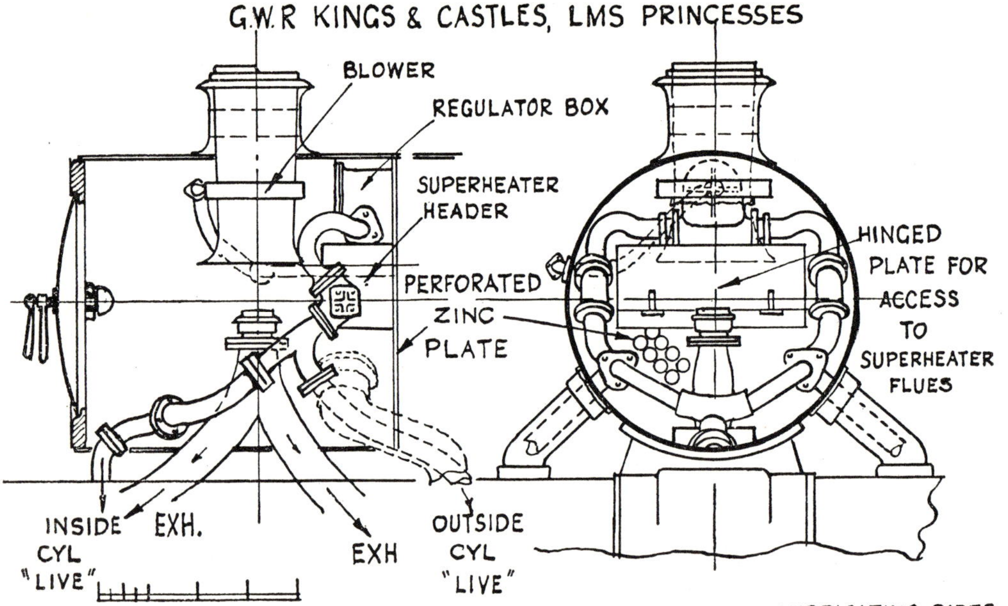

33 SMOKEBOX 4 CYL LOCOS (SIMPLIFIED)

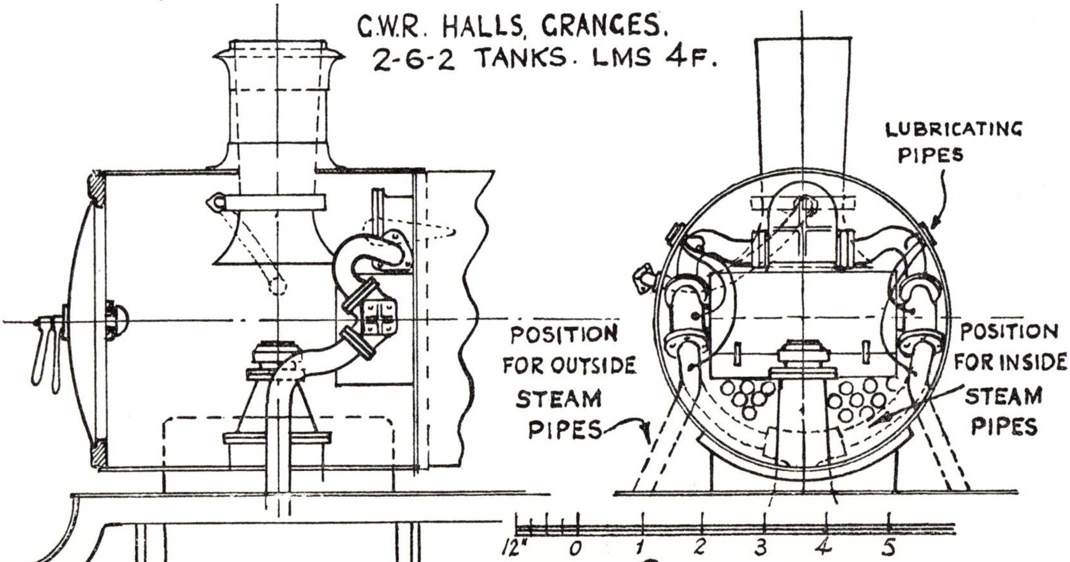

34 SMOKEBOX 2 CYL LOCOS

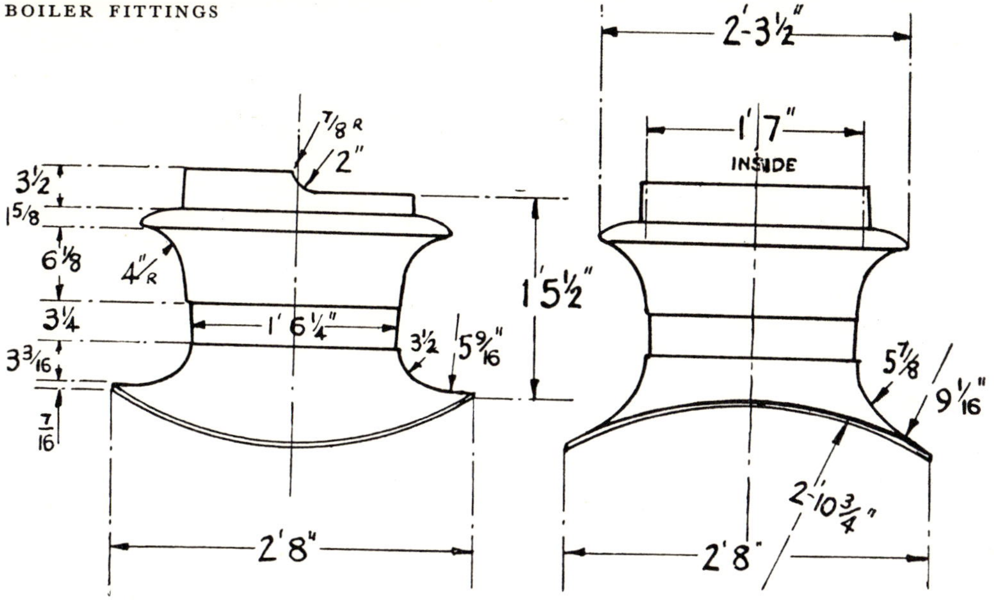

38 GWR chimneys—4700 class 2-8-0 mixed traffic loco

pensate for the latter reason. In the chapter on tools, it was recommended that a little jig be made to the drawing of the boiler fittings being made, and that this be offered up to the work while it is being turned. I am afraid that a lathe is really necessary to turn boiler fittings, and when we have discussed the little differences between the various types of boiler fittings illustrated, instructions will be given for turning them the easiest way. I am very much indebted to Mr. F. C. Hambleton for his collaboration in preparing several of the boiler fitting drawings and also to Mr. Kenneth Leech and the GWR. Every effort has been made to get them accurate, and to prevent anyone rushing into print taking me to task because this or that chimney or dome is too short or too long or was not fitted to this or that particular loco, let me hasten to add that they were the standard designs of the locomotive engineers mentioned. It was quite possible that they were lengthened or shortened to suit different designs; this is particularly applicable to the LNWR.

When modelling them it is the top and the bottom that matters, the bit between these extremities was lengthened or shortened to suit the loco, as shown in the drawing of the Stirling cast iron chimney. Those fitted to the earlier 8 ft. singles were longer than those fitted to the later ones, likewise the later chimneys had a modification introduced by Mr. H. A. Ivatt. The latter gentleman's chimney is illustrated in the chapter on jigs and tools. It will be noted that the drawing of the LNWR chimney has an undercut below the top lip. This should be incorporated in the model as it gives the characteristic sharp edge to the top beading. Opposite to this is the Stroudley chimney which had an undercut on the top lip. Little things like this are worth making in the model as they are obvious, and the larger the scale the more they will be missed if they are omitted.

The largest chimneys ever fitted in this country were on the old Broad gauge 8 ft. singles, and it will no doubt surprise readers to know that the polished copper top of this chimney was no less than 3 ft. in diameter! It was in perfect proportion with the rest of the engine. The GWR always fitted the largest chimneys, with the exception, of course, of the modern double

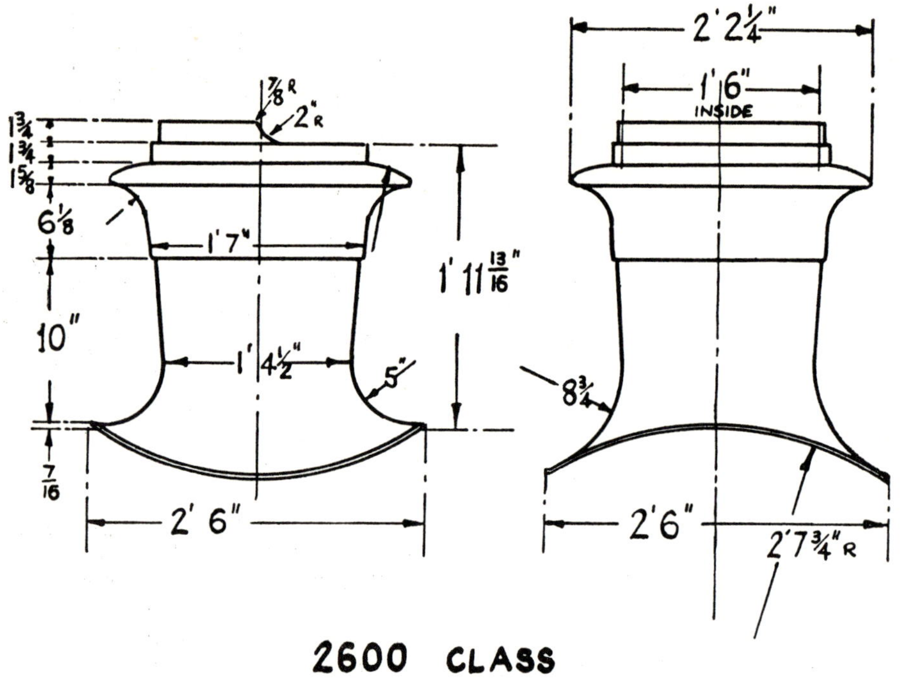

35 GWR chimneys—"Aberdare" class 2–6–0

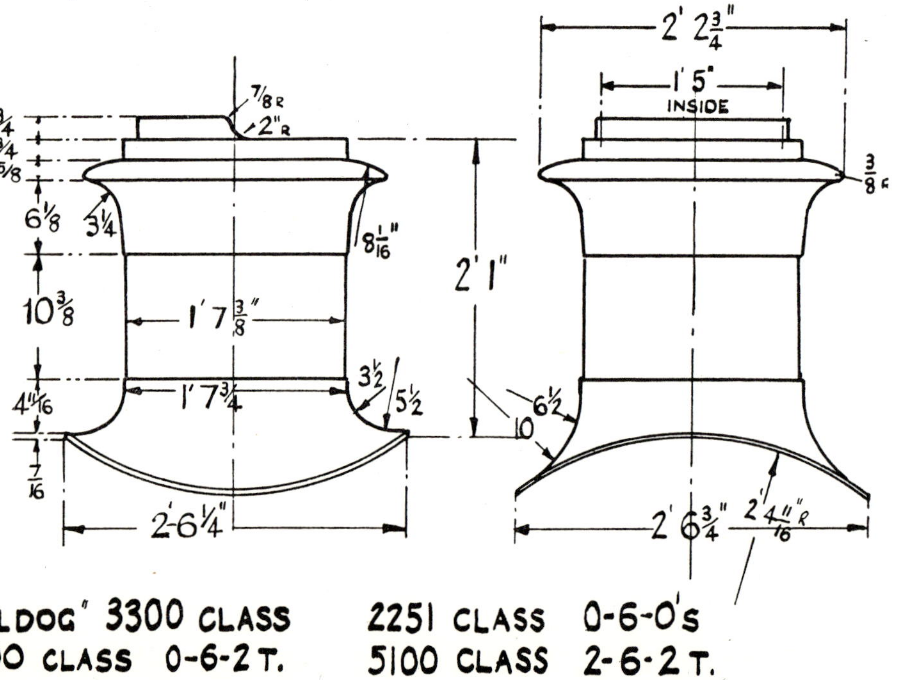

36 GWR chimneys

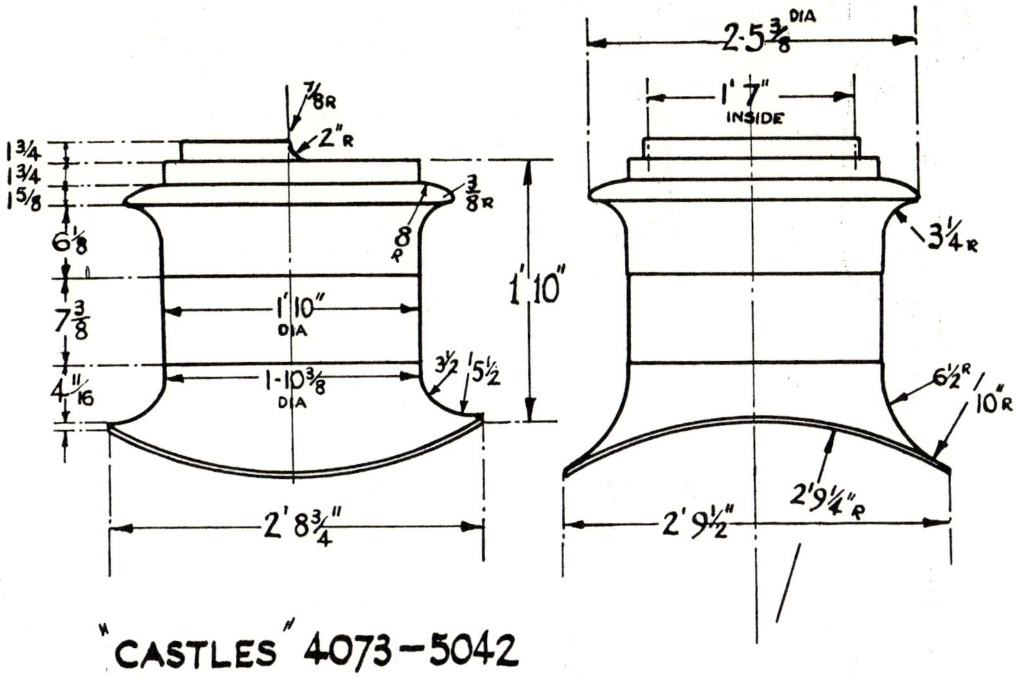

37 GWR chimneys—"Castle" class 4–6–0 to 5042

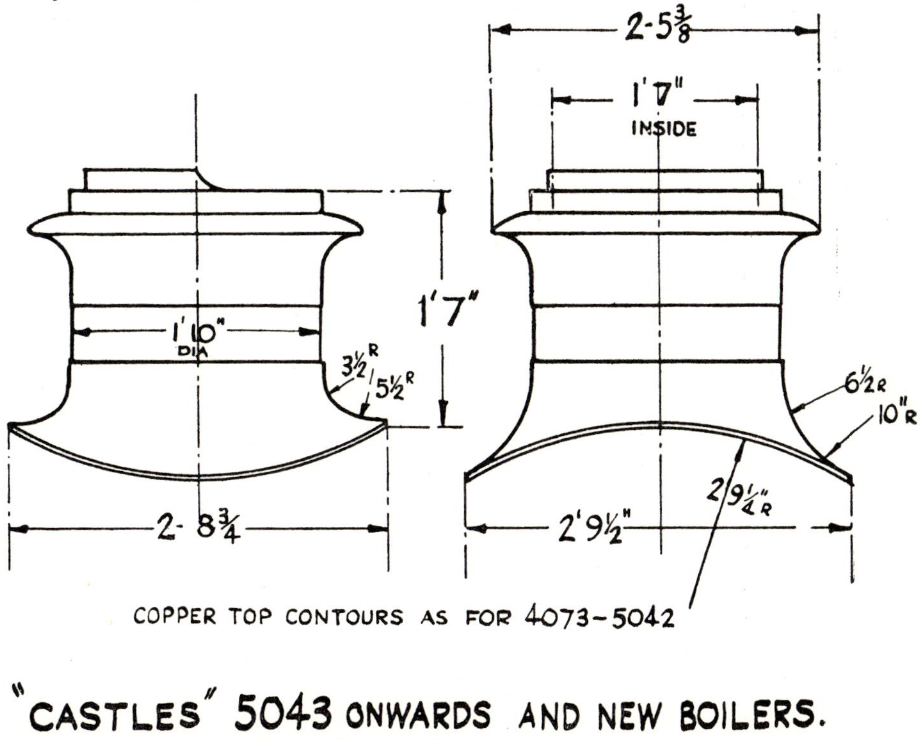

38 Chimneys on "Castle" class from 5043, and locos with new boiler

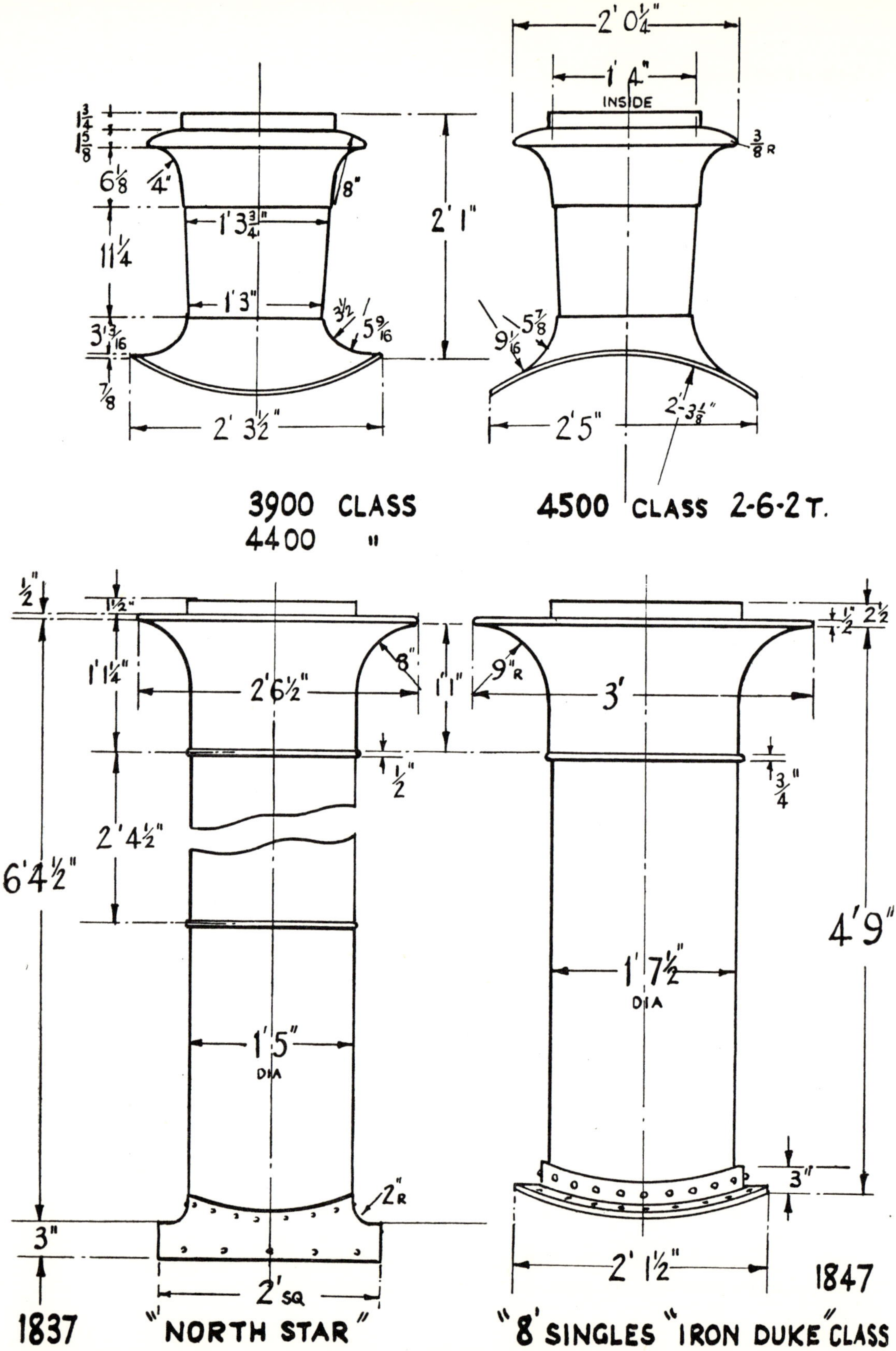

39 GWR chimneys—3900, 4400, and 4500 classes 2–6–2T; *North Star*, 8ft singles and "Iron Duke" class

chimney, and some dustbins that are fitted to the Nelsons and Schools on the Southern Railway. In passing it may be mentioned that there is nothing new under the sun—the method of fitting these large chimneys on the Southern is the same as that used on the old Broad gauge loco, that is angle iron round the base.

Particular note must be taken when turning domes and valve covers to get the curves correct. There were as many as five different radii on the GNR Stirling valve cover, and four on the Midland Johnson valve cover. Domes especially were very seldom parallel sided, as a glance at the drawings will show. In the case of the domes fitted with the Salter spring balance safety valve, it will be seen that these must be modelled properly to get the character of the fittings. Using pins and bits of wire simply will not do. They should be entirely turned in the lathe from the fitting on the boiler clothing to the adjusting nuts on the balances. The latter must look capable of being adjusted even if they are dummies ! The drawing of the Ramsbottom valve fitted to the GER engines will explain why there is always a dome shaped casing with a flat top underneath the valve casing proper. On LNWR casings it should be noted that these had tapered sides and they also had oiling holes in the centre to oil the centre spring anchor. Coming to the GWR chimneys, some of these drawings have been published before by Major Sparkes, Col. Templer, Sir Francis Layland-Barratt and others, so there is really no excuse for getting a GWR chimney wrong, but somehow or other some of us do ! I do not think a complete selection has been published before. The tall cast iron chimney is scattered indiscriminately among the Pannier tanks, with the parallel type, so either type is correct, but make sure that the No. of the loco corresponds with the chimney fitted. This also is true of the two corresponding lengths of the Castle chimney. These locos as they go in for a full overhaul emerge with the short chimney, which to the writer's mind, vastly improve the Castles. It makes them look bigger than they really are.

The Stanier Chimney (illustrated, fig. 40) has a marked GWR flavour and was probably derived from the latter Railway when Sir William Stanier became CME of the LMS. Here again the *top* and *bottom* curves are constant, only varying in height, as a glance at the two drawings of the standard 2–6–2 tank and the class 5 mixed traffic loco chimneys will show.

The Ross Pop safety valve (fig. 41) as fitted to the class 5 4–6–0s on the LMS is also illustrated, and it will be seen that there is considerably more than two bits of wire, which is the usual method of making these in the smaller gauges. The drawing of the LMS top feed (fig. 42) is also of interest as it gives all the necessary radii. It will be seen that the pipe to the injectors is not entirely outside the boiler as was usual on the GWR, but is sunk inside the lagging and covered only with a slightly curved piece of strip. Some of the later LMS types have reverted to the GWR style in that the pipe is quite outside the boiler and covered with the GWR type of curved cover half way round the boiler. The later LMS top feed cover was also slightly different in that it is domed right across, and is still more like the GWR type.

Now we come to the method of turning some of these fittings. It is the writer's usual method to turn these with the top of the chimney facing the chuck and the bottom of the fitting facing the tailstock. First find a piece of

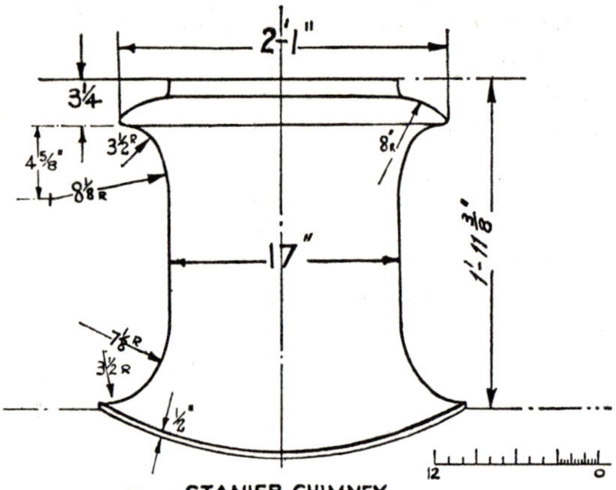

40 STANIER CHIMNEY
L.M.S. 2-6-2 TANK

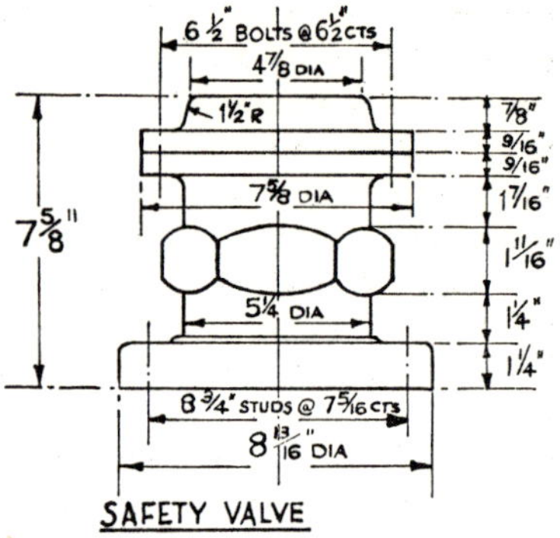

41 Ross pop safety valve for LMS 2-cyl mixed traffic loco

brass or copper rod, according to whether the chimney is plain or has a copper top, of slightly *over* the diameter of the bottom of the chimney or dome, set up in the tool-holder a bar of steel to act as a hand-rest, and turn the chimney entirely by means of hand tools. As this type of turning may come rather awkward to some it is better to experiment on a few pieces of scrap before the actual job is commenced. When the operator thinks he can tackle the job successfully, then measure off the drawing with a pair of dividers the distance from the extreme top to the extreme bottom of the chimney in the *side elevation*, and *not* in the front elevation, otherwise the chimney will be too short if the front elevation is used as a basis (do not forget it has to be saddled over the boiler).

Having arrived at this dimension, subtract from the height half the distance between the front and side elevations of the bottom. The reason for this will be apparent when the writer's method of saddling these is used, i.e., tapping on the top with a hammer over a piece of steel the diameter of the boiler. It will be seen during this process that the front and rear of the bottom of the chimney will curve upwards and the sides will curve downwards, therefore the fitting will be the correct height when it is saddled. Now having got this dimension with a pair of odd-legs or dividers, while the lathe is running scribe a line from the bottom of the bar right round it. This line will represent the top of the chimney. It need hardly be said that the bar must be faced off before this operation is carried out. Dimension lines representing the top lip, top flange, top beading, etc., can now all be scribed on the bar, and there only remains to go ahead and worry it to shape with the hand tools. Make sure the hand-rest in the tool post is a little below centre, and the hand tool must be worked at centre height, do not, in your hurry to get the job done, take great bites out of the metal by holding the cutting edge too far below centre otherwise it will dig in and the fitting will be ruined. Make haste slowly is the best advice one can give in hand-turning.

The shape of the hand tool is important, the writer usually uses a round nosed tool throughout, only using a parting type of tool for the top lip and parting off. Nothing has been said so far about the internal diameter, as this depends on the modeller and his method of fitting the chimney or dome to the model. Some prefer to screw them on and others prefer to solder. The writer uses the soldered method. In the screw-on method, it is only necessary to drill a hole the tapping size of the screw used, and when the chimney is parted off this hole can be opened out the full bore for so far as the modeller wishes, while being held on a mandrel, and the remainder of the hole tapped with the fitting screw. In the soldered method, the full bore may be drilled out before the outside is shaped. In both cases the bell-mouthed aperture of the bottom must be turned out either before or after the outside is formed.

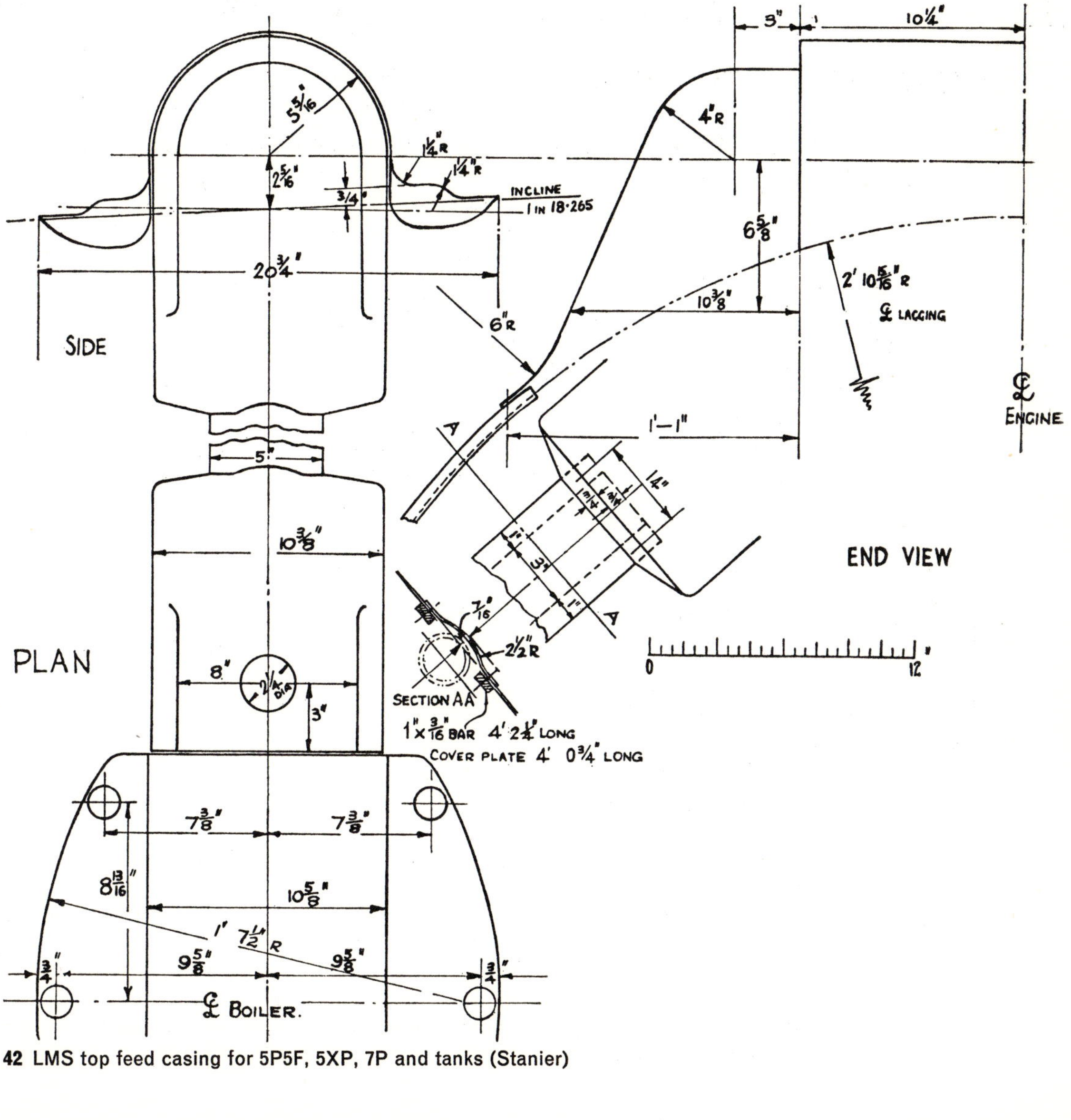

42 LMS top feed casing for 5P5F, 5XP, 7P and tanks (Stanier)

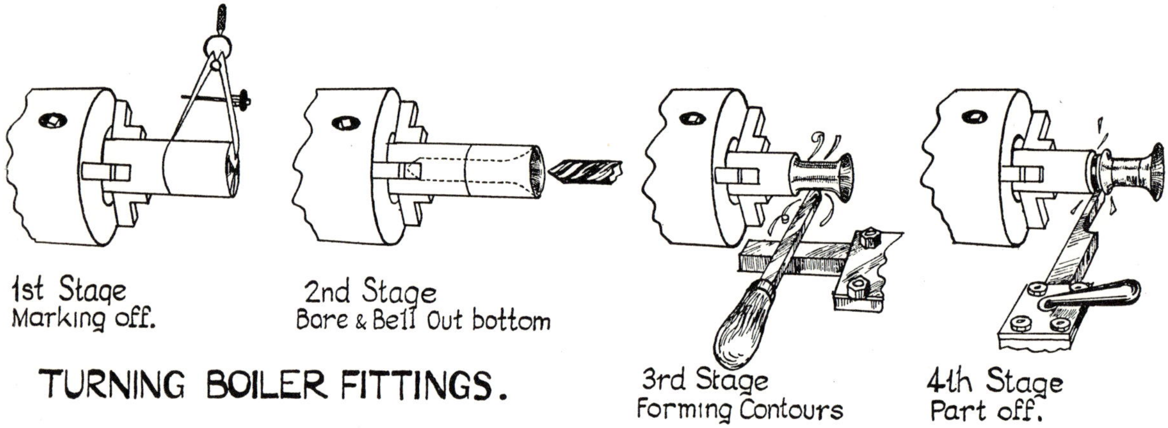

43 Stages in turning boiler fittings

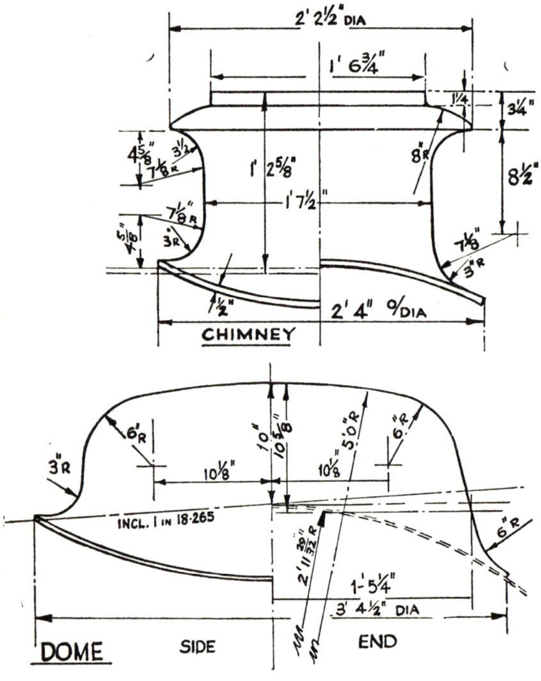

44 Chimney and dome measurements for LMS 2-cylinder mixed traffic locomotive

It does not matter which way it is done, but if the bell-mouthed aperture is turned out first, great care must be taken not to go through this with the outside turning tool, otherwise the bottom will fall off and you will have to start again.

The writer has never had the misfortune to do this, so I do not think it will happen to others. We have a sort of sixth sense which tells us when the bottom is getting too thin. The illustrations will, I think, make all this clear.

The next item is to saddle the fitting to the boiler. To do this, first anneal the fitting by holding it in a bunsen flame for a few seconds until all the brightness has faded away. Take care not to hold the fitting long enough

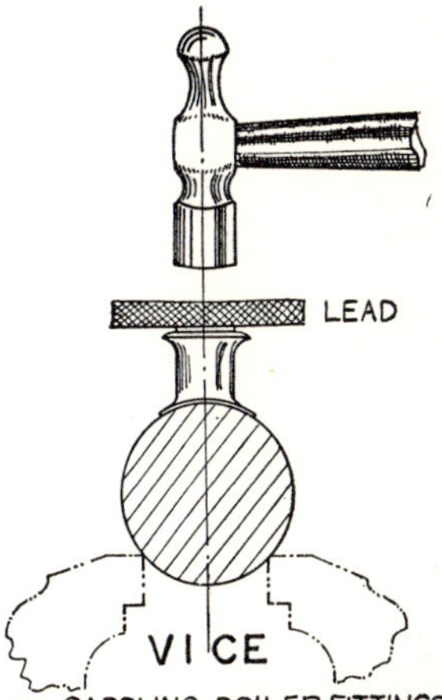

45 SADDLING BOILER FITTINGS

in the flame to get it red hot; this is not necessary. Now obtain a piece of steel or brass bar the same diameter as the smokebox, and place it in the half open jaws of the vice. There is no need to screw it in the vice. Now obtain a piece of lead or hard wood, place it on the top of the chimney and gently tap with a hammer until the chimney or dome seats itself over the former. Take care to tap it directly on the top, and in a straight downwards direction, otherwise the fitting will saddle itself crookedly.

If the operator is at all afraid of being unable to strike with the hammer straight up and down, then a peg, the diameter of the internal bore of the chimney, can be forced into the former, and the chimney placed on that, then proceed as before. This cannot, of course, be done with domes unless they are very tall, so care will have to be taken to get them saddled straight. With a taper boiler this is not so important as if they are crooked then it will be corrected when placed on the boiler the right way round.

Safety valves are a plain, straightforward turning job and should not need any explanation, with the possible exception of the Ramsbottom type, which had a domed shaped cover at the bottom. This is treated as a dome, The Stirling, Midland, and early GWR type are treated as chimneys when it comes to turning and saddling them. It may be stated that the foregoing method of turning and seating boiler fittings can be used up to 1 in. scale. The writer has turned chimneys for this gauge, with perfect success, so why go to the bother of hand filing the base for hours to get it saddled on the boiler?

I have often been told that my method of making boiler fittings is not possible in the larger gauges because they never have that "close to the boiler" look of the full sized article, but I retort that neither has the filed method. They all look as though the modeller has got fed up with filing, and there are great thick walls of metal at the sides of the dome or chimney, where it seats on the boiler. I will say, however, that the GWR dome of Dean vintage which was almost 3 ft. in diameter, and seated on a boiler only just over 4 ft. in diameter, was a sticky problem when it came to saddle it. I got over it by practically making the whole fitting hollow, by boring out the inside and making the walls in the vicinity of the bottom a uniform thickness, and by making the bottom of much larger diameter than necessary, trimming it to the correct diameter by filing round before soldering it to the boiler.

The LNWR square base chimney calls for comment here. The base of this must be made of much larger diameter than necessary in order to be cut square after the saddling process. In other words the base must be a circle outside the square.

We now come to other methods of making boiler fittings. A favourite, method, sometimes used by the trade, is to cut a circle of metal the diameter of the base, curving it to fit the boiler, then turning the chimney or dome without a base, and soldering it direct to this, filling up the radius at the bottom with solder. This is quite all right if the model is to be painted. The writer has a rooted objection to filing solder as it ruins the files; there is always the feeling that it is a tired way of doing the job. In the smaller gauges where a cast white metal smokebox is used, this method cannot very well be a success as the melting point of solder is very near that of white

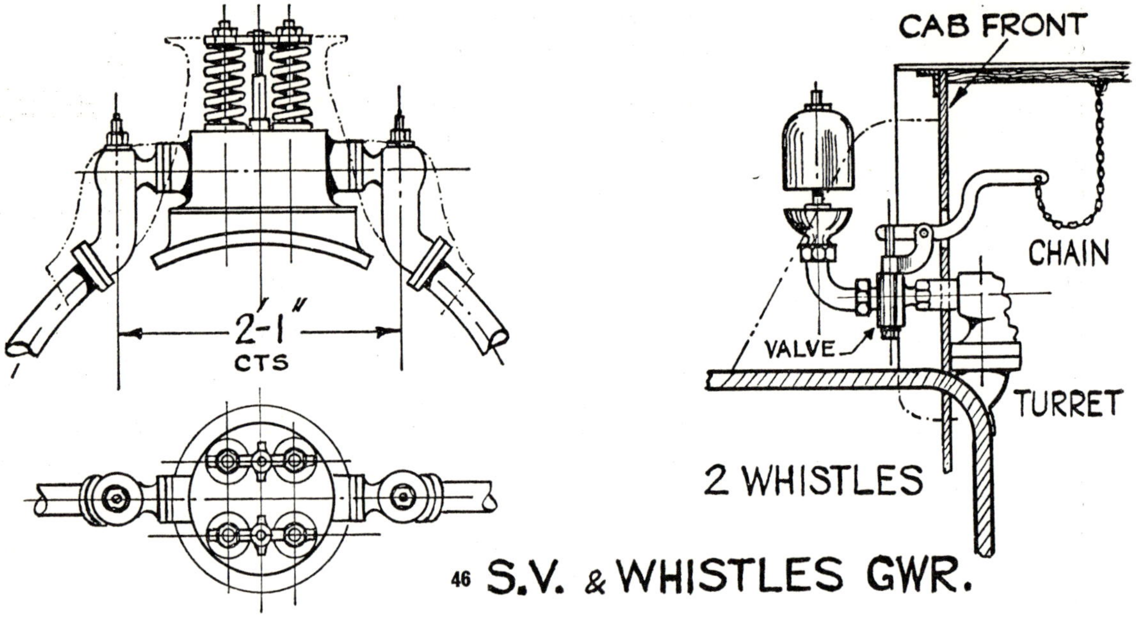

46 S.V. & WHISTLES GWR.

metal, and the smokebox has a habit of fading away at the soldering stage !

The other method is the filing method of saddling them. Then, of course, the fitting can be turned the other way round, i.e., the top of the chimney towards the tail stock. When all the radii are complete it is parted off in the usual manner. Then the real work commences. A peg is put in the former, and chimney threaded on this and the bottom surplus metal filed away until it seats nicely on the boiler. Great care must be taken over this, as one cannot put back metal that has been filed away, until a scientist invents a putting no tool! Yes, I know welding is a putting on tool, but we have not all got welding outfits and I would like to see someone welding a OO gauge chimney !

In most gauges castings can be obtained of boiler fittings, but if only one engine is being modelled I do not see the necessity of cleaning up a casting. To do it properly it has to be chucked in the lathe, and while one is doing this, one may as well turn all the chimney. After all most of the other jobs on a steam loco are lathe jobs so why jib at turning the chimney? When turning the chimney on a large model, the extreme top lip is left off. This is really the top of the inner chimney and petticoat pipe, although it can be turned on the actual chimney and the petticoat pipe turned from thick-walled brass tube tapered to fit the jet of steam from the blast pipe. This pipe is fitted to the boiler, properly lined up, and the chimney forced over it. The latter can then be removed at any time for polishing the top, or to fit an outside blower when raising steam.

In the smaller models, when turning Ross Pop valves, always leave a portion of spigot at the bottom for threading on a nut inside the boiler, having first threaded the spigot 10 BA. While on the subject of safety valves, do not forget it is a safety valve and not just a cover, and please put at least an imitation of the top of the valves inside the cover. GWR modellers are the chief offenders in this respect, some of them even going so far as to leave the top of the cover solid ! This is definitely bad as I should like to be as far away as possible from a County with a 280 lb. pressure boiler with a solid safety valve ! The sketch should put this right for most of the GWR fans.

Before drawing a locomotive for modelling purposes a thorough knowledge of the machine should be mastered, and if an official drawing does not show these details then the draughtsman can put them in from his own knowledge.

Before leaving boiler fittings there are one or two fittings seen on modern locomotives that were not seen before. In the later LMS class 4 2–6–0s, the steam turret that supplied the boiler backplate fittings, formerly inside the cab, is outside the cab and the whistle was mounted on this in a horizontal position. The pipes from the turrent to the cab fittings went through the cab front plate. The regulator gland, formerly inside the cab, is also outside on the side of the boiler, and is connected to the regulator by a long rod like a handrail. Footplates as we knew them of yore have disappeared, in the later designs. The last locos had none at all only two walking plates attached to the boiler, Continental fashion.

The first loco not to have footplates was the Southern Q1 and is known among the Cornish enginemen as the "Flying Dustbin". Needless to say these men are real dyed-in-the-wool Great Westernites !

It is a great pity as the GWR was the only railway to retain its Victorian outline in locomotives, while keeping the innards up to the most advanced designs.

To return to Boiler Fittings, in one of the drawings the proportions of the bell type whistle will be noted. This is seldom modelled properly, inasmuch as there is usually no provision made for working it ! Yes I know it is a dummy, but the pipe from or to it should be at least put in. The only engine which had a whistle with no visible means of operation was the old LNWR. In that case it was mounted with its bell only protruding through the cab roof, and all the pipes and valves were inside the cab, but in modern types, the whistle is usually mounted in front of the cab, and the gland and pipe are also outside the cab, only the chain operating it is inside. The sketch will make this clear.

Salter spring-balance safety valves as fitted to Victorian locomotives, are very clearly shown in the drawing and do not require much description. Suffice to say that the spring balances should be properly made and they will look as though they work. They should be turned throughout in the lathe, and should be of brass, but the levers at the top should be made of *steel*, and polished. Here again the top of the valves should be put in the casing—one cannot have two levers from the spring balances operating nothing ! The drawing will make this clear.

Before leaving the subject of boiler fittings, a word may be said here about lagging the boiler, and the retaining bands. I think it is fairly safe to assume that models in 4mm. and 7mm. scale are never properly represented when it comes to the boiler lagging and its bands. If anyone has ever had the pleasure of climbing on top of a locomotive they will see all sorts of openings and little covers in the lagging that are never put in a model. They will also see that the boiler bands in tank locos are joined on the *top* but no one ever thinks of joined bands in a model—*why not*? Even in a model with a high

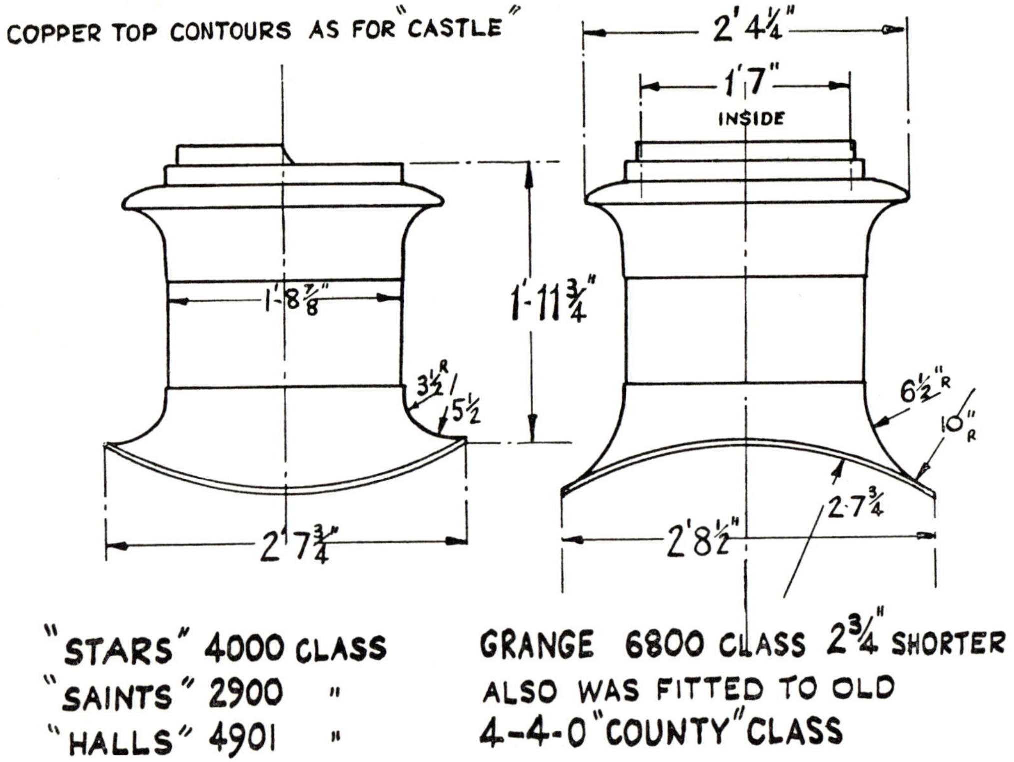

47 More GWR chimneys

boiler well off the footplate, perfect in every detail even down to every rivet and nut, the boiler bands are still stuck round the boiler and the ends lost in some way or other ! They should finish in two little right angle lugs which are nutted together. Some boiler bands have a rivetted lug attached to each end, and the adjusting is done by a small tommybar which is left in position. In tank locomotives this can be seen on the top of the boiler.

In modern locomotives with a large boiler the finishing of the lagging bands is not so obvious, and can be left off where they are not seen, but at least one band near the front can be seen with its fastenings under the boiler. The breathing holes in the boiler should always be drilled in the model. There are usually two near the top in the vicinity of the firebox, just behind the dome, and two more in the front just behind the first lagging band. The *top* of the firebox has also holes in it but these are usually covered with a little circular plate and hinged like the dome shaped covers over the washout plugs. The lagging itself should show a join somewhere on the top of the firebox, I am referring to Belpaire fireboxes, of course. In a small box it could be joined down the centre, and in large ones by two joints, one each side, just above the turnover of the sides, making virtually a large flat square plate on the top of the box. These joints should be shown by a scribed line, deep enough to show through the paint.

The LMS large fireboxes have joints all down the sides, one just above the handrail, and joined by small screws, which can be imitated on the model by little blobs of thick paint when the model is painted. There is another join on the side, where the specially flanged plate joins the curved portion with the flat portion on the large Pacifics.

A riveted smokebox also has rivets in the top, so if you are imitating rivets do not forget that the smokebox is really a flat plate bent in a circle, and has a join somewhere ! It is usually on the top on the centre line of the chimney.

The flanged band covering the top feed pipe has already been mentioned, and now we come to a real bone of contention among model-makers, the boiler bands themselves. Before someone throws the jug at me, let me hasten to add that these are 2 in. wide and $\frac{1}{16}$ in. or $\frac{3}{32}$ in. thick. Now will someone "tear me off a strip" for emphasising that these should be put on in paper after the model is finished, because one cannot get metal thin enough in 4 mm. or 7 mm. scale to make them look less like a fence sticking round the boiler. I have examined scores of photographs of models with metal boiler bands and they all stick out a mile and spoil an otherwise excellent model.

Modellers have taken me to task because they say that to mix paper up with a model made of metal is bad model-making and bad engineering. Well to these folk I say why not carry the thing to its logical conclusion, and use the correct materials throughout? That rules out nickel-silver motion work, brass footplates, etc., nickel-silver too, brass funnels, domes and safety

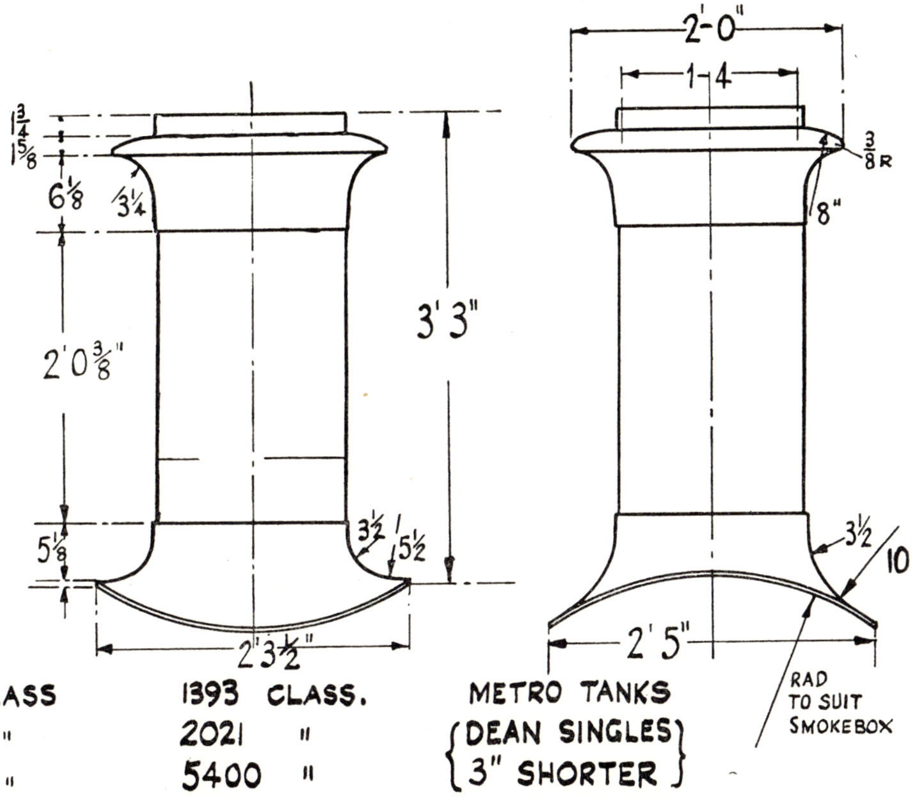

48 GWR chimneys

49 GWR chimneys

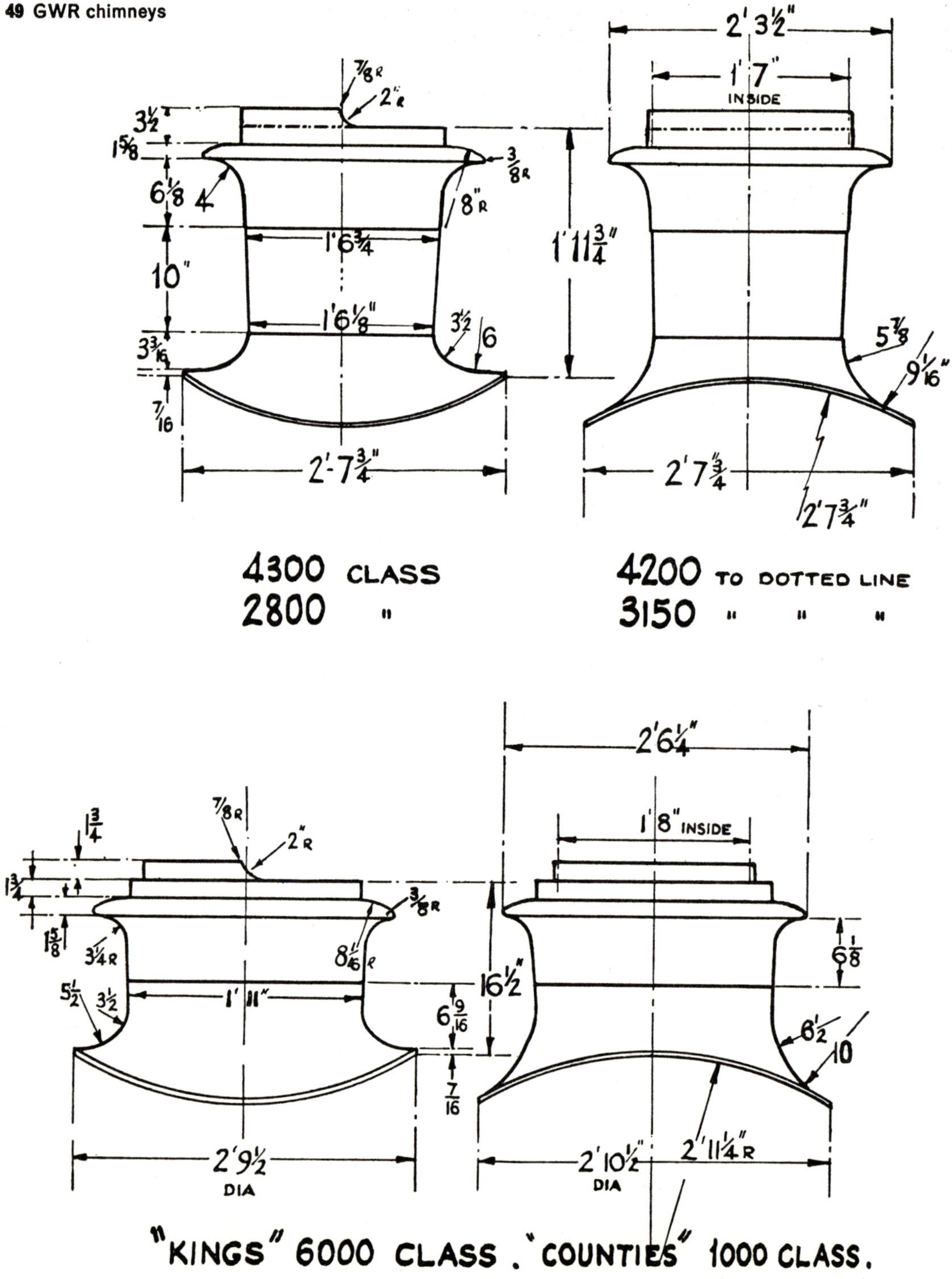

valves and all the other subterfuges that we employ. In fact build the model of steel throughout (in tinplate form) for the superstructure, steel for the motion, fine steel foil for boiler bands and do them up with a nut and bolt underneath in a proper manner because one cannot solder these fine metal bands in position and then scrape the solder away without damaging the band on its edge somewhere. Apart from this difficulty, there is the painting stage to consider and getting round these boiler bands *in situ* is about the worst condition met with (in a Stroudley engine in its old colours). Is it not easier to line and paint these bands in the flat and stick them round the boiler. When the model is varnished they will never come unstuck. I have a model of a Dean single that is 12 years old—not in a glass case—which has kicked around all over the place, but the boiler bands are still in place and not unstuck. So to blazes with the critics and make them of parcel tape.

Well I think this clears up all the points about the boiler fittings, lagging, etc., and we now pass to the cab fittings. It is not intended in this book to draw out lots of cab fittings for locos, as this would be an impossible task, and space would not allow it, but rather to give diagrams and views of the standard fittings that are found on all locomotives, such as injectors, brake valves, water gauges, regulator or throttle glands, reversing gear lever, and reversing gear screws, firedoors. The way they are arranged in the cab, etc., is a matter of observation. The reversing screw would naturally be on the same side as the reversing rod. Yes, I have seen them on opposite sides ! The firedoor and throttle gland are in their usual positions, but the brake valve is placed according to whether the engine is right, or left hand drive, in other words on the driver's side of the locomotive. The driver's side of the loco is the one on which the reversing lever is placed and all the fittings appertaining to his particular field are on his side, such things as lubricators, speed indicators, ATC gear, etc. The fireman has injection controls, water gauges, etc.

Cab Fittings

Before leaving the boiler, there remain the cab fittings to consider. In early days these were very simple, consisting merely of the firedoor, throttle gland and regulator, reversing lever, pressure gauge and water gauge. These fittings are still with us, but there are many more and fittings in the modern cab have come to be rather over-elaborate these days, leaving the layman appalled at the array of gadgets.

In modelling cab fittings it is much better to model properly the *essential* fittings enumerated above, than to fill the cab with a lot of "bits and pieces" with no semblance of the originals, connecting them up with a lot of meaningless bits of copper wire, with no resemblance to a *pipe*, which is what the bits of wire are supposed to represent. Remember a pipe has flanges on it somewhere, and a union nut where it connects to a fitting. It is not just pushed into a hole in a lump of shapeless metal. A few sketches are given just to show what is meant by the foregoing remarks.

It will be realised that to give readers a representative selection of cab fitting drawings would fill these articles to the exclusion of all else, and space would not allow it, but the sketches show the essential fittings without

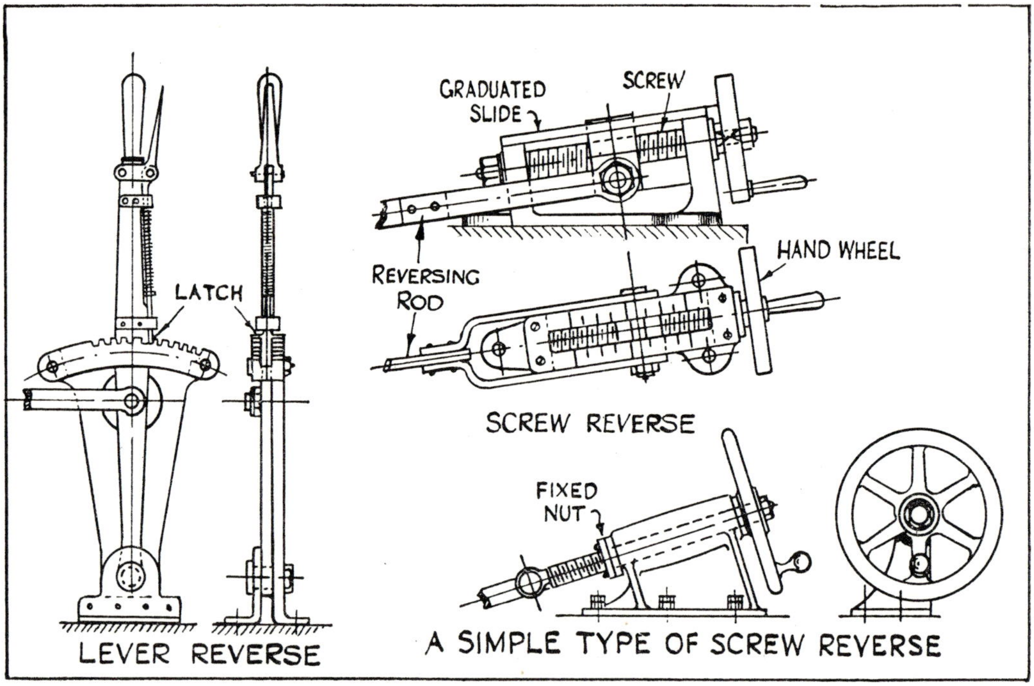

50 Reverses

51 GWR firedoor

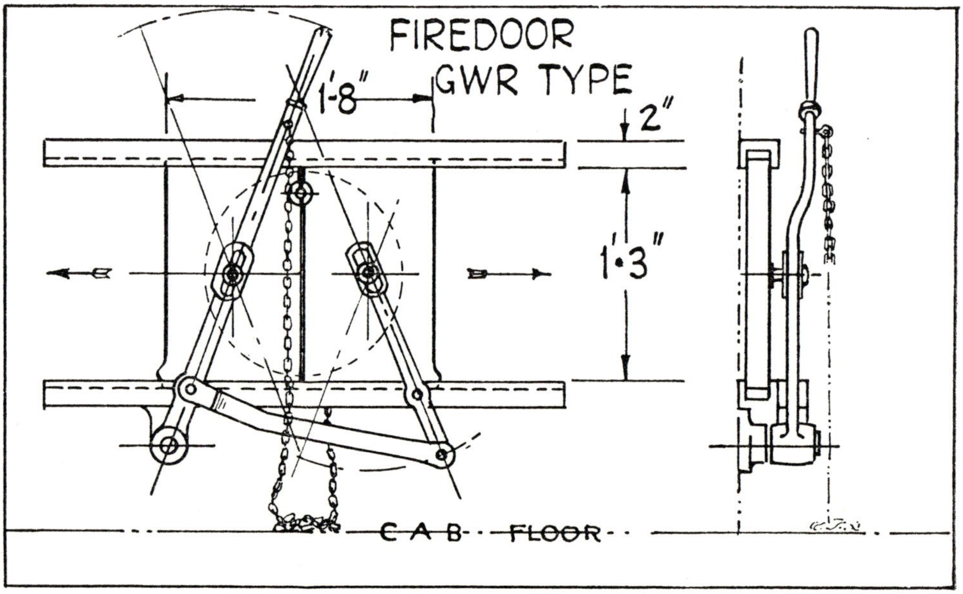

which a locomotive would not run. In small models, in O or OO gauge these are about all which can be got in to look right. To try and add more would only overcrowd the cab, and detract from its neatness.

In dummy locomotives not using steam as a motive power, the cab fittings are best built up on a separate plate bent up into a right angle, the upright portion representing the back of the firebox, and the horizontal portion the footplate, each part being filed to its proper shape. Do not forget to add sides to the firebox back, as these show through the windows of modern cabs. Also add a beading which is usually polished, and here we must not forget to add washout lugs in the corners. For some reason these are nearly always left out of model fireboxes. They are very conspicuous and should be put in.

When modelling reversing gears, make sure that the locomotive you are modelling has the correct type. There are two types: screw and lever. These are shown in the sketches. The simplest type of screw reverse was that fitted to the old LNWR locos. This type can be modelled for a modern locomotive, as after all only the actual wheel is seen from the rear of the cab, the sides of a modern large firebox covers up the rest of it. Of course, if the model is a small ex-LNWR type then it will be seen, and care must be taken to make it properly. For models which are electrically propelled with AC current the reversing lever will make an ideal reversing switch, and the writer has seen this done with a large model German loco. To the expert there is no limit to what can be done electrically in the cab. The regulator can be made into a starting switch, with an isolating position, so that a loco can be stood on the track without interference to others that are running, and without injury to itself. A small lamp can be put into the back of the upright portion of the firebox (the backplate) behind the firedoor and covered with a piece of red cellophane. If the firedoor is modelled in the open position, we now have a real fire. All the wiring for these added bits of realism can be hidden behind the back of the firebox, and when the complete fittings are screwed in, there will be nothing to give the game away. Think how nice it will be to say to your friends, "Look at the cab fittings, and they all work !" Except (sotto voce) the water gauge !

There remains one other item, the dials of the gauges. Do not attempt to model these actual size. It is much better to draw them out several times full size on drawing paper. If the modeller does not fancy his skill as a draughtsman, perhaps some draughtsman friend will draw them for you. They must be drawn complete with the gauge needle in the appropriate position. Do not have the needles all in the zero position, unless your model is to be a glass case one. The pressure gauge should be at boiler pressure, and vacuum gauge at 30 inches of vacuum, and speedometer (if fitted) at between 40 and 70 according to the type of locomotive. We all know that a model locomotive runs considerably above either of these speeds, particularly in 4 mm. scale. One hears a lot of the arguments that still rage among model railway enthusiasts regarding this vexed question; in fact it seems it will never really be solved. The writer recently saw a working OO gauge layout in which the models seemed like a lot of agitated ants running about, expresses doing about 100 mph, and goods trains the same, with the poor trucks taking a flying leap over a point or crossing, running off the track for a considerable distance and jumping on again. Most unrealistic—

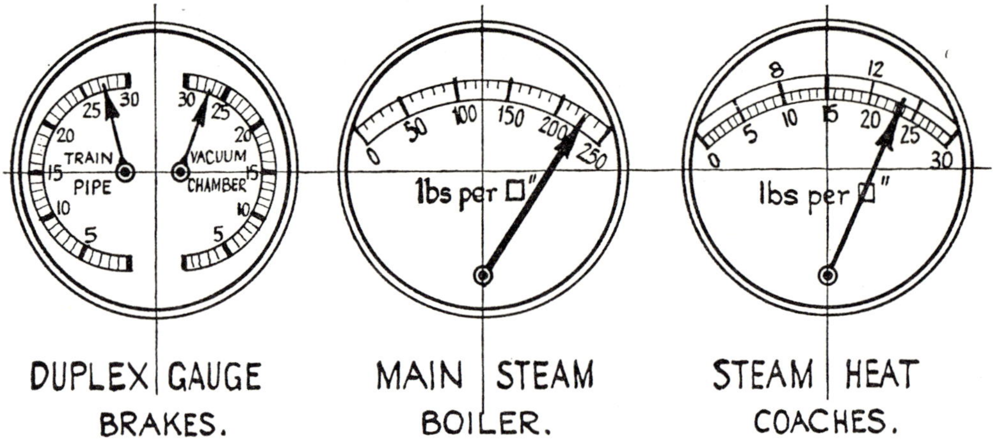

CAB GAUGES

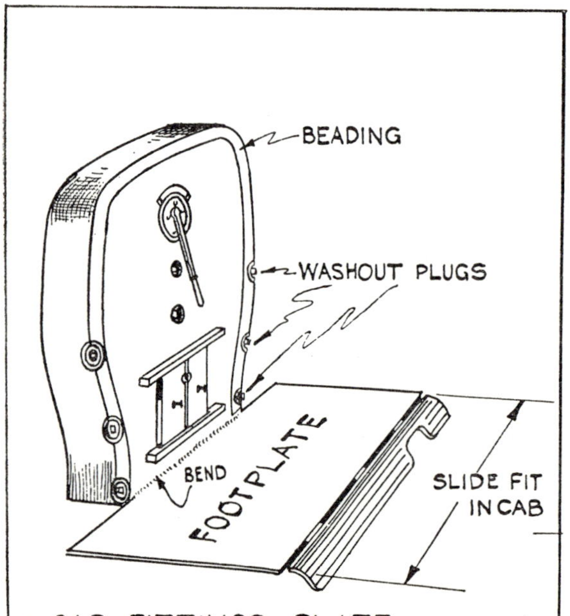

CAB FITTINGS PLATE

PROPORTIONS OF WATER GAUGE

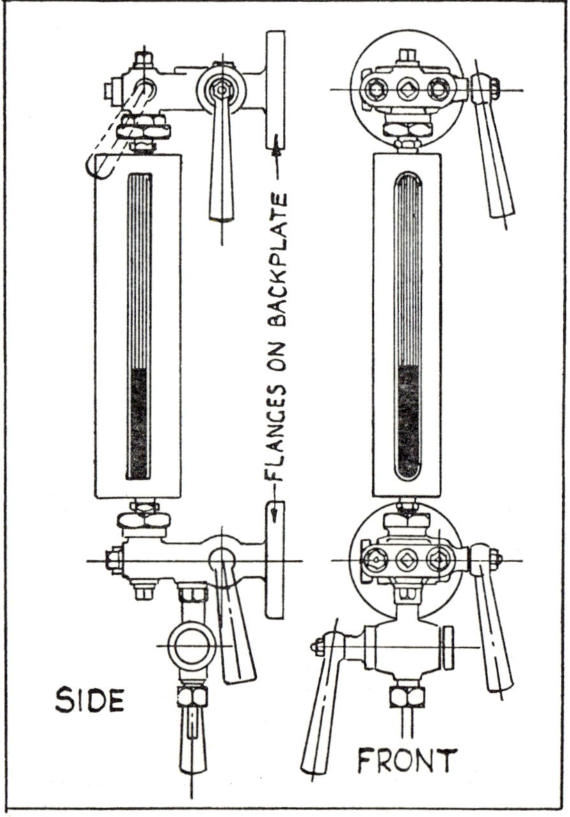

and not very good propaganda for the model railway hobby—when one considers the amount of realism that is put into lineside accessories! Or is this the reason why enthusiasts take up this gauge, in order to spread themselves out on buildings, embankments, stations, water works, gas works, etc., the trains themselves being put in as an afterthought! Think about it and consider the position!

Well, after that digression we must get on with our dials. If they are drawn out several times full size, they can be photographically reduced to the size of the model. By this method the dials on a OO gauge loco can be seen and read. Get them photographed on to glossy paper and there will be no need to put anything in the dial to represent glass. To represent water gauges in O gauge and large models, glass tube can be obtained from medical sources, $\frac{3}{64}$ in. in diameter, which is just right for the job. Enthusiasts who are doctors should find no difficulty in obtaining this as it is used in blood transfusions! Any hospital will supply this glass tube as it is only thrown away after the operation. Several thousands of people during the war had this operation performed on them at some time or other, and all railway enthusiasts should have stuck to the tubes! With this tube it is only necessary to model the top and bottom fittings with the necessary shut-off valve handles as shown in the sketch.

I think this about completes our boiler, and it is now ready to go forth into the erecting shop.

The Prototype

The choice of prototype has quite a lot to do with the success or otherwise of a model locomotive; the writer cannot for the life of him see why model railway enthusiasts must have a Pacific, or a long wheelbase 4–6–0 like the GW Kings, when they have a small layout with sharp radius curves. The obvious choice of a locomotive to operate this sort of railway is a 4–4–0 for express work, and small wheeled tank engines for all other purposes.

There are many excellent examples of modern 4–4–0s like the Southern class V (Schools) the Midland compounds, and the beautifully proportioned 4–4–0s of the Irish railways. These can always be painted in the enthusiast's own colours if he does not favour any of these railways. One of the most ideal prototypes for sharply curved railways was the ex-GNR Atlantic. This engine is scarcely modelled at all today. Why?

There is every reason why the GWR is popular amongst model-makers; the Castle class engines are fairly short for a large locomotive, and the fact that the cylinders are over the rear bogie wheel gives a little more latitude in clearance (for bogie wheels) than the usual position in the centre of the bogie. GWR prototypes did not alter much over a period of years and a locomotive built 40 years ago was still modern by GWR standards in 1948. The Castles are a 60-year-old design with a larger boiler, and improved details such as superheater and pressure, which does not concern electrically driven models. But why, oh why, are they all Castles and Kings that one sees about?

The French Compounds were the most beautifully designed and daintiest locomotives ever run on a railway, and ideal for sharp curves in that they had the added advantage of only two pairs of driving wheels. The trailing truck could be given unlimited side play owing to its inside gearings, and the outside cylinders being small (they were the high pressure ones), were well above the centre line of the bogie wheels, thus allowing more than the usual side play. In fact the locos were ideal in every respect from a model-maker's point of view.

And in passing, what about the Broad Gauge fliers? The GWR gave the world efficiency and standardisation in its locomotives, at the same time keeping a neatness of outline, but its model-makers are far behind, and there is no reason why a third rail should not be added to run broad gauge trains on a layout. There were several miles of cross sleepered broad gauge tracks about long after the gauge was abolished in 1892. I have a picture of *La France* hauling a train over mixed gauge track, which had not been taken up, so there's precedent for it !

A similar loco *Alliance* can claim to be the Father (or is it Mother?) of the modern 4-cylinder classes, as she had all the features of modern engines, including the Top Feed, De Glehn Bogie, Four-Cylinders with divided drive, and Walschaerts Gear. These features had never been seen all together in one engine in England until Mr. Churchward introduced them after studying the French engine construction. Even the safety valve cover has a faint resemblance to the modern article ! So any GWR fan who is modelling a history of GW locomotives is only half doing the job to leave any of these locos out. Drawings of the larger French engines were published in the *Loco Magazine* of 1906, and in the *Engineer*.

Coming to the Northern lines, why is there such a dearth of models of the ex-NBR Atlantics?, another favourite prototype of other days. These again have all the features to make a successful model, even though they were "coal eaters", and despite this a modern locomotive engineer has put forth the dictum that the function of a locomotive is to burn coal ! So why the quibble? His most successful revolutionary design is a prolific coal eater, but they can run and run to time. They were a revolutionary design for their period with the largest boiler ever seen up to that time.

Coming to passenger tank engines, there are many excellent prototypes that are seldom modelled. What about the ex-LTSR 4–4–2 tanks? There are many LTSR enthusiasts but they do not make any models of the locos, at least they seldom seem to come out into the open with them.

There were the many excellent prototypes of the Caledonian—all tank locos. One in particular—a 4–6–2—being a particularly handsome locomotive. The North British also had many handsome types of tank loco. What about the ex-LBSCR which had finely proportioned express tank locos? Also the GER had many handsome blue tank engines.

Well I think enough has been said regarding the choice of prototype without recourse to the eternal Pacific, Castle, and King, without mentioning the very seldom modelled numerous pretty little tank locomotives of the GWR. All one sees of these is the common Pannier in model form.

Now that the steam locomotive has vanished and all these grand old names but a memory, it is the time to perpetuate the memory of British Locomotive history by modelling some of these handsome prototypes. They are all we have left to remind us of the past efficiency and glory of the British railways at their best period.

The Erecting Shop

We now commence the interesting part of our model locomotive and the part that requires the most care, for no matter how beautifully we make the boiler, the model will not run properly unless we take the utmost care in fitting our wheels, making our frames nice and square, and giving adequate freedom of movement for bogies, pony trucks, etc.

It is not proposed to give details of how to get a Pacific round a dinner plate. A Pacific should not be built if it is desired to get it round curves of this radius; that is more in the line of toys than models, and these can be bought ready made. The purpose of this book is to improve the breed, and a thing of beauty is a joy forever in models as well as in full size engineering.

After all we *are* model engineers, and the engineering part of our model is the running gear. Even the most dumb newspaper reporter who sees a model locomotive properly built cannot write it up as a toy train when it is so obviously far from such. It is when he sees a Pacific lurching round a 3 or 4 ft. radius curve, with the bogie wheels outside the frames altogether, and the tender coupled a scale 3 ft. away from the engine, that he writes articles about us playing with toy trains. It is up to modellers to educate this fraternity by making locomotives look right, and work correctly, thus having our hobby designated rightly on radio, and in newspapers, as "Mr. So-and-So's miniature trains which were a delight to behold . . .".

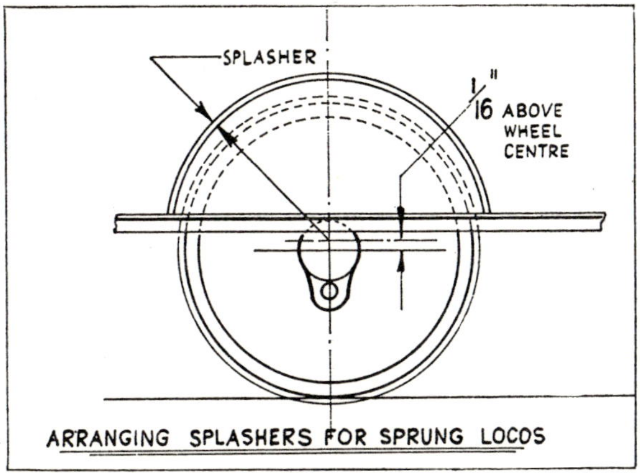

53

The drawings show the frames for a GWR City class 4–4–0, and the drawing is representative of all GWR double framed engines. It will be seen there are double frames, two inside and two outside. The frames on the inside in the vicinity of the bogie are narrowed inwards for clearance of the leading bogie wheels, and in a model these may have to be further narrowed below the footplate line. The correct narrowing is shown on top of the footplate. There is no objection to this fake; it is when the wangling is done in broad daylight that it becomes such an eyesore, and when it is necessary to do this, don't model the loco at all, but choose a prototype that will go round curves of your radius.

This drawing should also make clear several features that may have been a mystery to modellers of GWR prototypes of the double framed variety. To mention a few, the box-like structure in front of the smokebox sides is

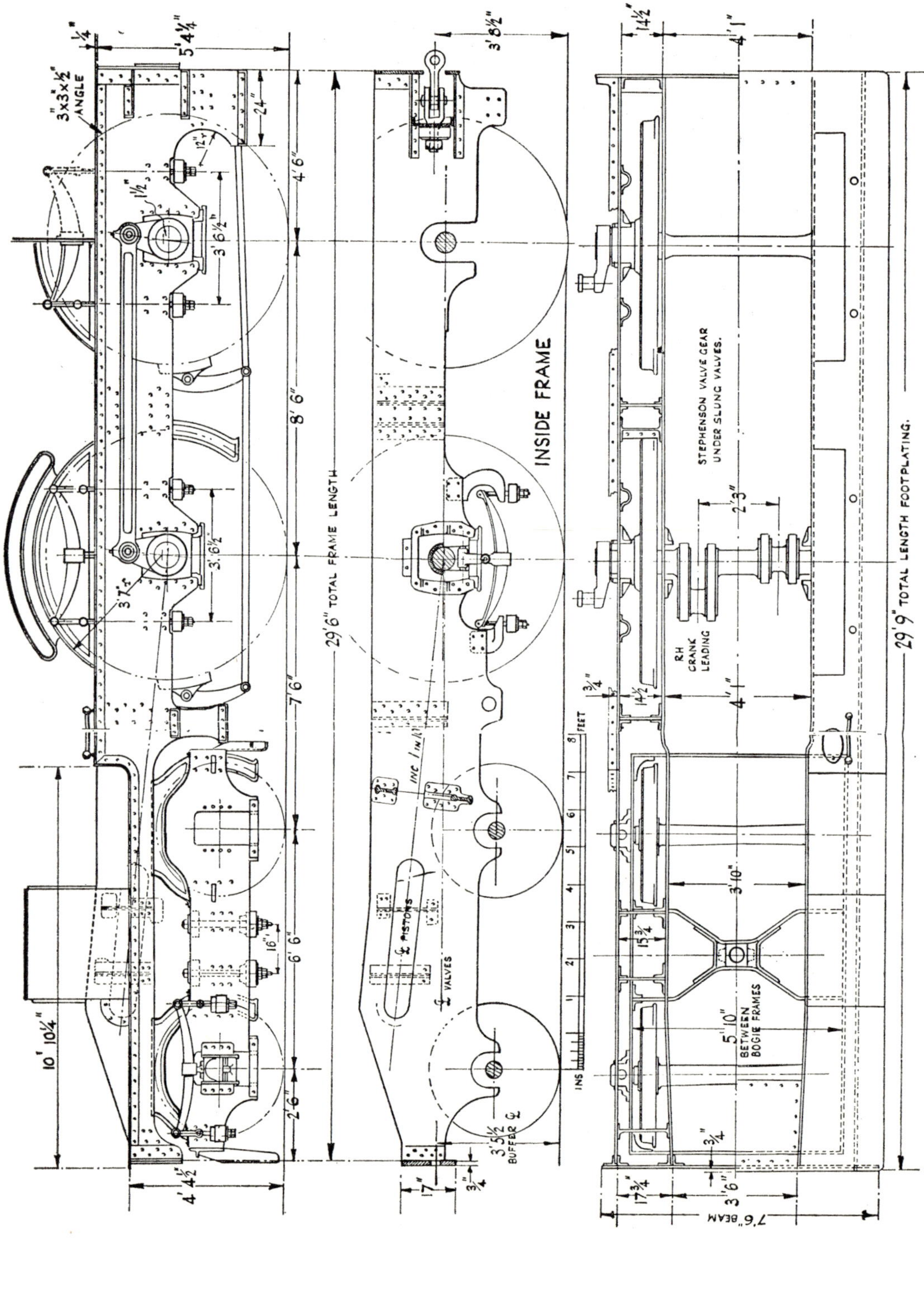

54 Frames for GWR "City" class 4-4-0 loco

really a casing over a hole in the frames; the upward sweep of the frames behind the smokebox, familiar on all Dean engines from the Singles to his last 4–4–0 design, was necessary to obtain strength in the framing owing to this large hole. The main axle boxes were on the *outside* frames, and not on the inside as is popularly supposed, and the inside boxes were shallow ones supporting only a portion of the weight of the engine. These were only on the driving axle, and not on the trailing axle. The larger rear spring should be noted, and lastly the rear drawhook. For a full-sized loco this has a remarkable model look about it.

A word here on springing should be noted. The radius of a splasher top, is always struck from a centre slightly higher than that of the driving wheel, and *never* from the same centre—a common error in drawing locomotives. This is to allow for the rise and fall of the springs, and if a model is to be sprung this difference in centres should be observed. In the engine under review it is 1½ in. The supplementary sketch should make this quite clear. In O gauge the difference should be at least $\frac{1}{16}$ in., and OO about half this amount.

We now come to the thickness of frames. In a model this has to be slightly thicker than scale to obtain strength, but where the frames show above the footplate, they should be thinned to scale thickness. The average thickness of a locomotive frame is about 1 in. The GWR use comparatively thick frames, these being 1¼ in., while the LMS in their Pacific engines use frames of 1⅛ in. in thickness. A lot depends on the tensile strength of the steel. A steel of high tensile strength can be thinner in section than that of a low tensile strength.

The distance apart of the frames themselves varies according to the thickness. The back to back distance of the wheels cannot be varied owing to the rail gauge, therefore the thicker the frames, the closer they are together. This is usually 4 ft. 1¼ in. to 4 ft. 1½ in., the GWR being different from anyone else, use a distance of 4 ft. 1 in. between their frames. This is where we get into a sticky mess with a model. The gauge of 1¼ in. for O gauge is far too narrow, and of course 16.5 mm. for OO gauge is quite outside the pale! This latter is all wrong and no one in this wide world can build anything but a toy for this gauge, because the whole thing is a fake from beginning to end; the beginning being the frames, and the end having the appearance of a very fat Babu on a knock-kneed donkey! The solution of that problem is to build narrow gauge prototypes to a scale of 4½ mm. per ft. and call it a 3 ft. 6 in. gauge railway, or use a gauge of 18.25 mm.

The arguments for and against this gauge have gone on for years and it is not proposed to go into them here. It is only to be hoped that commonsense will win in the end and the scale go back to 3½ mm., and 16.5 mm. gauge and 18 mm. gauge for those who still want the 4 mm. scale. The scale was ideal when introduced with steam roller wheels, and other coarsened details, and the result was "Hornby Dublo", the acme of perfection in toy railways, but when we introduce fine scale standards, it is nothing short of the sport of gilding the lily and introducing unnecessary complication. For an illustration of the futility of building a miniature locomotive in this gauge try building a single-wheeler, at one end of the scale, or a large wheeled Pacific at the other. In both cases you will find that you have to have the driving wheels running *inside* the boiler instead of outside!

In O gauge we can get very near to scale proportions in the matter of frames, if we use the fine scale distance of 29 mm. back to back when putting on the wheels, spacing our frames at 3 ft. 9 in. apart. This is 4 in. under scale—rather a lot, but not noticeable. This will give a clearance of $\frac{3}{4}$ mm. behind the wheels, and if they are put on true they will not rub on the frames. Of course, this standard is not attainable in any locomotive other than a Single or a 4–4–0. Directly we introduce a third pair of driving wheels we are up against it again, as one pair of driving wheels, usually the centre pair, will have to have a little side play. For heaven's sake don't remove the flanges—one of the worst eyesores ever! The frames will have to be narrowed to 3 ft. 8 in. or under (about 26 mm.). If we make our frames $\frac{3}{4}$ mm. thick about 22 gauge steel, we should have no trouble on a 6 to 8 feet radius curve. For curves under this modellers should stick to the Greenly standards of 40 years ago and not attempt to mix up fine scale standard and 4 ft. radius curves in O gauge; they will only get into an unholy mess!

These standards were carefully thought out and we all owe a lot to the late Henry Greenly, although we have always grudgingly admitted it. Only now do we realise how carefully thought out they were, now we are in a morass of fine scale standards on railways that were laid to the old standards, including the gauge which remains the same; this should have been standardised at $33\frac{1}{4}$ mm. before we started juggling with fine scale wheels!

The Greenly standards were derived from the *outside* of the loco. The distance from the *face* of the wheel to the *face* of the wheel the other side formed the basis of his calculations. The wheel tyre and flange were coarsened to suit the lower standard of workmanship of modelmakers of other days, which gave a distance of 27 mm. back to back, later increased to 28 mm. The space that was left, after allowing for clearance on curves, was available for frames. This worked out at 1 in. or 25 mm. over the outside of the frames, and this is what it will have to be in a model using 4 ft. radius curves, so we come back to the old standards after all, fine scale or no fine scale!

The Frames

While we are making our frames, before we put them together, we must decide now how far they are to be apart; we have already proved that we cannot fit them the scale distance apart owing to the model gauge being under scale, and the fact that model wheels do not fit tightly to gauge as do the prototypes, by this is meant that the scale clearance of a prototype in the matter of back to back distance and the gauge cannot be scaled down as it would be too small to be practicable in all but show case models. This has all been worked out by the late Henry Greenly and in later days by the BRMSB, arriving at what we call the model standard back to back distance of the wheels, which in OO gauge is 14.5 mm., and in O gauge 29 mm. In $\frac{3}{8}$th scale it is 1.37/64, this latter is very near the scale distance as this works out at 1.43/64ths, in the $\frac{3}{8}$ths scale.

A sketch (fig. 55) is given showing how to arrive at the clearances required. This shows a LMS 2–6–4T—one of the longest engines to be met. It is really

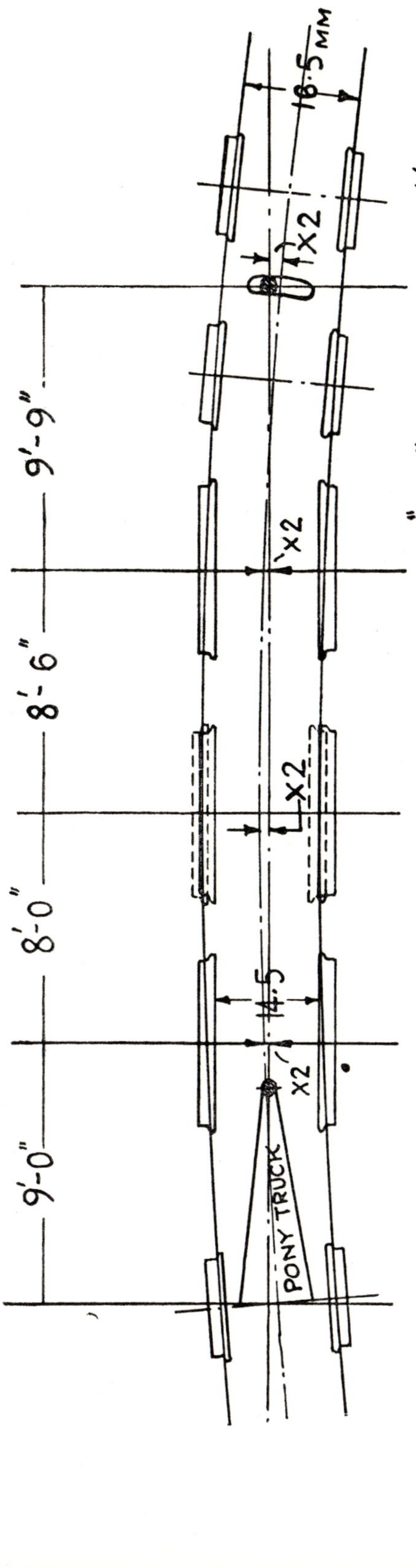

55 LMS 2-6-4T ON 3FT RADIUS CURVE IN "OO" GAUGE. SCALE 1/1

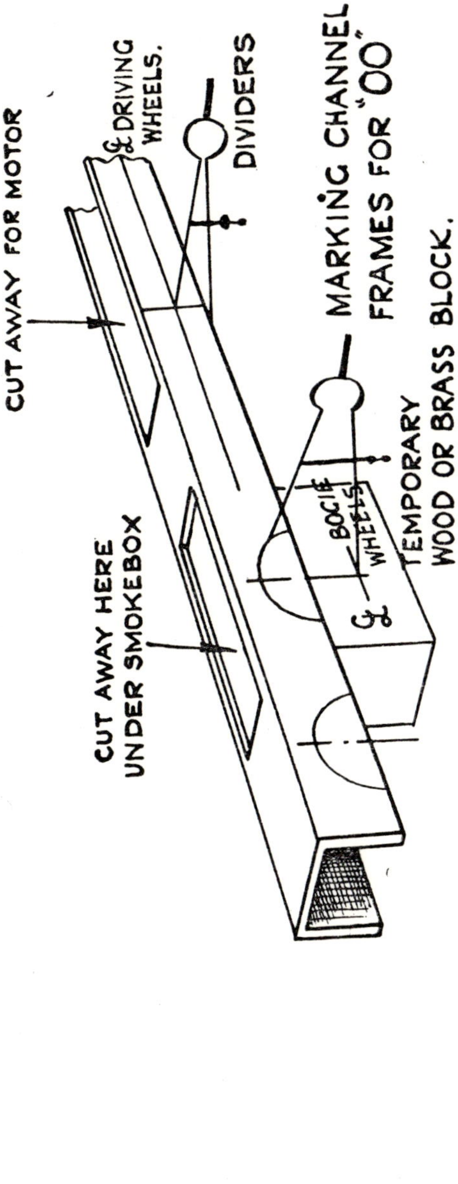

56

a Pacific in reverse and is an extreme case, but the same diagram can be used for all types of engines. First set out on a piece of paper your smallest curve (usually 3 ft. radius in OO), find the centre of this and draw in a centre line. Next draw out in plan form the wheelbase of your engine, and draw in also the centre line of the engine. Where the centre line of the engine and the centre line of the curve intersect the centre lines of the wheels, will be found the clearance required for each pair of wheels. This must obviously be multiplied by two as the clearance is required both sides of the engine, It will be seen that the play required in the centre pair of wheels is considerable, and when this pair are the driving wheels, it is difficult to allow such play without the gears coming out of mesh in the case of a spur driven engine. In the case of the worm driven model, the gears will bind. This accounts for the hum one sometimes hears in an electric model when rounding a curve, as the motor has a lot of friction to overcome. In a case like this, it is better to drive on the rear wheels. Having found the clearance required, the frames will have to be made to allow for it, and it is unusual to find frames in OO gauge much more than ½ in. over the outsides; in fact this is considered the standard distance for this gauge, and brass channel is usually used, as it dispenses with frame stretchers, the top of the channel acting as a stretcher. Details for marking this out are shown (fig. 56) and to find the clearance required to clear bogie wheels, place a scrap piece of the same channel up against the piece being worked on and centre pop the centre of the bogie wheel on this, a piece of wood will do, or a scrap brass block. Using the dividers as a pair of odd legs scribe the centre of the driving wheels along the side. It should be unnecessary to add that the channel should be perfectly straight and free from kinks. Scribe the arcs of the bogie wheel clearances allowing about 1½ mm. clearance. Centre pop the centres of the driving wheels, and repeat the dose on the other side. If the channel is perfectly straight and square, the centre pops on each side should be opposite one another. If there is any doubt about this happening do not use the full size drill for the axle when drilling, but use a smaller one. If the holes are out, they can be pulled into alignment with a small rat tail file, and the full size drill put through.

Anticipating a little, it is advisable to make the coupling rods at this stage or at least drill the steel being used for these at the same time that the frames are being drilled. This will ensure that they do not bind when fitted to the wheels. Another and even better way is to make the coupling rods first, and use these as a jig for drilling the frames. The rods will then be a perfect fit. Nothing is worse than coupling rods that require to be different for each side of the engine or rods that have egg shaped holes in them, resulting in the front or rear pair of wheels turning nearly a half revolution, without moving the remainder. This throws an awful strain on the rods and the motor, particularly if the rear pair are the drivers. It often results in binding the rods up and jamming the engine, and it won't start. A little care at this stage of drilling the frames and making the rods, will be amply repaid in better running.

Turning to O gauge, if a Pacific is being modelled, the frames should be 1 in. over the outside. The same diagram can be used to find the clearances in the wheels, and it will be found that in a 4–4–0, using 29 mm. back to back wheel spacing, the frames can be made nearer to scale. It is usual in O gauge to make the frames of steel plate, with stretchers between to keep the distance apart of the frames constant. The drawings show various forms of stretchers. In a real loco the cylinders form a frame stretcher, but as we do not fit cylinders in an electric model, it is usual to make a stretcher here to carry the bogie pin, or the pivot for a leading truck. The next stretcher is usually the motion plate, to which the slide bars are fitted in an inside cylinder engine. In the case of an outside cylinder engine, a stretcher is placed in the same position and the motion bars on the outside bolted right through the frame into this stretcher. Various minor stretchers are placed across the frames to carry air cylinders, brake cylinders, etc., until we come to the last main stretcher in front of the firebox. The last and final spacer is the drag plate and rear buffer beam. The drawing will make all this clear. One or more of these may be left out, according to the size of the motor, which, of course, is a stretcher in itself, as the motors designed for this gauge today are designed to go between the frames.

More will be said about fitting motors when we get to that stage, but allowance must be made now for them. The Reid Maxwell motor is 21.5 mm. over the frame but others are smaller and average width would be 18 mm. For sprung models using axle boxes and springs the smaller motor gives more room for these refinements. Springing can be indulged in using the Reid Maxwell motor if the axle boxes in the vicinity of the motor are made slightly thinner in section. When using the pre-war type of motor in which the frames are part, as in a 6-coupled or 4-coupled unit, it is usual to make auxiliary frames for the bogie and cylinders, and a pair of little frames at the rear, to carry the rear footplate. These are bolted to the motor,

57

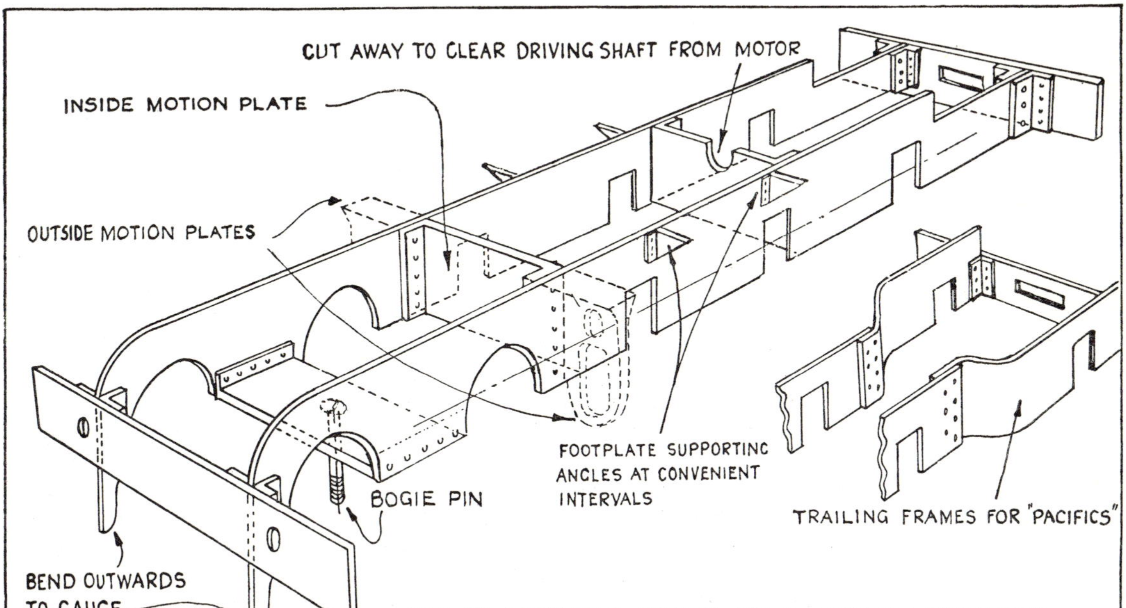

HOW TO ASSEMBLE FRAMES FOR A MODERN LOCOMOTIVE.

making a complete chassis. Never attempt to fit these pieces of frame to the body of the loco as it entails a lot of juggling, to get the motor in or out, when outside motion is used. The sketch should make this clear. In a 6-coupled loco part of the motor should be cut away as shown to avoid that blocked-in appearance where there should be daylight under the boiler. It also avoids a lot of unnecessary cutting of the boiler. In making a model electrically-driven steam locomotive, every effort should be made to get as much of the mechanism in the firebox as possible, even if it does protrude into the cab. With modern cabs with side windows this is not so bad as having to block in half of the boiler.

The construction of a model locomotive is a task often lightly entered upon and just as often laid aside incompleted. Amateurs working in spare time should consider the type they choose with a view to the amount of work entailed and the amount of spare time available. Where both are limited, it is better to adopt a small model in O gauge rather than to attempt a Pacific in OO. Strict adherence to every feature of a prototype often causes a lot of unnecessary work, although if spare time is unlimited it is well worth the trouble. In the matter of frames, so long as the external shape is preserved, the components may be simplified in many ways.

While sheet brass may be used for framing in OO gauge, for O gauge and larger, mild steel sheet is stiffer and generally a more satisfactory material. The thickness of the sheet used, should be approximately a scale equivalent of $1\frac{1}{4}$ in. or $1\frac{1}{2}$ in. If it is not intended to fit bushes for the driving axles in OO gauge, then the frame plate should be at least $\frac{1}{16}$ in. thick. It is always advisable to fit bronze bushes to all, even the smallest models for the driving axles. Turned bushes from commercial screw bar are worse than useless, as the wearing properties of these are less than that of the drawn brass frame material.

As far as possible the builder should avoid tapped holes in the frames. All holes should be plain clearing holes for the bolts and screws attaching the stretchers, brackets and other parts. Except in the smallest models there is no need to solder parts to the frames. Therefore steel is the best material to use, from this point of view. In a model, stretchers or distance pieces have no great duty to perform except to keep the frames the correct distance apart, and in small models of OO gauge and under the round bar type of stretcher shown in the sketch is quite efficient. Holes for taking these spacers must be drilled in the frames after they have been filed to shape and before they have been taken apart. In fact, all holes, whatever use they have, should be drilled while the frames are together.

Trailing frames for Pacific engines should be attached inside the main frames. Space is so limited between the wheels, that there is no room for attaching them outside as is done in some full size engines. Referring to the tapping of holes in the frames, it is quite permissible to tap holes in the frames for attaching the footplates. That can be erected from outside the engine, by first fitting the bracket to the frames, and then when the footplate is made it can be soldered to the brackets, and the whole lot removed as a unit. Buffer beams should be attached to the frames through the medium of angles both inside and outside the frames as shown in the sketch. But soldering parts of this nature should be avoided at all costs as this beam takes all the weight of the engine when it runs into dead-ends too fast. These beams and also the rear beam should be made the scale equivalent of $1\frac{1}{2}$ in. thick material. The angles should be riveted in O and larger gauges, and screwed in OO with counter-sunk screws, the slots must be filled in before painting.

4–4–0 engines are notoriously heavy at the front end and to move the

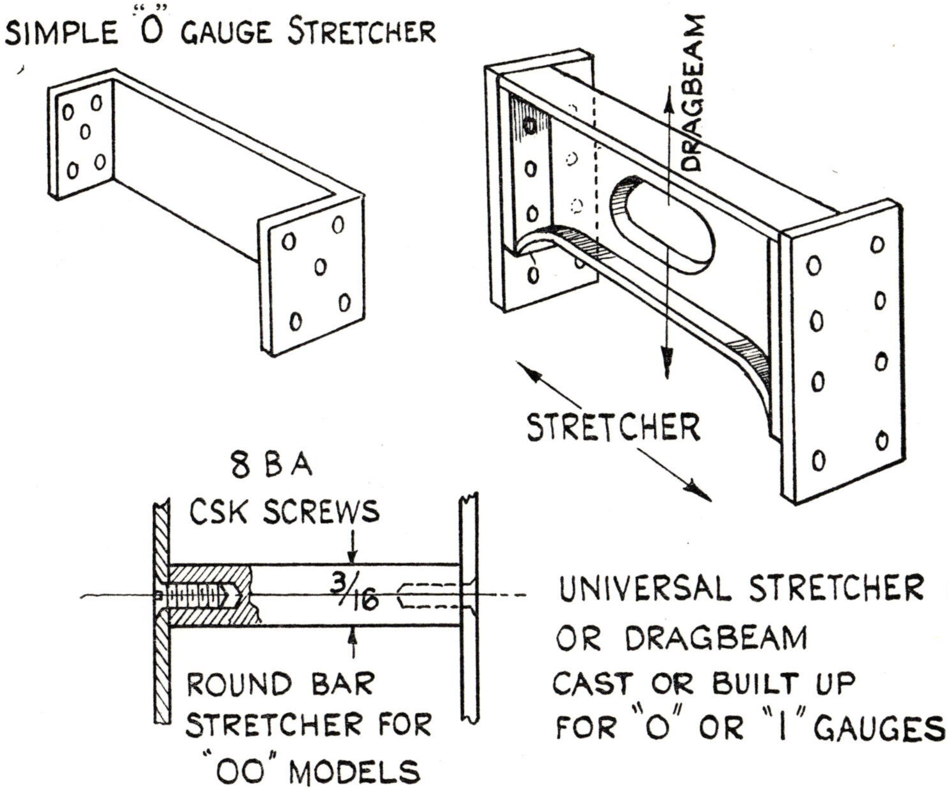

58

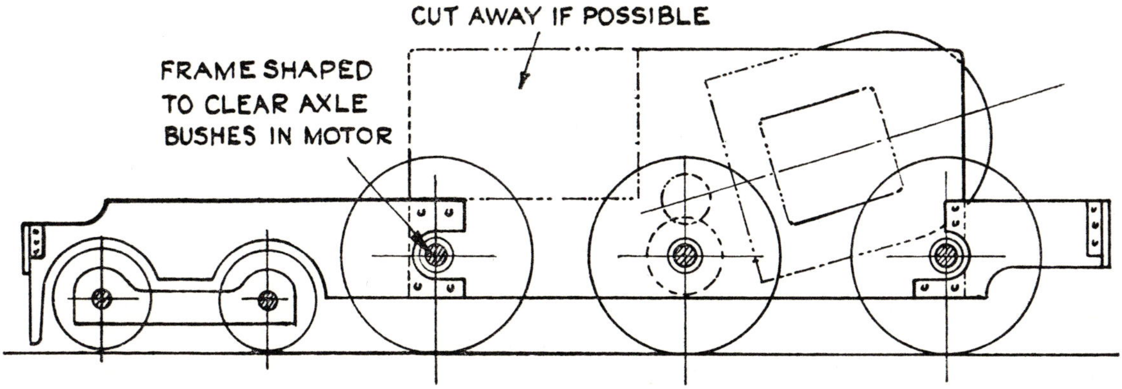

centre of gravity back it is usual to attach a heavy cast drag beam at the rear end which carries the footplate. A design for this type of stretcher and drag beam is given in the sketch. It is universal and can be used either way, i.e. vertical or horizontal, and a hole is shown for attaching the tender drawbar. In choosing steel for frames a planished plate or piece of strip should be favoured, and in cutting it care should be taken not to distort the plate by chiselling out the unwanted portions. Centre lines of the axles, bogie wheel clearances, holes for attaching parts etc., should all be marked out on one plate, and all the holes centre popped. The marked plate should then be attached to its fellow with copper rivets, and the two drilled, sawn, and filed to shape. The holes for the service rivets should be chosen with due regard to their future use if any. Usually the buffer beam angles can be attached here.

Springs and Axle Boxes

If the model is to be sprung, great care should be taken that the slots for the axle boxes are all of the same width. It is most annoying to have to fit separately each box to its proper slot, and then having to mark each one, besides entailing extra work. A good plan to avoid this, is to use a jig the width of the box, or make a box itself the jig, and file with a fine file until the box slides perfectly up and down without any longitudinal shake. When the frames are completed they can be taken apart. In the case of long locos required to traverse sharp radius curves the frames can be cranked just behind the rear bogie wheels, to give extra clearance. There is precedence for this in some Caledonian and North Western engines, also the GWR four cylinder locomotives of the Star class.

Guard irons are usually attached to the frames separately, but in a model it is better to try and make these part of the frames, as shown in the drawings. They are then less liable to get knocked off in service. Try to avoid the use of smaller than scale bogie wheels to get clearance on curves, as this practice savours of the toy shop type of job, and ruins the appearance of the model if it is of a definite prototype. It is better to have overscale clearance holes in the frames; these will not be noticed with the modern small scale flanges. One way of overcoming the large bogie wheel clearance in models such as the GNR Single and early LNWR 4-4-0s is to split the bogie into two, i.e., making the leading pair of wheels as a pony truck and giving the second pair plenty of side play.

We now come to axle bearings. In OO gauge and smaller scales, frames are much simpler and horn blocks dispensed with. In these sizes the practice is to cut out springing and bush the frames with turned bronze bushes as already mentioned. These may be of the single flange type, but where such bushes are used, care must be taken in the sequence of operations in assembly, otherwise the wheels may be difficult to get in place. A much better scheme is to use a double flanged bush fitted into a slot, the top circular portion of which should be accurately placed and formed by drilling a plain hole through both frame plates before slotting. The keeper plate is a continuous strip of metal about the same thickness as the frames which is screwed to the main frames below the bushes. The wheels and axles can

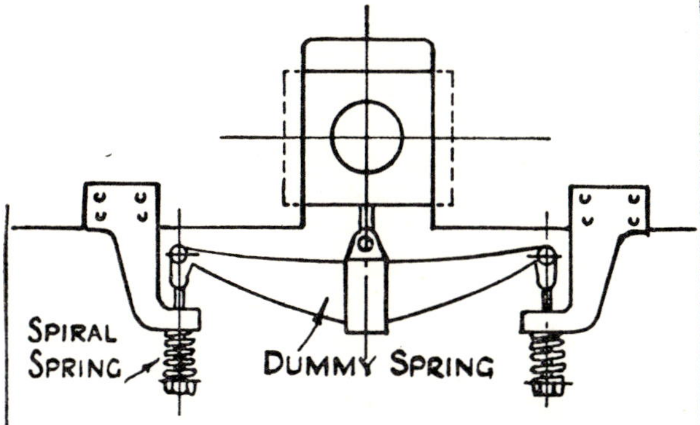

59 A MORE ELABORATE METHOD APPROXIMATING THE PROTOTYPE.

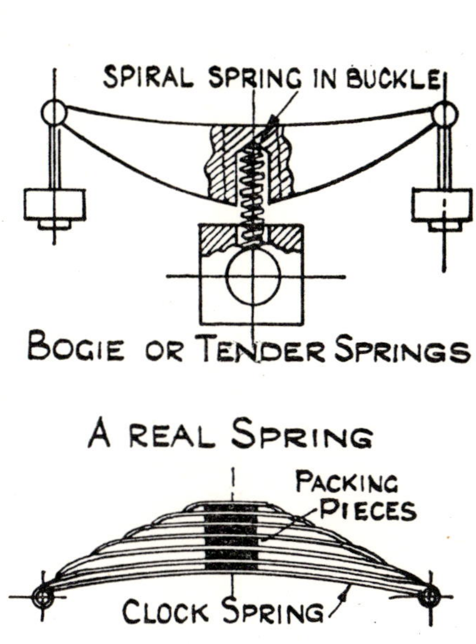

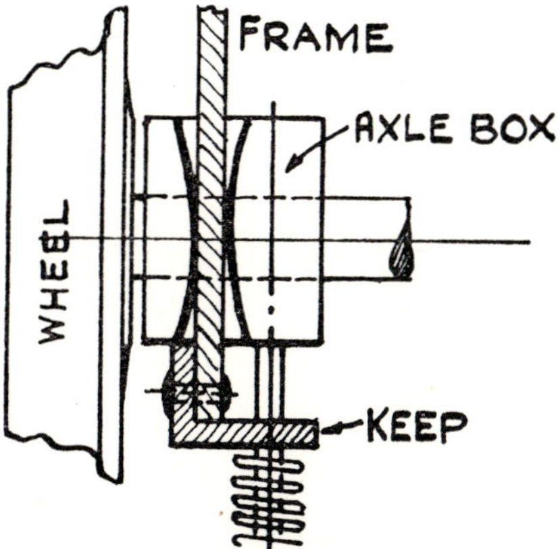

60 ALLOWING FOR CANT UNDER ACTION OF SPRINGS.

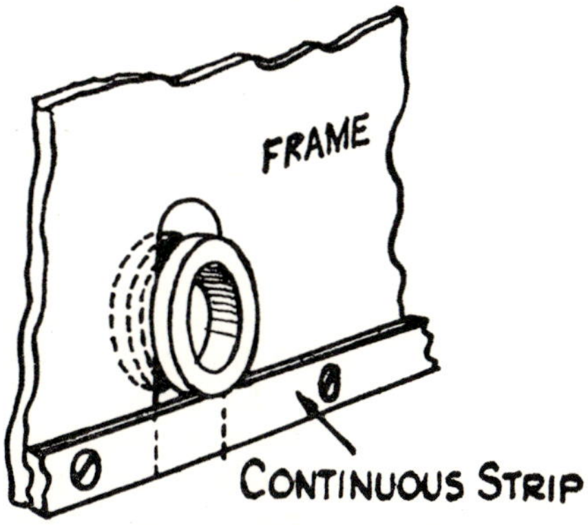

61 A BUSHING DEVICE ALLOWING WHEELS TO BE REMOVED.

then be finally fitted together, independently of the assembly of the frames and foot-plating, as in the case of a locomotive built on the orthodox plan with sprung axle boxes. The bushes also can easily be renewed when they are worn. This method is recommended when the driving wheels are forced on their axles, as in the case of driving wheels which are insulated at the hub as in some OO gauge models. Of course, there is no reason why a 4 mm. model cannot be sprung, providing the skill of the worker warrants such an expedient and a method of springing a small model in this gauge is shown in the sketches, clock spring being used. The springs must be very delicate as the lightness of this small gauge stock is a serious consideration, and attempting to overcome it by heavily weighting the locomotive beyond what it needs for adhesion, detracts from hauling power.

A simple type of axle box for O gauge is shown. The frames are slotted and axles restrained from moving in a fore and aft direction by the slot, the axle box governing the vertical movement. This form of box is more useful for bogies, and similar cases where the distance over the outside of the frames is not important. A hornblock of more orthodox appearance is shown in another sketch. Here the axle box slides in the hornway, and not in the frames; this gives more width between the latter. When making axle boxes, the slots which slide between the frames should be relieved a little to allow the box to cant under the action of the springs as shown in exaggerated form in the drawing, particularly is this necessary when a vehicle enters a super-elevated curve from the straight. A close approximation of the real thing in locomotive springs is also shown in which the real springs are of the spiral type and are placed under the hangers of the dummy spring. Another method is shown which would be applicable in tenders and outside framed trailing or bogie wheels, such as Pacific trailing ends, and outside framed engines of the GWR type. In this a spring is concealed in the buckle of the dummy spring, and the top of the axle box is drilled for the spring to seat itself. The writer uses this method for springing tenders, and has also used the clock spring method of making a real working spring as shown in the final sketch. The old broad gauge locos of the GWR used this type of spring, but it can be used for a modern loco wherever there are laminated springs. This spring consists of leaves of a clock or watch spring punched in the middle with a small hole, and one of the leaves turned up at each end to form an eye. The leaves are packed out with brass packing pieces as shown. This type of spring is quite sensitive if properly made, and care must be taken in punching the centre holes without softening the spring too much or losing its temper.

Returning to axle boxes, the bearing edge of the frames is quite sufficient for all practicable purposes. Where hornways are desired such as in a large model in No. 1 gauge, or a steam model, they should be made from the same material as the main frames. In fitting any spring borne axle box, the box should not be too rigid a fit laterally. As remarked earlier, it is always better to have some side play to allow the box to tip slightly as it rises and falls. No play, however, must be allowed in a fore and aft direction, otherwise coupling rods will bind, and the whole object of the springing be lost. This object is to obtain better and more realistic running, better hauling power, and freedom from derailments. Bearing bushes, or axle boxes, as a general rule should have a length of bearing equal to the diameter of the axle. Coming to springs, the spiral type is largely used in model locomotives. To determine the correct size for a given model is somewhat of a drawing office problem, with various fundamental rules regarding compression and deflection. It is usual to resort to trial and error methods in very tiny models such as OO and O gauge. The usual diameter for OO is between $\frac{1}{16}$ in. and $\frac{3}{32}$ in., and about $\frac{1}{4}$ in. to $\frac{3}{8}$ in. long. The thickness of the spring is about 26 swg and the material phosphor bronze. Small electric motor brush springs make good springs for this gauge.

Coming to O gauge, springs are between $\frac{1}{8}$ in. and $\frac{3}{16}$ in. diameter, $\frac{3}{8}$ in. and $\frac{1}{2}$ in. long and the material 22 or 24 swg spring steel wire. The number of coils does not affect the safe load, but only the deflection. The less number of coils the harder the spring is, and the more the coils the more sensitive the spring becomes. Laminated springs, if made to scale, will have little or no deflection, certainly not sufficient for the purposes of a working model. Where, for the sake of external appearance, they should be used and the methods shown in the sketches must be employed.

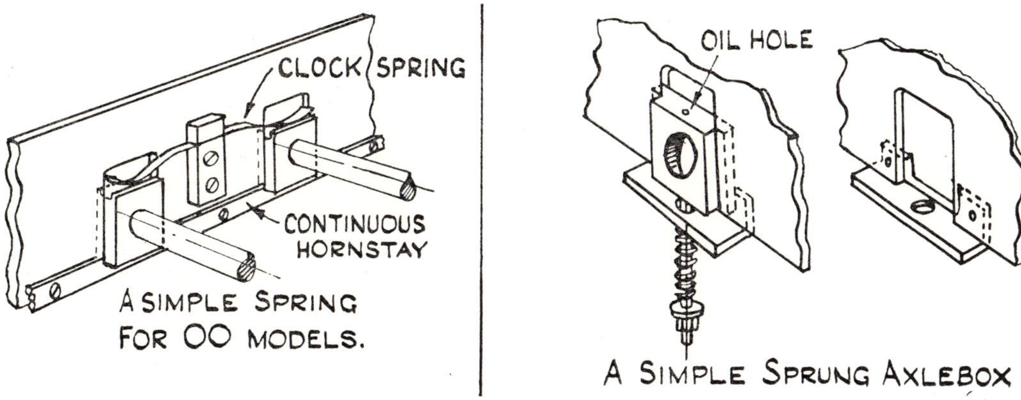

62

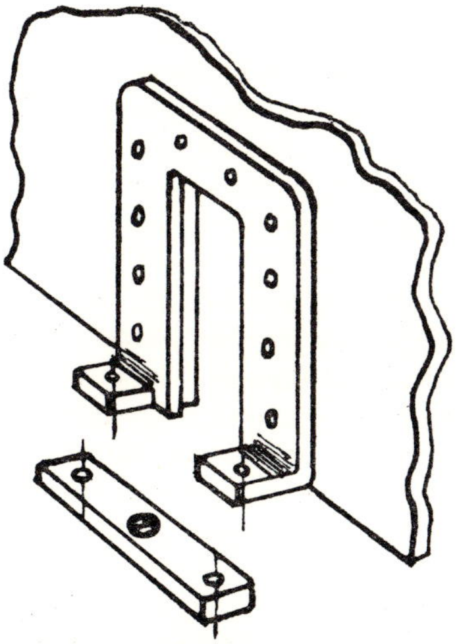

A SIMPLE HORNBLOCK AND KEEP FOR SPRUNG MODELS 63

Wheels and Axles

Having got our frames erected, we next must tackle the problem of wheels. These are of three types: (a) driving wheels, (b) coupled wheels and (c) carrying wheels. Except for the different positions of balance weights there is little difference between the first two classes. In actual practice wheels are made in two parts, the centre casting containing the spokes, and the tyre. The tyres are shrunk on and sometimes fastened with retaining rings and studs. In model practice one piece cast-iron wheels are usual, and a good range of castings containing the correct number of spokes for a given prototype is available from the trade. There is no excuse whatever for an incorrect number of spokes in locomotive wheels at the present time, particularly in bogie wheels. The days of the 8-spoke bogie wheel are over.

If a certain type of wheel is not available, instructions have already been given on an early page for making one's own patterns.

The balance weights of the prototype may be copied exactly if the builder makes his own patterns, and a balance equal to the original will be obtained in a steam model if the same number of cylinders and cranks are employed, but in an electric model, an over-balance will result since the prototype balance weight does not balance the coupling rod alone. In a sprung model, if the modeller considers it worthwhile, the balance weight may be blind drilled at the back to reduce the revolving mass to something nearer the weight of the coupling rod and connecting rod (in an outside cylinder model). In an inside cylinder model, the face of the wheel is often coned outwards, so that the maximum length of axle-box journal is obtained.

In modern outside cylinder engines the face of the spokes is usually quite flat, as the available width for the outside motion is limited. Balance weights, however, are arranged to project beyond the face of the tyre as shown in the sketch, so that the plane of these weights more nearly coincides with the masses they are counter-balancing. OO gauge driving wheels fall down badly in this respect as the balance weights are always the wrong shape and recessed in from the face of the tyre. However, there is one advantage; for the modeller may superimpose the correct shaped balance weight and rivet or araldite it in place. The metal, composing these wheels cannot be soldered.

Most wheels on the market, for OO gauge, are already in the finished state as far as the price will allow, but they may require a little trimming up with a knife edge file to clear away any casting flashes. The spokes near the centre require to be filed nearer to the boss, as there is considerable flash here. One cannot expect the trade to do this job as it would entail a considerable amount of handwork causing the cost to be rather prohibitive. A little trouble in trimming the wheels in this manner vastly improves the appearance of the finished model.

When the modeller turns his own wheels for O gauge and larger sizes, due regard should be paid to the features of the full size wheels. At exhibitions one can see that not one model in five had any indication of the tyre machined on the wheel face, and not one in ten had the same indication on the back of the wheel. There was also a common failure to produce the bevelled edge of the tyre on the front. The sketch of a portion of a driving wheel will make this clear. Another common fault is the high polishing of the tread of the tyre. In

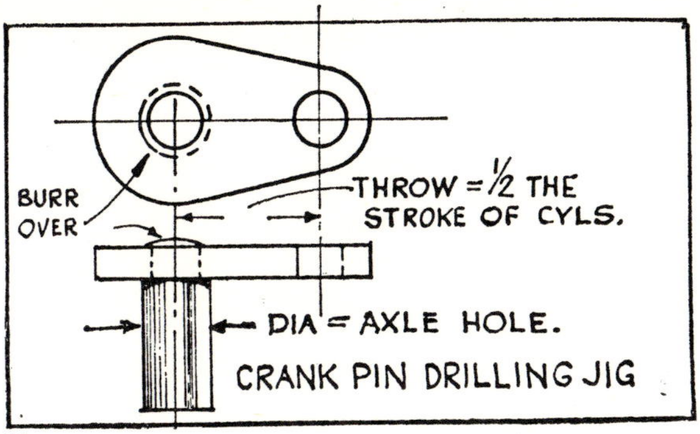

64

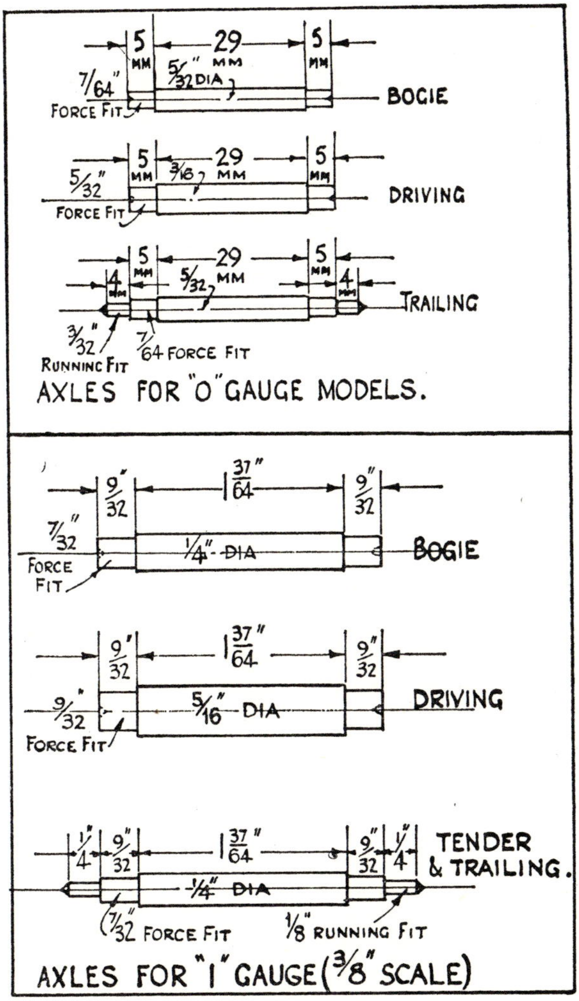

65

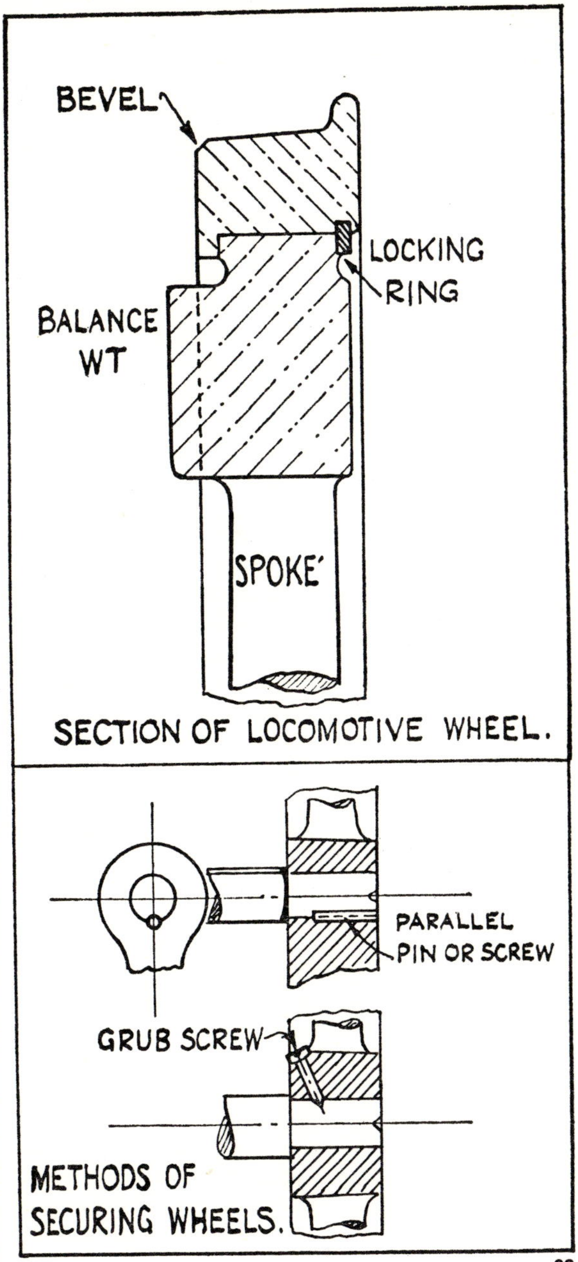

66

TYPE	GAUGE 18 & 16·5 MM.	1¼"	1¾"	SCALE ½"	¾"	1"
	DIA IN INCHES			DIA IN INCHES		
DRIVING & COUPLED	1/8"	3/16"	5/16"	3/8"	9/16"	13/16"
BOGIE & TENDER	14 SWG	5/32"	1/4"	9/32"	3/8"	9/16"

SIZES OF AXLES IN THE VARIOUS GAUGES & SCALES.

67

a model locomotive this is unnecessary as it causes wheels to lose their grip on the rail. If the model is to do a lot of running, a highly polished wheel tyre picks up dirt from the track; the pre-war nickel plated wheel was a source of trouble in this respect. It is better to leave the wheel tyre as finished by the tool. By this it is not meant that it should be left like a ploughed field ! but rather the finish left by a roundnosed tool.

In turning wheels the casting should be fettled up, so that on chucking it by the tread, back outwards, it runs reasonably true. Anyone who has had considerable experience of turning cast iron wheels will know that they are anything but round, except by accident ! Having got the wheel running reasonably true, as previously remarked, and having put it in the chuck *back* outwards, the edge of the flange may be turned nearly to size (but square), the back of the wheel and boss being faced and the hole for the axle bored. *Never* drill small wheels from the face side. Gauges should be made so that all similar wheels have the same bore, at least within half to a quarter-thousandth of an inch. The wheel may then be reversed in the chuck and finished off. When drilling the axle hole, the writer always uses a small drill first, in case there are any hard spots in the centre which would throw the drill out of true. If the full sized drill is put through and it wanders, there will be a few words of railroad Esperanto and a ruined wheel, so safety-first is the rule in machining these small wheels. In any case the hole should be reamed to the correct size, and never left as a plain drilled hole. because should the operator have the misfortune to break a drill and it is reground, or another one obtained, the chances are that it will be larger or smaller, in spite of the fact that they are all labelled the same size ! Check it first with a micrometer and if a piece of broken drill is embedded in the wheel boss, the act of getting it out may enlarge the hole, so always *ream* the axle holes to size.

Having now machined all our wheels, there are now the axles to make. Full size locomotive axles are made of a high grade steel which will stand shocks, and have collars next to the wheels and journals. These may be copied in the model, but reliance should not be placed on such collars for taking lateral loads as the wheel boss face provides much better surfaces. The ordinary model axle is not subjected to such heavy stresses as in a real loco, but wear and tear is greater on outdoor lines due to the presence of grit and dust. The drawings show typical axles for O and 1 gauges. Axles should be forced into the wheels and be $\frac{1}{2}$ to $1\frac{1}{2}$ thou. larger than the hole according to the size of the axle. The increase in size should be slightly greater at the back than at the front, but this does not mean that the fitting at the latter point should in any way be loose. Centres should be left in the axles so that the wheels may be skimmed true. The distance between tyres is so important that accuracy must be observed in all lateral dimensions of wheels and axles.

Bogie and carrying axles require no fixing other than that provided by the force fitting, but driving wheels, if of large diameter, should be secured by pins or keys. The most satisfactory method is a screw or parallel pin driven axially half in the wheel and half in the axle. Screwing wheels on to axles is only adopted in small commercially made toys, and a locking device must be provided to adjust and maintain the correct 90 deg. angle of the

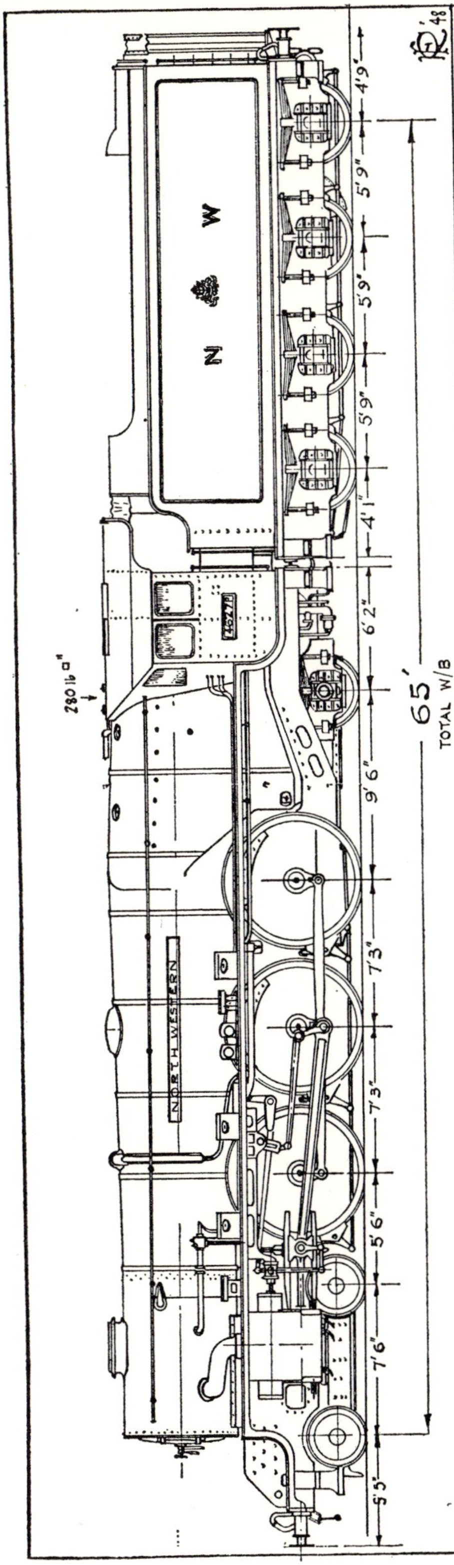

L.M.S. "DUCHESS" FITTED WITH CORRIDOR TENDER.
FITTED WITH 6'-6" DRIVING WHEELS & 280□" BOILER PAINTED AND LINED IN EX L.N.W.R STYLE,

89

crank pins. Other methods of fixing wheels to axles such as square holes, and squared axles, slotted locking nuts, etc., are only found in 4 mm. scale and do not concern the larger modeller. Even in these gauges force fitting is possible, and indeed is indulged in for carrying wheels. It may be used for driving wheels, if the method of a continuous hornkeep, previously mentioned, is used. The wheels can then be removed at any time for servicing or motor adjustments. The sizes listed are recommended for axles in the various gauges, the exact dimensions of wheel seats, etc., being determined by the design of the axle, with due regard to the dimensions of standard reamers, used in the wheel holes.

Further notes on wheel turning are given on page 181.

Cranks and Crankpins

The next job is the crankpins, and they depend for design on the size of the loco. For OO and some small O gauge engines, shouldered screws are quite satisfactory. The sketches show the standard practice of today for amateur built O and 1 gauge engines. Do not attempt to improve on full-size practice by dispensing with the nut, and using a washer held in place by a split-pin, a fault which spoilt some of the finest trade models of a well-known maker. It is not only bad engineering practice to rely on a split-pin to hold a coupling rod in place but it is also incorrect.

In larger models there is no objection to using a splitpin, if the nut is *screwed* on as well, and the pin put through the lot. This is standard practice on some lines. When making the leading crank pin, due regard should be paid to the clearance required for the connecting rod. Special devices are indulged in for retaining the rods and a few of these are shown in the sketches. In any case the nuts retaining the rods in place should fit tightly, and should have little work to do in holding the rod. There are several small fibre insert locknuts on the market which can be used on the larger models. Changes in diameter of crankpins (and axles) at the shoulders should be protected by corners of ample radii, to guard against failure or bending.

A simple jig is necessary to ensure that all the crankpin holes in the wheels are exactly alike, and a method of making this is shown in the sketch. The spigot which goes into the axle hole of the wheel should be riveted or burred over, into the jig, and the whole should be made of tool steel and case hardened, if a lot of wheels are being worked on at a time.

In models fitted with inside motion, appearance rather than actual work is usually the reason for indulging in the joy (or otherwise) of making a cranked axle. These are peculiar to this country, they are seldom found abroad except in compound engines using three or four cylinders. The making of a model cranked axle, no doubt, deters many amateurs from adopting an inside cylinder prototype if inside motion is desired in an electrically-driven model locomotive. For those who have a lathe, it is better to turn the complete axle entirely, but cranked axles can be built up by brazing the parts together, or even force fitting them. They have little work to do, as they are turned by the motor instead of the axle turning the wheels, as in a steam model. Two methods of making these are shown in the drawings. The writer used the built-up method in his King and Castle class engines. When making the centre piece do not forget to place the eccentric sheaves in place before fitting the other pair of webs. Stephenson's valve gear requires four eccentrics, and inside Walschaert's gear, two. Other forms of valve gear will be described when we come to that section. Both single and double throw crank valve axles may be turned from mild steel bar of a section the same size as the webs. The centre portion of a double throw axle should be bent hot after turning in the rough, and throw plates for the ends are required to get the best results. A good operator on a power lathe, should be able to make a cranked axle in about three hours. When the axle is complete, ready for forcing on the wheels, be sure and pack out the webs with pieces of steel plate to prevent distortion during the forcing process. We have now covered the driving part of our engine, and must next turn our attention to bogies and pony trucks.

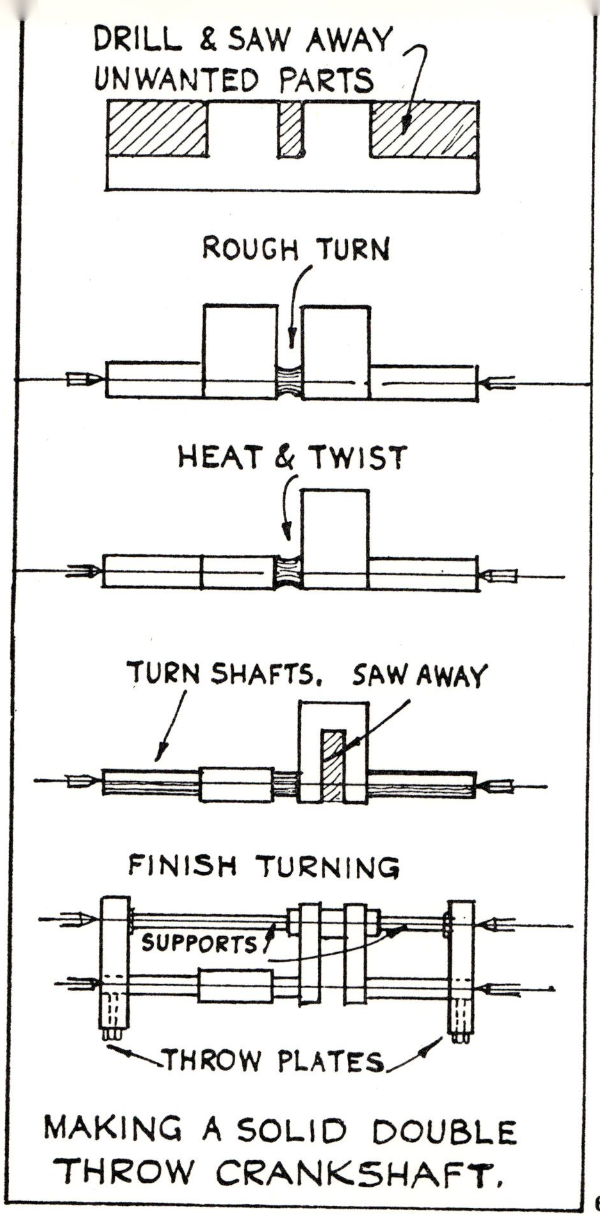

69

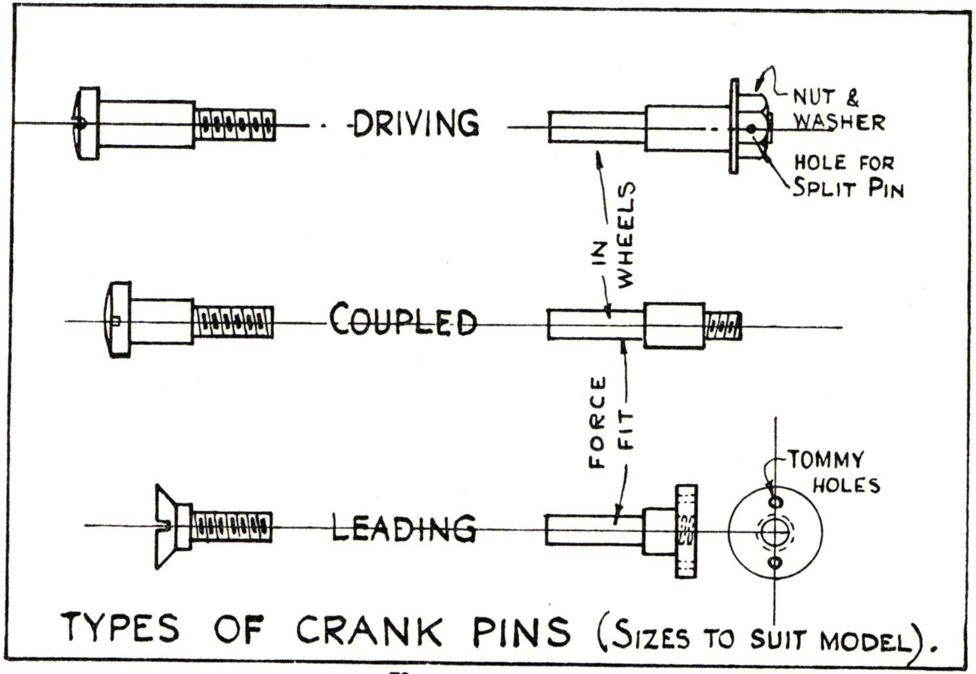

70

71 Built up crankshaft

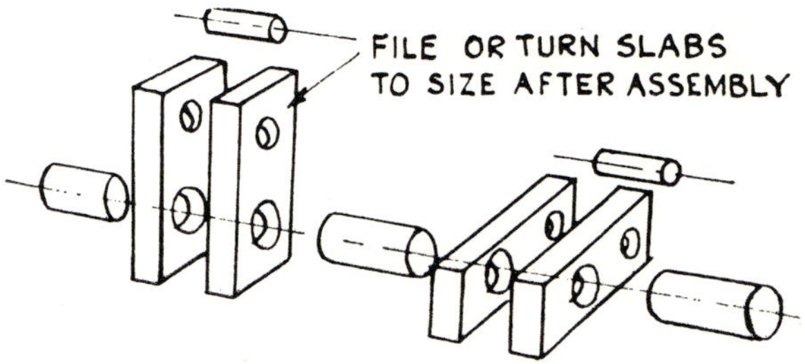

Bogies and Pony Trucks

The bogie of a steam locomotive is usually carried on four wheels of relatively small diameter. It provides the necessary support for the front or rear end of the engine in a manner which renders the whole wheelbase of the locomotive much more flexible on curves than if the frames were carried on rigid axles. As a rule a four-wheel bogie is much preferred to a two-wheeled truck or any other form of radial axle at the leading end of an express locomotive. A bogie also fits very naturally under the cylinders. The placing of a four-wheeled bogie truck on a plain central pivot does not entirely fulfil all the functions of a bogie forming part of a locomotive which has any portion of its wheelbase rigid and parallel to its main frames. This will perhaps be better understood by a reference to the diagram given of the LMS 2–6–4T on a curve (fig. 55). It will be seen that the bogie must slide laterally on its pivot as well as turning round it. It is also desirable that the sliding box, or pad-piece into which the bogie pin fits, should be controlled by springs or some equivalent device which will tend to keep the truck central.

Before we pass to bogies and pony trucks, a little more must be said regarding turning and fitting driving wheels. Earlier, when dealing with this subject, I purposely refrained from giving concise instructions for turning and fitting, for the simple reason that no two lathe workers use the same methods. I did however give *my* method, and Mr. Michael Longridge has given *his* method, totally at variance with mine (see page 182).

This book is not intended to be a treatise on lathe work, as many modellers have no lathe. The subject of wheel turning has been amply covered by such writers as L.B.S.C. in the *Model Engineer*, Henry Greenly, George Gentry, and scores of others and in every case their methods are different. The fact is that wheel turning is treated according to the operator's own methods in turning; all I can do is to give a few hints and don'ts.

I do not recommend using form tools for a one-off job. Modern O gauge wheel castings are very delicate and form tooling them causes chatter and consequent breakage. A form tool is only used for profiling and should not take off more than a shaving, as I mentioned. I said never drill small wheels from the face side. I was, of course, referring to bogie wheels, which have the spigot cast on the face side.

Herewith are a few sketches showing my method of turning these wheels. I have literally turned hundreds and not had a breakage, or a wobbly wheel. I always turn all the wheels required for a loco completely from the front and drill them for axles, not necessarily right through the spigot, but only so far as is required. I then change tools and back them all off together, exposing the spokes. I think I can claim to have used every make of lathe under the sun from Drummond to South Bend in all sorts of workshops in England and abroad, but I will say here that the best type of lathe is one which has a box type revolving tool holder, in which all the tools for the job can be set up. It only needs a turn of the holder to bring the correct tool into use. This feature is found on the South Bend lathe. Many modelmakers fit a tool post of this type themselves; it is far more useful than the pattern supplied with the majority of English lathes. The smallest lathe I have ever used was a Boley watchmakers lathe for turning bogie wheels, and the largest a huge affair with a 10 in. chuck. The latter lathe was about 10 feet long. I forget its name for the moment, but I used it for turning a pair of 8 ft. drivers in O gauge!

Now for a few words on fitting wheels on their axles. I have already given the forced on method and details of pinning them if necessary. Where the wheels are required to be removed frequently for servicing the motor in an unsprung loco Mr. Longridge's method may be used. It will, of course, be obvious that the gear wheel on the axle should be a sliding fit, and pinned

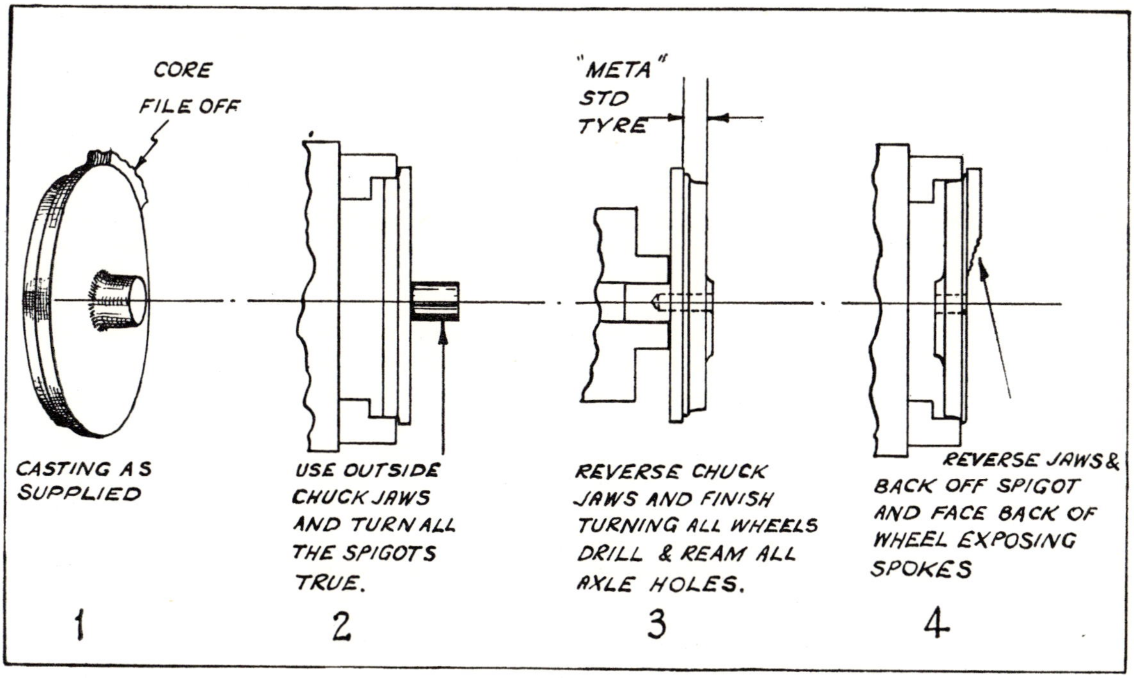

72 Wheel turning

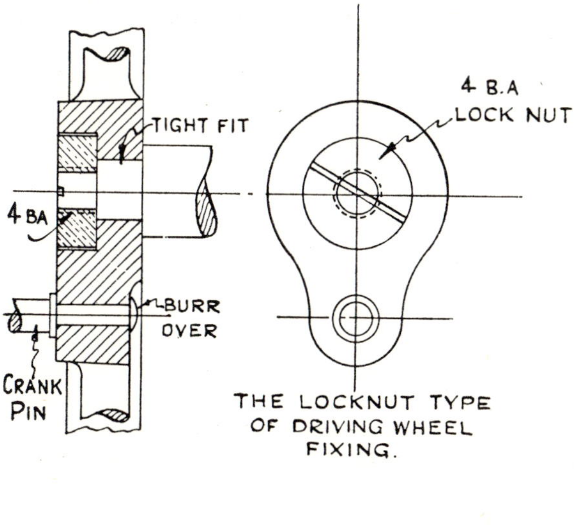

73

to the axle with a grub type screw, in order that when one wheel is unscrewed, the gear wheel can be loosened, and the whole axle and the forced on wheel withdrawn. Another method of fixing wheels is shown in the sketch. This is a partly forced and partly screwed method. Yet another is the squared axle and squared hole in the wheel method. Great care must be taken in squaring the hole in the wheel, and the axles of course may be purchased. It is not advisable for the amateur to make these himself without a milling machine, but such wheels can be purchased complete in 4 mm. scale.

The advantage of this method is that a dead correct 90 deg. angle of the crankpins can be obtained. In an electric model it is not necessary to quarter the wheels at 90 deg. to the nearest thou' as it would be in a steam driven model. A very accurate method of quartering wheels is to do it by eye through the medium of the spokes. Place both wheels on their axle until they are a friction fit (not too tight), hold them up to the light, and turn them on the axle until they are approximately at 90 deg., and get all the spokes opposite one another, until both wheels appear as one.

If the crank pin holes have been accurately drilled, the wheels will be at 90 deg. for all practical purposes in an electrically driven model. They may be even 90.5 deg., but so long as they are all alike it is all that matters. When forcing or screwing bogie and tender wheels on their axles, it is also advisable to get the spokes opposite one another. The model will photograph better than if the wheels are put on with their spokes staggered, making it appear as though they are Bicycle wheels when daylight shows through across the engine. A glance at photos of full size locos will reveal that the spokes of the wheels are opposite one another.

In the locknut method of fitting driving wheels to their axles, the lock nut should in no way be a sloppy fit; it must fit tightly into the recess provided. The slot can be filled up with plastic wood before painting, and it will not be noticed. Always put all the slotted nuts on the same side of the engine.

Frames and Running Gear

As there is interest in GNR Atlantics, I give some drawings of these famous locomotives. The coming of 4 mm. scale on 16.5 track was a help in modelling an engine of this type. The superstructure can be modelled dead to scale, including the correct width across the splashers in this gauge. The trailing wheels and the leading pair of bogie wheels can be given side play, making the remainder of the wheelbase rigid. The total wheel base is only 26 ft. 4 in. In 4 mm. scale this would work out at a little over 105¼ mm., or 4$\frac{3}{16}$ in. I do not think that the standard 3 ft. radius curve used in OO gauge would put an undue strain on that! Colonel Templer's method of making dummy frames above the footplate would have to be resorted to in order to reproduce the correct smokebox saddle. These frames would have to stop short at the commencement of the driving splashers. It will probably be found that the flanges of the driving wheels will foul the boiler, but as this has to be cut away to incorporate the motor, any difficulty from this source would disappear. With careful workmanship there is no reason why the cylinders should not be fitted to the main frames, making a complete chassis from front to rear beam. Making the cylinders as part of the super-

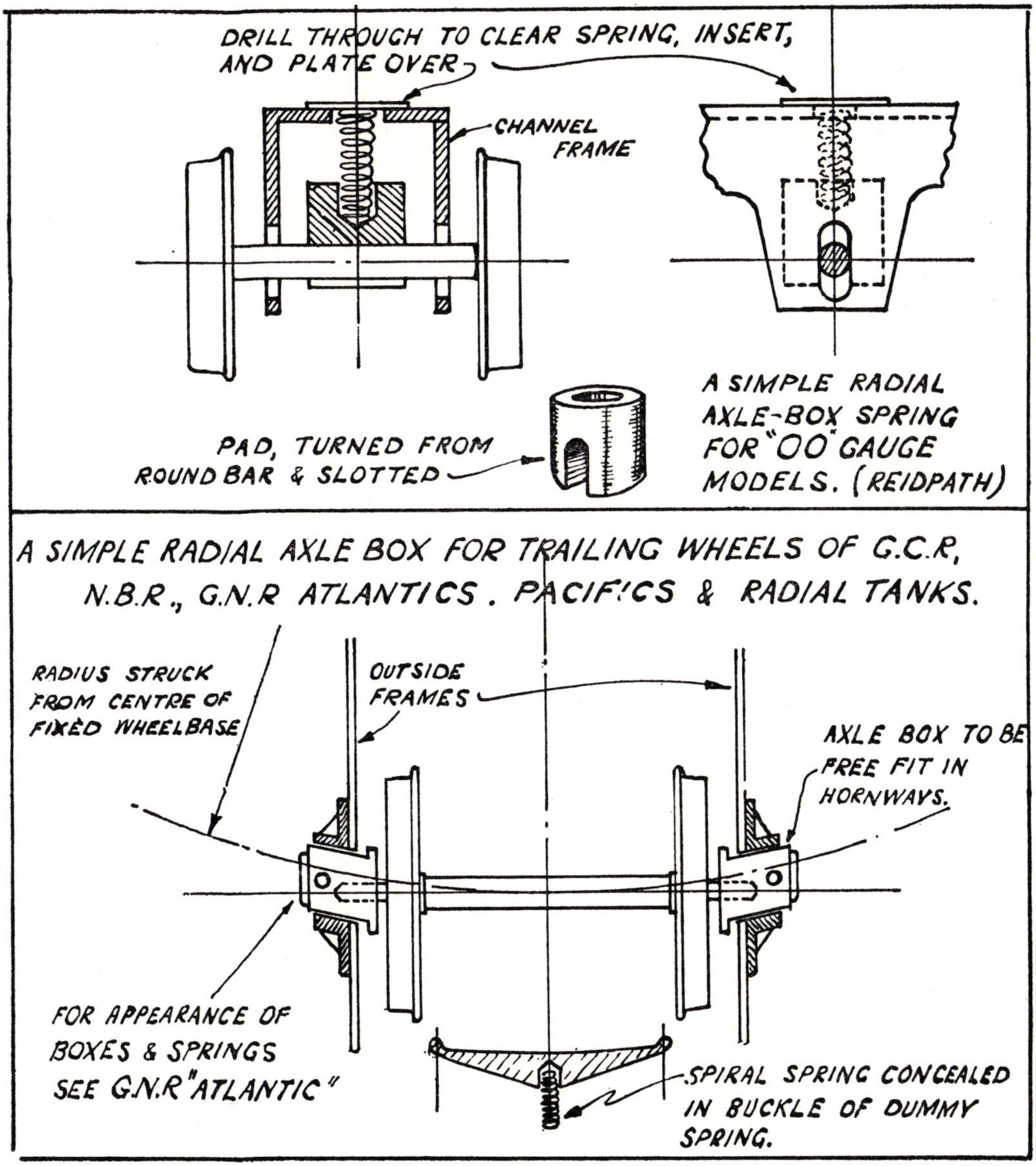

74 Making axle boxes

structure is a fiddling business when it is necessary to remove the power unit. In making the chassis, the front of the main frames should be set in a little in order to avoid cutting any clearances for the bogie leading wheels, as if this is done there is very little metal left. This wangle will be hardly noticed as there is a large plate attached to the valance which will hide it.

Coming now to the coupled wheelbase, the official drawings show the

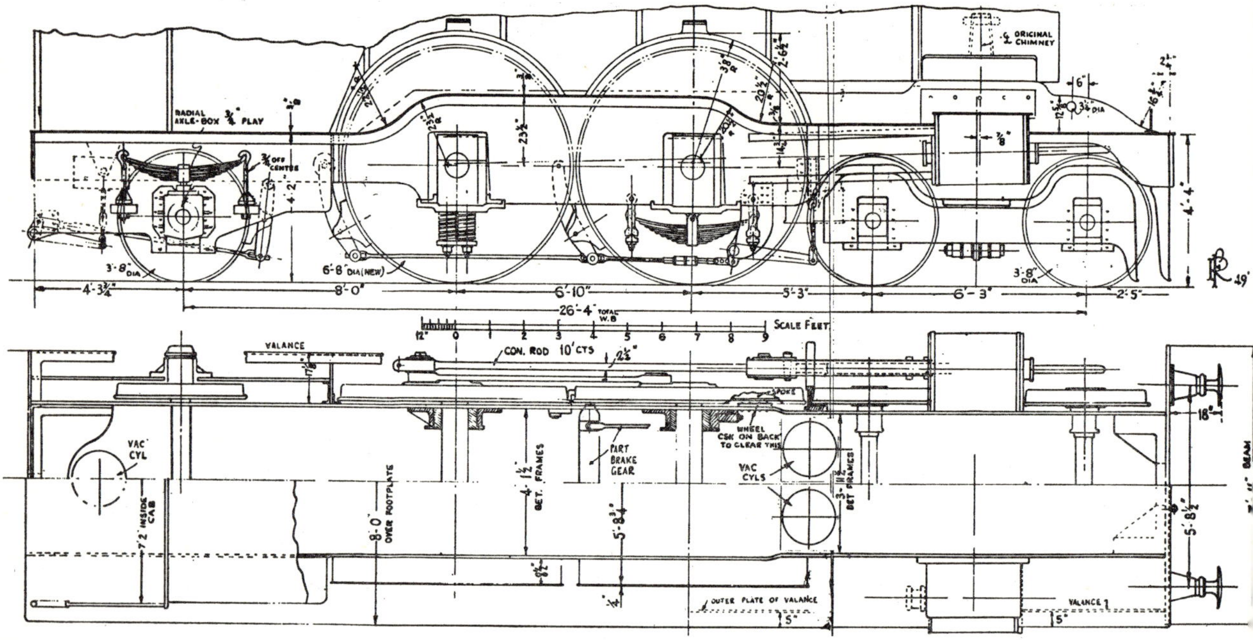

75 Ten-wheeled (four-coupled) express passenger locomotive, Great Northern Railway

wheels as stated 6 ft. 8 in. (new), the word new being in brackets as shown. Official descriptions of this loco state the wheels as 6 ft. 7½ in. so readers can take their choice! They were placed at 6 ft. 10 in. centres. This must be preserved in the model at all costs, and the wheels reduced in diameter until the flanges clear one another by about the thickness of a visiting card. I feel it is unnecessary to state that there must be no sloppy fits in the driving axle holes or boxes! The brake hangers to the leading coupled wheels were *inside* the frames, and were joggled outwards below the main frame to accommodate the block, and the rear brake hanger was made in the normal way.

All other details will be apparent on perusal of the plan view, including the slight narrowing of the main frames at the leading end to a distance of 3 ft. 11½ in. apart, the remainder of the frames being 4 ft. 1½ in. apart. I should very much like to see a good model of this locomotive complete with the famous GNR clerestory teak coaches; these too have almost disappeared. I have a model of one of these coaches in 3½ mm. scale which is a dining car, and completely fitted internally, even with a chop in the frying pan!

While on the subject of pre-Grouping prototypes that have disappeared, I was sorry to see the last of the famous Premier Line locos have gone to their Valhalla. If only we had a Wagner to compose a symphony to the passing of these great friends of man, which built up our railway system to the pitch of excellence it enjoyed during the years of their heyday, when the competitive spirit was seen in their cleanliness, their race against time to beat their opponents of the GNR. In the traffic for the north, they were always rivals, in a friendly way, these two, LNWR and GNR.

If a model of a GNR Atlantic is modelled then we too should have an Experiment or a Precursor to keep it company.

Here again, in the case of the Experiments we had a prototype that was not often modelled in earlier days owing to its close coupled wheelbase, but using our modern fine scale standards in both O and OO gauge we can make an almost perfect miniature of this famous class.

From reference to Mr. Platt's drawing, it will be seen that the main frames were spliced at the front end, and also again narrowed in the vicinity of the leading bogie wheels. This splicing of the main frames at the front was a feature of all LNWR engines of Geo. Whale's design, and some of Mr. Bowen Cooke's. The main frames proper were cut short just behind the leading steps, and additional frames were riveted behind them to the front buffer beam. This feature was taken advantage of in the old method of construction where we had our wheels attached to the motor frames in O gauge. Little dummy frames were soldered to the front of the superstructure, to butt up against these motor frames. In the modern method of construction, we make our frames all in one piece, including those over the bogie; these frames can be narrowed to a greater extent than scale according to the curves we have to negotiate. The correct narrowing can be shown by scale thickness frames soldered above the footplate, or bedplate as we used to call it in model parlance. Again, in this loco, avoid if possible, cutting the main frames to clear bogie wheels. This savours of toyshop practice, and looks awful if our flanges are too much over scale, besides leaving very little metal above the wheels. In the Precursors luckily, smaller bogie wheels were fitted later in their life, although it rather spoilt their typical LNWR flavour. In the author's opinion, fitting smaller than scale bogie wheels to an LNWR loco is on a par with fitting the wrong shaped chimney; it entirely spoils their appearance. However, we can now alter all these earlier faults common to models of these GNR and Premier Line locos if we build to modern standards. Some beautiful models of LNWR locos have been built in O gauge, HO and OO gauge and they *all* work! I have built many little LNWR engines in HO gauge, and in O gauge for a well-known trade firm, and many beautiful models of LNW locos were built in O gauge by Miller Swann, in pre-War days. To return to the subject, on further reference to Mr. Platt's drawing, and my own of the GNR Atlantic, it will be seen that in the former case the splashers were only 8¾in. wide over the beading, and as the wheels were 5⅜ in. from the face, to the face of the main frames, we have not much room to increase the thickness of the wheel, but if we add to this the narrower than scale distance of the main frames apart, we can use slightly thicker wheels without making our splashers over scale regarding the distance from face to face across the loco. The distance apart of the splashers of the GNR engine was 5 ft. 9¼ in. or 5 ft. 8¾ in. plus a ¼ in. thick beading each side of the engine. Again owing to our wheels being slightly thicker due to the frames being under scale apart, and also the gauge being under scale in both O and OO gauges, we can still make our splashers correct. Both locos can be made dead to scale, and still work properly if all the wheels are sprung, and scale flanges used, and—most important point this—the track is properly laid. So many modellers blame the loco, the wheels, the firm who built it, in fact everything but their own track laying.

So many aids to track laying are now on the market in both gauges, that there is little excuse for badly laid track, and point construction. OO gauge in itself is too small to allow of much inaccuracy in track laying, and in fine scale O gauge the same applies. This is the chief reason why these standards were introduced, because our track laying has improved from the coarse, and tinplate standards of former years.

Locomotive Kits

While we are on the subject of erecting the loco, a few words may be said about locomotive kits now on the market. These kits are a boon to those like myself who have no workshop facilities, and only a few hours of spare time. I have to work for my living like anyone else and all my models have been built in spare time.

The last model I built, a GWR Castle, took the best part of two years using other peoples workshop facilities. I have never had a workshop of my own! Having got that off my jolly old chest let us proceed.

On receiving the kit, a good deal of cleaning up is necessary to remove flashings due to the dies not meeting properly. One cannot expect a trade firm to do this as it would make the cost prohibitive. A great deal depends upon how this is done. Great care exercised at this stage will be amply repaid when the painting stage is reached.

When the body is cleaned up to the modeller's satisfaction, provision can now be made for any additional detail not included with the kit. A word here about the split pins supplied for handrail knobs. The instructions say push these into the boiler and open out inside, but if it is done like this the handrail will fall out when the loco is stood on its smokebox, as action of opening out the prongs of the split pin also unfortunately, opens out the eye of the pin, I cross the prongs inside, reference to the sketches will explain this. This will close the eye of the split pin, and hold the handrail firmly.

We now come to the tender. Care again must be exercised in the cleaning up.

Now a word about the wheels. First clean them up with a knife edge file, and—most important this—drill right through the wheel with a No. 66 drill at the crank pin hole. If this is not done, the tiny 14 B.A. screws supplied for crank pins will break off when they are only half screwed in.

Kits can be a very creditable effort in the right direction and a great deal of thought goes into their production. If as much thought goes into the chassis (if marketed), we will have a very inexpensive little model of a very famous prototype. I realise a great deal of capital has to go into a product of this sort, and the producers have to work in the dark as it were, as English enthusiasts have so many favourite types that it is impossible to please everyone, and the market is therefore limited. The kit system of railway modelling is far more advanced in America than in this country, but American locomotives are all built by outside firms to a more or less standard pattern, and putting them up in kits is therefore considerably simplified, from the humble 0–4–0 switcher to the mighty Mallet Compounds, and they make perfect models. I have seen one of their loco kits, and the whole thing is a marvel of ingenuity and packing. They are put up in a box with dozens

An S gauge, 3/16in to 1ft scale, model of an ex-LSWR Adams' radial tank built by Bernard Wright

A 7mm scale model of the LNER (ex-GER) class G4 0-4-4T built by Ken Leeming. The only commercial parts used in the construction were the electric motor, the gearing and the transfers. This model won the Chairman's Trophy at the Model Railway Club's competition in 1967

A standard Tri-ang B.12 class 4-6-0 which has been super-detailed and repainted by E. N. Bellass. A far more realistic appearance can be gained with a little work on many of the proprietary range of locomotives

A 4mm scale (00 gauge) model of an LNER (ex-GNR) class J6 0-6-0 goods locomotive. The model was built by Frank Dyer for his Borchester layout and uses Romford TT gauge wheels and is fitted with a Romford Terrier motor

A superb model of an ex-LSWR class T9 4-4-0 built by Bernard Wright for his S gauge layout

Another locomotive from the Borchester layout built by Frank Dyer—an ex-GNR class 02, 3-cylinder 2-8-0 goods locomotive. A Zenith 004 motor has been fitted into the spacious boiler. Note the fully working Walschaert's valve gear

Lord Rodney, a 4mm scale model of the SR Lord Nelson class 4-6-0, scratch-built by Alan Taylor

An ex-LSWR class M7 0-4-4T entirely hand built by Bernard Wright to 3/16in to 1ft scale (S gauge). This is a sister locomotive to the one shown on the dust jacket

A view showing the realism that can be obtained using proprietary locomotives and plastic kits in a 4mm scale locomotive depot. Part of the realism has been obtained by suitably dirtying the loco to simulate the working appearance of the 1960s

An unpainted 4mm scale model of the GWR King class 4-6-0 that has been constructed by Alan Taylor. Note the rivet detail on the cab and on the smokebox

Another view of the very fine model, coupled to its tender

of compartments, each having its own little part in their order of erection. It appears quite impossible to go wrong and I hope to have the pleasure of putting one of these kits together in the near future. All power to the elbows of their British counterparts in putting kits on the market, but here a word of warning, *do the job thoroughly*, and get together with other trade firms marketing parts other than your own. META (Model Engineering Trade Association) was formed for that purpose. There is still too much rivalry and backbiting among the trade; to quote an example, I recently put together some goods wagons, in which the body parts were perfect, but somebody else's chassis was used, consequently the body was narrower than the chassis, ruining the whole thing. In cases like these not one firm suffers, but two or three, or more whoever goes to make up the kit. I am in favour of a central clearing house, to which all firms send their parts to be made up into kits, by this 'marketing board' and everything that does not fit is thrown out. This would keep the trade on their toes and the public satisfied, especially the beginner, who is the one who really suffers. The standards are specifically laid down, i.e., 4 mm. 16.5 gauge and 7 mm. 1¼ in. gauge for all kits. All the trade has to do is to work to them, but apparently they cannot! How else do we get a chassis a scale 8 ft. 6 in. wide to go with a body only 8 ft. wide, which latter is the correct dimension for open wagons. An experienced modelmaker can put any sort of kit together, good or bad, but that is not the market to cater for. There is a vast, untapped market in this country and abroad, for kits of parts to suit the young student of transport, who has little skill, but likes, during the long winter months, to make something that works. Model aircraft firms have shown us the way, now it is the turn of the model railway trade to get into this market. The perfect kit should require nothing but a screwdriver, a tube of adhesive, a pair of pliers, and a razor blade, with possibly a pair of tweezers and a ruler, but this should be a luxury if the kit is properly made, and a proper drawing supplied. The drawings I have seen in some kits appear to have been made by a first year apprentice in the drawing office.

The GWR Bar Frame Bogie

Well we have strayed far from our theme of modelling locomotives and we must get back on the main line again. Col. Templer mentions breaking down the superstructure into several component parts for painting purposes, I admit I led him to assume that I favoured this method, because I built a model Castle class loco like this, which he has seen, but I do not think I have favoured this method in my articles. If I have, then I am sorry to have been misleading others. I built the model in this fashion more or less using steam locomotive methods as the engine was originally intended to be steam driven, but being moved around so many times in India I gave up the idea, and completed it for electric propulsion, intending to fit a motor when I came home.

Be it now understood, once and for all, that this book favours building the superstructure as a unit, particularly in gauge OO. In gauge O the footplates can be built separately when it is of complicated construction, with a lot of bits in it of different levels, or it is attached to the boiler high up, like the B1 of the LNER and the 2–6–0 of the Ivatt design on the LMS. These footplates are built separately and attached to the boiler anyway. In earlier prototypes, and tank engines, the footplate can be made as a Bedplate and the necessary clearances for frames etc. cut away. This will be made clear when we deal with the platework of the superstructure.

Regarding the paragraph of Col. Templer's about painting, I am afraid it is myself who is heading straight for the nearest mental institution, along with the people who send me models to paint, because, contrary to Col. Templer's hope, they only too frequently send me models to paint with the wheels, motion, etc., all *in situ*. That is why I think I have never given spray painting a real trial—I have never been able to do it! One hesitates to take down other people's models, even if that were possible, because if anything goes wrong with the works, they are sure to blame me and that is why, along with the Colonel, I favour screwing or bolting things together. Some people are far too fond of the soldering bit and hammer, and have a passion for rivetting ! So the next time you meet Napoleon in the aforesaid institution, it will be myself, and I shall tell you fervently that I retreated from Moscow, not on a horse, but on a model locomotive with the wheels, motion etc., all rivetted up and soldered !

Regarding the remarks of some people regarding frame widths the scale width at the front of the model can be preserved in the matter of frames by fitting dummy frames above the footplate, but so far I have described locos with narrowed in frames at the front end, including the GWR Stars and early Castles and 4–4–0s. In these cases there is no reason why the frames should not come right through the footplate. It is only with modern prototypes, having frames the full 4 ft. 0 in. or more apart throughout the locos, that we get into trouble at the smokebox end. Of course it is possible to remove a built-in motor without taking down the motion, providing that the aforesaid motion is attached by means of auxiliary frames to the front of the motor, a method which we should all use, and naturally we rigidly adhere to steam outlines in the superstructure if we are building a model of a steam locomotive. As a draughtsman myself I have some wonderful schemes that work on paper, but somehow or other they do not look or work half so

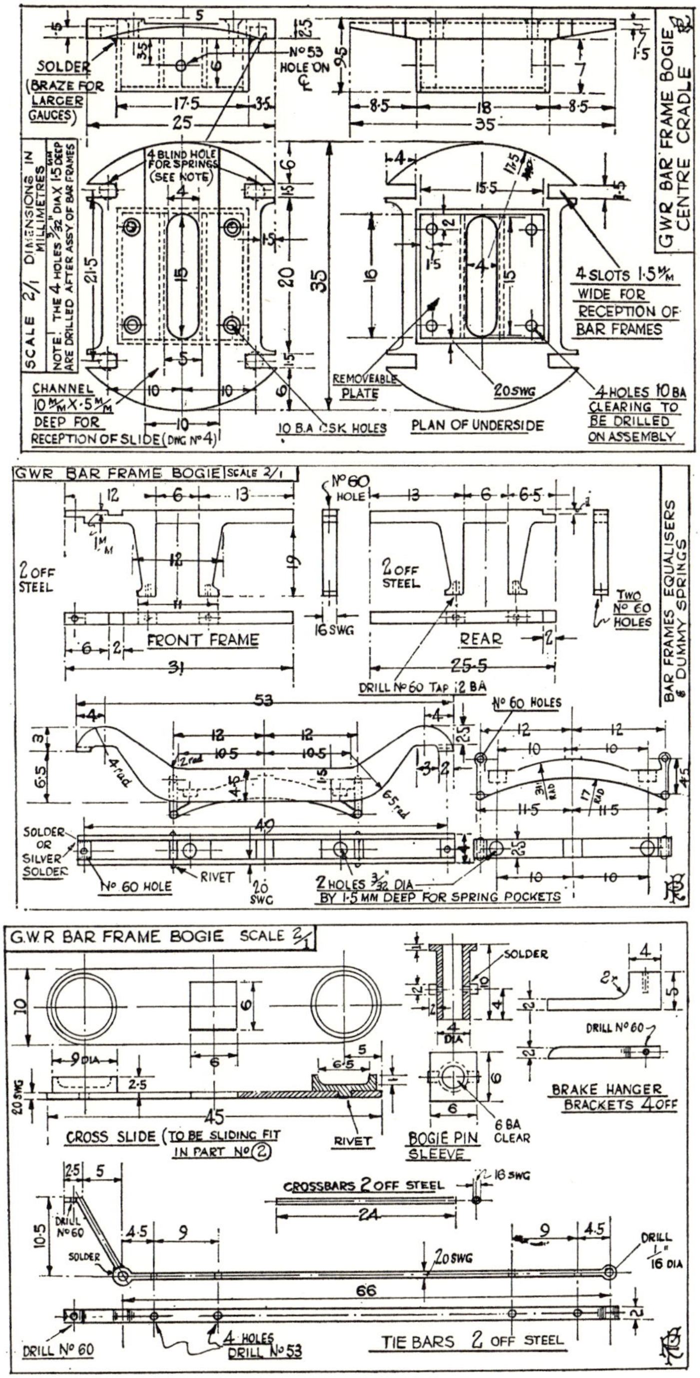

76 GWR bar frame bogie detail (actual size, 7 mm scale)

77

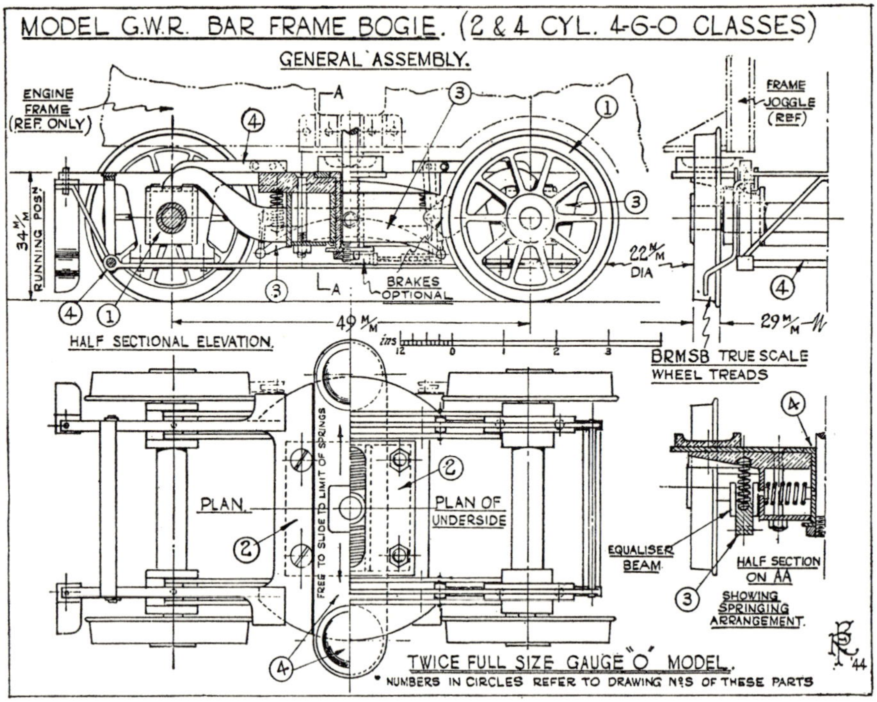
MODEL G.W.R. BAR FRAME BOGIE. (2 & 4 CYL. 4-6-0 CLASSES)
GENERAL ASSEMBLY.
ENGINE FRAME (REF. ONLY)
FRAME JOGGLE (REF)
34 M/M RUNNING POSN.
BRAKES OPTIONAL
22 M/M DIA
49 M/M
29 M/M
HALF SECTIONAL ELEVATION.
BRMSB TRUE SCALE WHEEL TREADS
PLAN.
PLAN OF UNDERSIDE
FREE TO SLIDE TO LIMIT OF SPRINGS
EQUALISER BEAM
HALF SECTION ON AA
SHOWING SPRINGING ARRANGEMENT.
TWICE FULL SIZE GAUGE "O" MODEL.
NUMBERS IN CIRCLES REFER TO DRAWING NOS OF THESE PARTS
'44

78

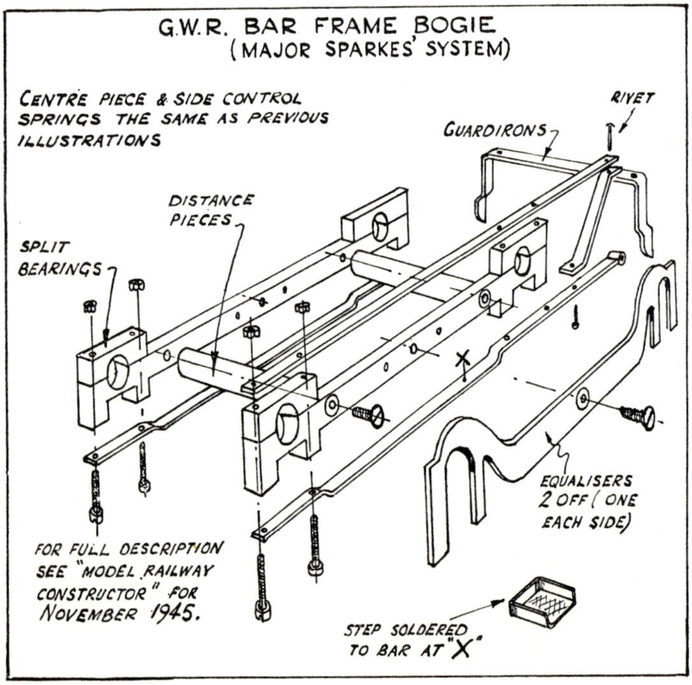
G.W.R. BAR FRAME BOGIE
(MAJOR SPARKES' SYSTEM)
CENTRE PIECE & SIDE CONTROL SPRINGS THE SAME AS PREVIOUS ILLUSTRATIONS
RIVET
GUARDIRONS
DISTANCE PIECES
SPLIT BEARINGS
X
EQUALISERS 2 OFF (ONE EACH SIDE)
FOR FULL DESCRIPTION SEE "MODEL RAILWAY CONSTRUCTOR" FOR NOVEMBER 1945.
STEP SOLDERED TO BAR AT "X"

well in practice. In the course of my work I do a lot of experimenting, and I would not dream of putting on to paper things I know would not work. Very little is ever made in the works exactly as it is designed in the drawing office. Years ago in the model steam locomotive field we had some wonderfully powerful locos worked out mathematically on paper, but when they were built they would not even haul themselves, but that is outside this particular field, as we are dealing with electrically-driven steam outline locomotives.

We now pass to bogies and pony trucks and other carrying wheels of our locomotive. In the drawings will be seen a typical GWR bar frame bogie, simplified for model purposes. A complete set of drawings is given, drawn exactly as I made the bogie in 1944. The brake gear is not shown as this was removed from most of them during C. B. Collett's regime. The drawings are fully dimensioned for 7 mm. scale. This bogie need not be so elaborately made in OO gauge as long as essential features are retained externally.

Also shown is another method of making this bogie for which I am indebted to the late Major Sparkes. This method would be ideal for 4 mm. scale. A full description of these bogies was given by the late Major Sparkes in the November 1945 issue of the *Model Railway Constructor* to which readers are referred. The swing link gear is omitted from the model in both cases as it was thought this is not necessary on a model, but a spring box is incorporated underneath the author's version, to accommodate a side control spring. The lid of this box is removable by undoing the four nuts to service or replace the spring any time this is necessary.

Next, one or two other types of bogies will be shown, and will cover all the types that were in use on British Railways. The reason for giving them is primarily to show that the bogie is a necessary part of a model locomotive, and should be made properly. In OO gauge it should have a certain amount of weight in itself, besides carrying a portion of the locomotive's weight, and if it is made properly it should function properly and not derail as it often does.

The Bogie

It will be seen on reference to the drawings that bogies are anything but bits of bent tin, or bits of channel brass with four holes and a so-called slot across the middle, a sloppy fit on a pin. Of all the parts of a model locomotive, bogies or pony trucks seem to get the least attention. It shows that the function of a bogie is not properly understood, and I will briefly repeat it here. It facilitates the movement of an engine round a curve. The weight of the leading end of the engine is spread over four wheels instead of two, and the bogie's business is to consolidate the road bed in advance of the driving wheels. They are only fitted on locos designed for high speed, and are fitted at both ends on expresses. Free-lance designers please note that there is an empirical rule which states that the wheelbase of the bogie shall be half as long again as the gauge is wide, 6 ft. to 7 ft. is usual in this country, but bogies are made up to 9 ft. and even to 10 ft. in India and Russia, where the broad gauge is used. If the bogie is quite free to traverse across the engine, it can do nothing to guide the engine on curves; for this reason

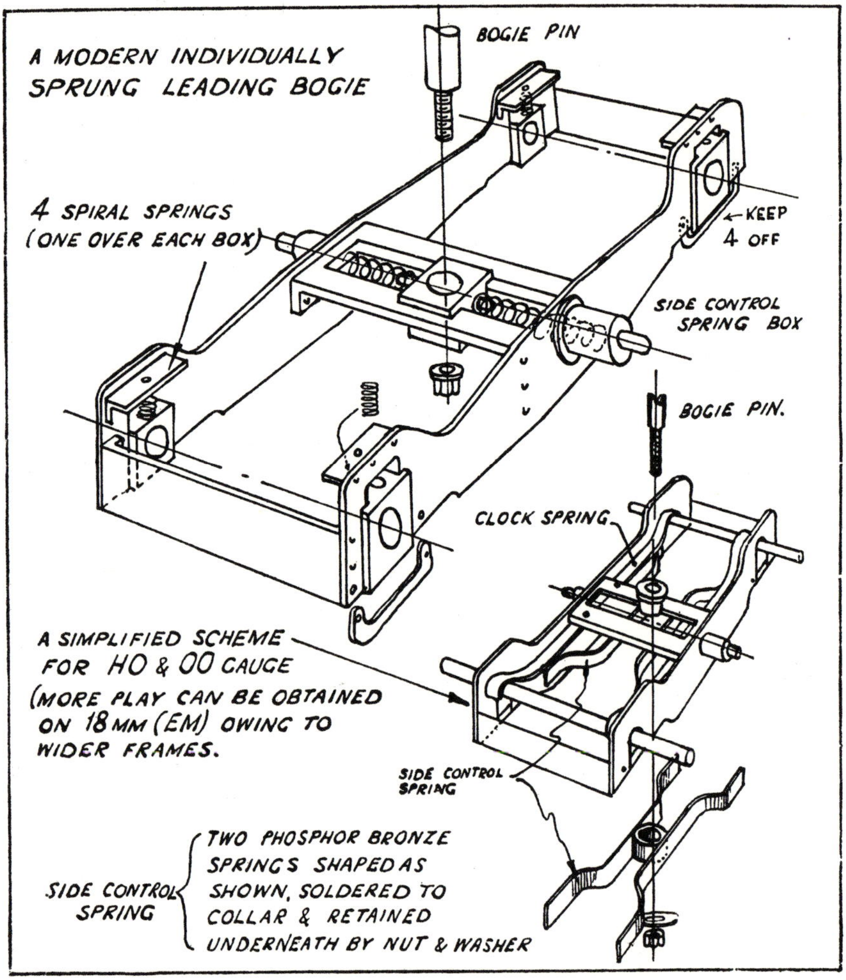

79 A MODERN INDIVIDUALLY SPRUNG LEADING BOGIE

it is never quite free. It is always returned to the central position by means of swing links, or side controlling springs. To do this the engine exerts an effort over the bogie; in popular language, the bogie has to overcome the centrifugal force of the engine which tries to pursue a straight line tangential to the curve.

In a more marked degree all this happens in a model, as the speeds are usually in excess of the scale equivalent, and curves are sharper, so unless the bogie has something to do besides slop around a pin the loco will derail, as nearly a quarter of the engine's length overhangs the curve before the driving wheels hit it with tremendous force. Far too often we do not have transition curves on a model railway, and the train of events is usually the following: the bogie, having nothing to do, tries to pursue a straight course tangentially to the curve and off it comes and is fouling the motion somewhere. If this does not happen, the quarter or more of the loco's length left without support is thrown on the leading pair of driving wheels. This overhanging

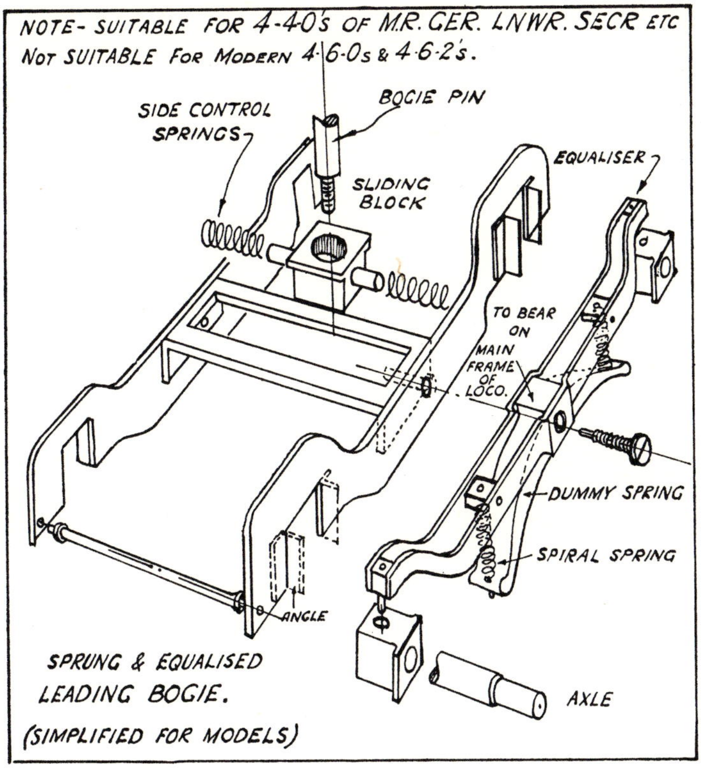

80 Simplified sprung and equalised bogie

weight coupled with centrifugal force causes the whole lot to come off or at least overturn. One has only to watch a child's clockwork engine hit a curve from the straight to see what tremendous forces are set up.

Returning to the model, the whole trouble seems to be due, in a large measure, to the fetish of weighing down the engine with lots of weight, and apprehension is felt that if the bogie carries any weight, the model will haul one less coach or something. This is sheer rubbish. No amount of weight in a model will compensate for a poor motor, or low gearing. The more weight that is put into a model, and the less support the bogies and pony trucks give it, the more liable the model is to derailments, as the loco becomes like a four-wheel tramcar of our youth, a long body on a short wheelbase, and one can remember how prone they were to bucking about and derailing. So when we make a bogie let us remember all these things, and give it something to do.

In O gauge and larger models the bogie wheels can be sprung either individually or by means of an equalising bar sprung at the centre. In OO gauge the bogie can be made compensating in itself by pivoting the side frames at the centre in much the same way as a carriage bogie. When we model a front coupled tank of the 0–4–4 variety we have to spring the bogie to throw the weight further forward, so why boggle at doing this on an express loco? The usual model of an 0–4–4 is always a better road holder than the model express engine, I have always found it so, and it is surely

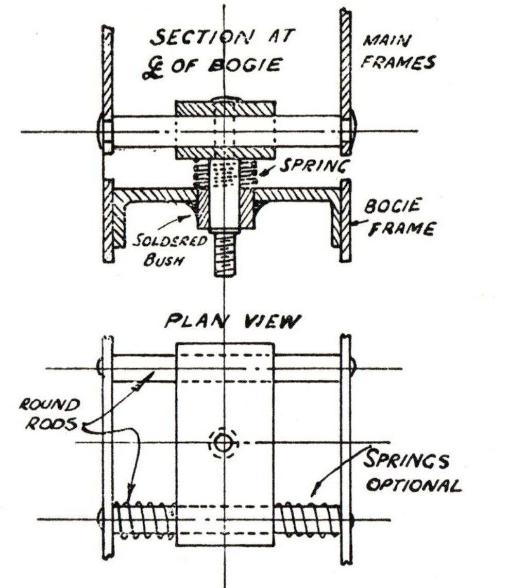

ANOTHER METHOD OF MOUNTING BOGIES FOR 4-6-4 & 4-8-4 LOCOS.

due to the fact that the bogie carries part of the weight of the engine. Most of us fit some sort of spring, usually of the spiral type, on the bogie pin to force the bogie down on to the road. This in itself is a good idea, but it is only half good enough. A side controlling spring should be fitted also, and the sketches show some ways of doing this quite simply in OO and O gauge.

Pony Trucks

We now come to pony trucks. Here again we have a similar state of affairs in a more marked degree. In all the models I have examined there seems to be total ignorance of their functions. They are usually made in the simplest possible form, just two holes in a piece of metal, with a long tail attached, and fitted to the engine anywhere they can be wangled in, without any regard to the correct pivotal position. When the loco is lifted off the track, the pony truck falls downwards with a rather forlorn air, reminding one of a chicken hanging up in a butcher's shop! I give in the sketch a simple method of finding the pivotal position of a pony truck. Never mind if the collector or some other gadget comes in the way, take it off, and fit it somewhere else because if the pony truck is fitted on the hit and miss principle there will be nothing but derailment until it is fitted properly. Here again we must provide for it to carry part of the weight of the loco, and it should be sprung, by means of either a central spring like the GWR, or by means of two little springs, over each box, as in the Southern locos.

Methods of springing pony trucks and radial axle boxes as fitted to 2–4–2T type locomotives are shown in the sketches. The method of springing a radial axle box is a novel method for which I am indebted to Mr. A. S. Reidpath. It was used by him and myself for many years on HO models with perfect success. Coming to radial axle boxes, they can be made in

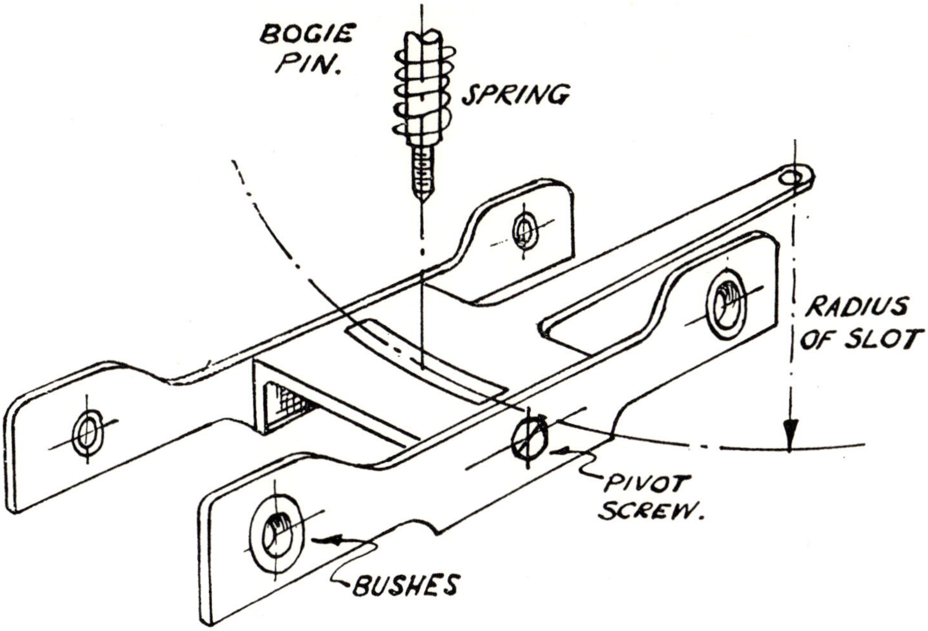

82 The pony truck

model form. It has been done in $\frac{1}{2}$ in. scale models, but owing to our comparatively small radius curves, they are rather difficult to make properly, and require a lot of lubrication to work freely without grinding.

The sketch shows the function of the boxes, although they are simplified for model purposes, but if they are made carefully, they will produce a very steady riding engine. They were used for many years by Mr. F. W. Webb on the LNWR, and to a great extent on the GER by Mr. J. Holden, in his radial tanks. They are fitted at the present time chiefly to the trailing wheels of Pacifics and what are left of the GNR Atlantics.

The axle boxes are sprung in the normal manner by leaf springs on top of the box. This spring can be made of solid material, and a spiral spring concealed in the buckle as shown in the sketch.

It will be found that when a model steam locomotive is properly constructed, with all the salient features of a steam locomotive, even though it is only electrically-driven, the finished model will be quite heavy enough in itself to get it to haul a train without resorting to loads of lead. So far we have only described bogies that turn on a central pivot. A type of bogie very useful in model form, although not often used nowadays in full size practice, is the Bissell bogie. In this truck the pivot is placed behind the rear wheels of the bogie, so that the centre of the truck virtually slides and turns. Its action is only suitable for one radius of curve, which makes it eminently suitable for model railways in 4 mm. scale.

The frames act as equalisers, being pivoted to the crossplate. A central post with a spring should be fitted to a convenient frame stretcher to limit its movement, and to provide for vertical springing.

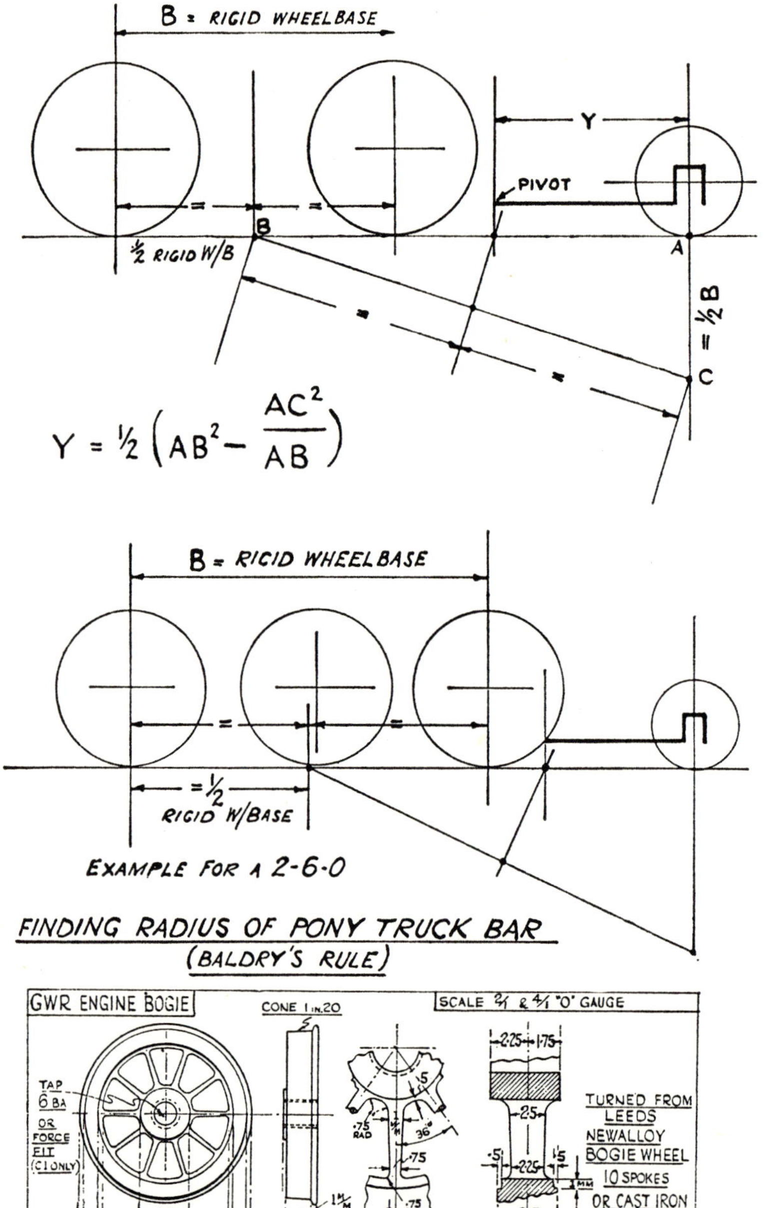

83 *FINDING RADIUS OF PONY TRUCK BAR*
(BALDRY'S RULE)

84

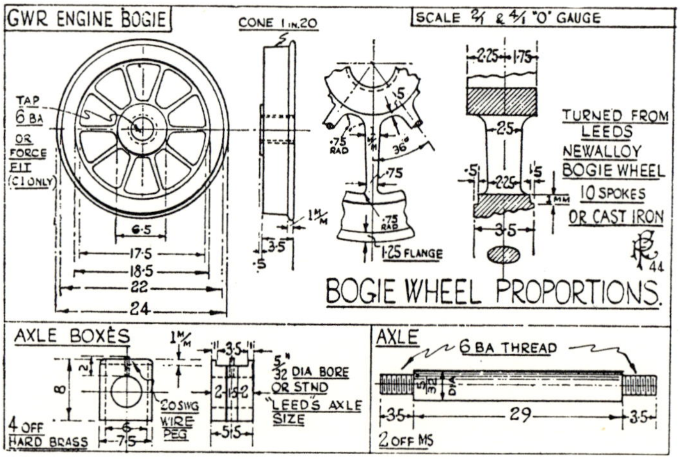

The action of Bissell truck on a curve is the same as that of a pony truck, and to find the length of the arm, the same formula as given on the drawing, i.e., Baldry's Rule, can be applied, treating the leading pair of wheels as a pony truck.

Another method of giving a steadier riding engine with a bogie at both ends is shown in a further sketch, this consists of two bars riveted across the frames, and a sliding block carrying the bogie pin being free to traverse across the frames. Springs may, or not, be fitted on the bars, at the discretion of the modeller. If springs are fitted their tension can be found by trial and error on the track. Mr. Longridge has applied this system to a two-wheeled truck.

I think we have now covered the subject of bogies and pony trucks fairly well, and so we can pass on to cylinders and motion. Even greater care should be expended on this part, as in modern engines it is all on the outside, naked and unashamed. We have progressed far from the simple coupling rod of earlier days. In OO gauge care should be taken not to get the outside gear too heavy in appearance. Owing to the fact that we have more room in 16.5 mm. gauge due to the gauge being under scale, the main rods can be made of fairly thick material in a horizontal plane but kept to scale in a vertical plane. In modelling Walschaert gear, care must be taken to study the prototype and to find out whether the engine has inside admission or outside admission piston valves or slide valves, as the gear is arranged differently for all three systems. In the author's series of drawings this will

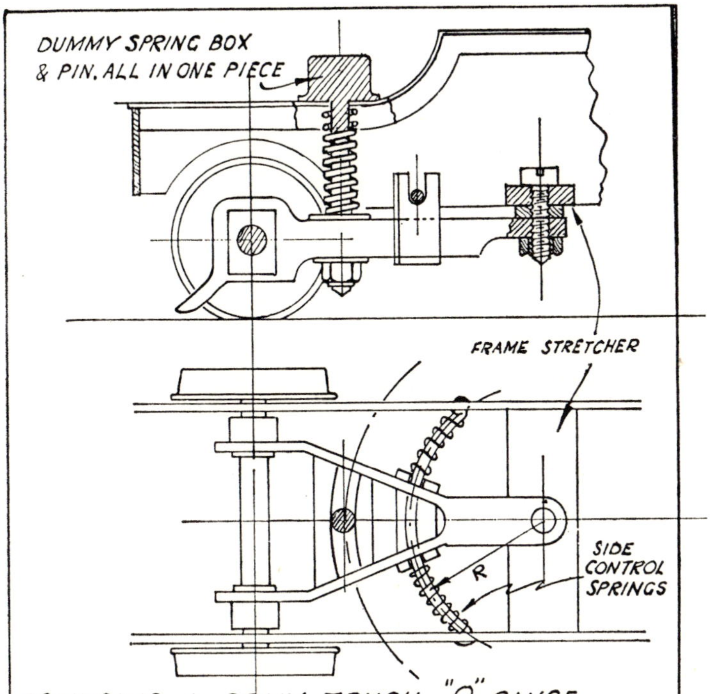

SPRINGING A PONY TRUCK. "O" GAUGE.

85

be pointed out on the drawing. The chief and most obvious difference is the positioning of the return crank outside the big end of the connecting rod. For inside admission this is offset towards the front of the loco. This is the more normal position, used by engines built with piston valves. For outside admission the return crank is offset towards the rear of the loco, this is the case with the Southern Railway Remembrance class. These engines were rebuilt from the LBSCR Baltic tanks, and they had piston valves, but it must not be inferred that all engines with this arrangement have slide valves. There are outside admission piston valves also. The pro's and con's of the two systems do not concern us; suffice to say that both systems were in use in this country and abroad, particularly on compound engines.

86 Cylinder casings for LMS 5P5F class locos

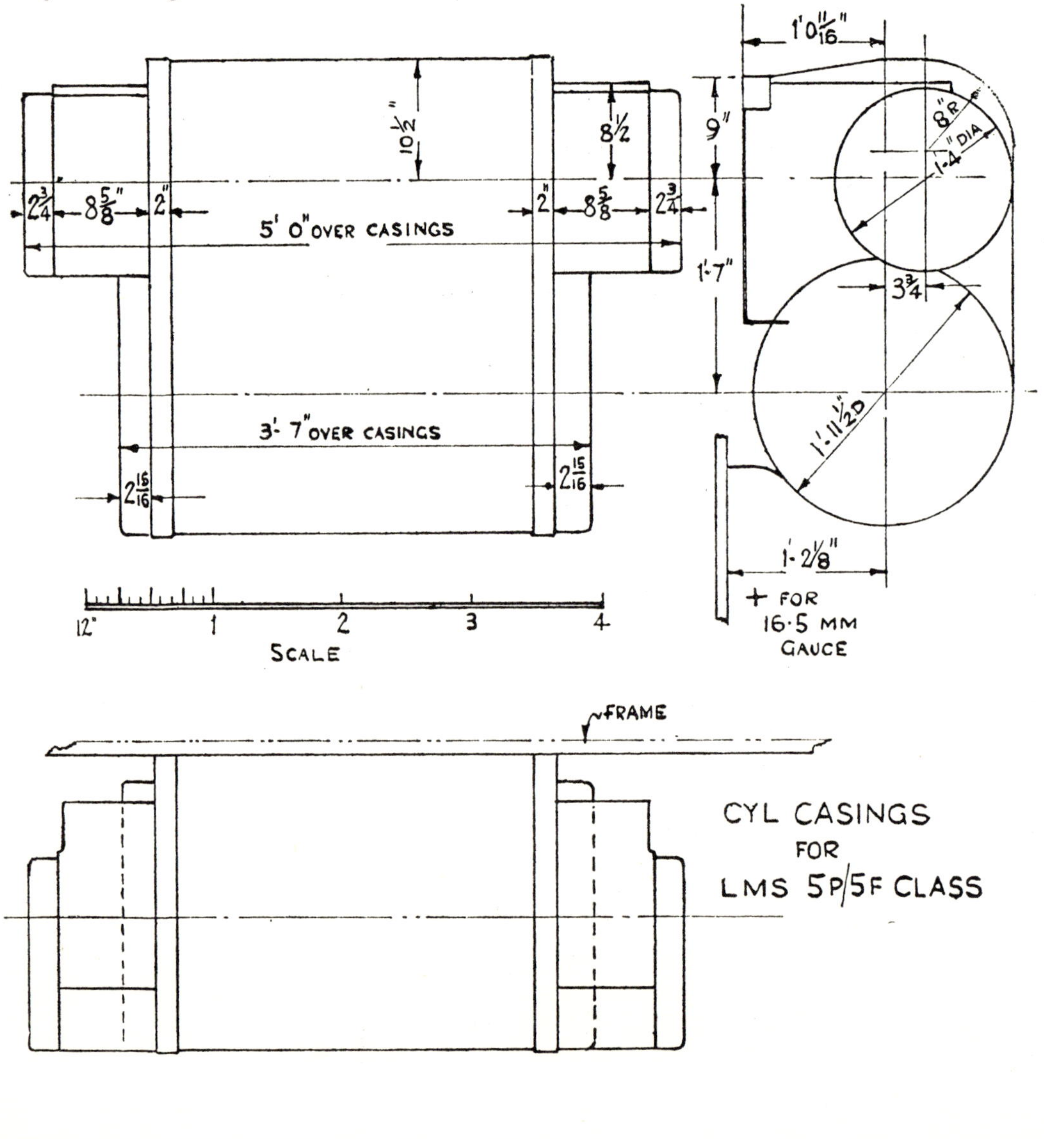

The other difference in the Walschaert gear due to the above two systems, is in the attachment of the valve spindle to the combining lever, in relation to the valve rod which is attached to the link.

In outside admission valves the valve rod is attached to the combining lever *below* the valve rod, and in inside admission it is attached *above* the valve rod. So even though our model is electrically-driven, remember it *is* a steam locomotive. If a model is shown in an exhibition, and the gear is wrongly connected for the type of valves used on the prototype, then considerable points will be lost, because the judges are qualified engineers as well as model makers themselves. I shall shortly be giving some drawings of Walschaert gears showing all these variations together with the names of all the rods and levers, which will clear up these points.

Before we pass to valve gear construction we must make the cylinders. In the drawing (Fig. 86) will be found a dimensioned sketch of the cylinders of the LMS mixed traffic 4–6–0. They are representative of all modern outside cylinders. The distance from the centre line of the cylinders to the outside of the main frame would be greater in a model owing to our frames being under scale—more so in 16.5 mm. gauge—and the amount should be added accordingly to that given on the drawing.

Coming now to the subject of queries, as they are of general interest I will deal with them here. First the GWR pony truck. Col. Templer has cleared up these queries and provided the sketches (figs. 87 and 88). The method of suspension is clearly shown, and the truck is of the most modern design having been modified to take A.T.C. pick-up gear. This is not shown in the sketch as it is thought that model makers would not fit this gear owing to the possibility of it fouling the centre rail pickup, but it could be fitted to two-rail operated locos.

Secondly the GWR 4-wheeled bogie. My drawing of this was modified for modelmaking purposes, and I now reproduce, again from a sketch by Col. Templer (fig. 89), the correct shape of the bolster (1), but one point I must mention is that the transverse dimensions are approximately under scale, by 1 mm., owing to narrower than scale frames, in O gauge. The second sketch shows the modern pattern strengthened bogie (2) and the end view of the dumb iron, showing the correct shape, and (3) shows a suggested modification to the model spring, so that the bogie wheel may mask the spiral spring. Note the modern type flat spring and new hanger shown; ends of the spring are entirely behind equaliser, only parts showing being the top and bottom of shackle bolt.

Earlier was illustrated a four-wheel pony truck. This is really a model adaptation to obtain a large arc of travel for sharp radius curves, and was extensively used on earlier toy engines. It is, in the author's opinion, a much better arrangement than splitting the bogie in two, making two of the wheels to traverse and the other two part of the fixed wheel base; this wangle is very obvious when the model traverses a curve, whereas the 4-wheeled truck looks and works better. I do not know of any locomotive fitted with this type of truck in full size practice at least in the British Isles, but I believe it was used in America in the very early days of the Civil War, but was soon discarded in favour of the bogie as we know it in this country.

Most of the Midland engines have been adequately dealt with by Mr. F. C.

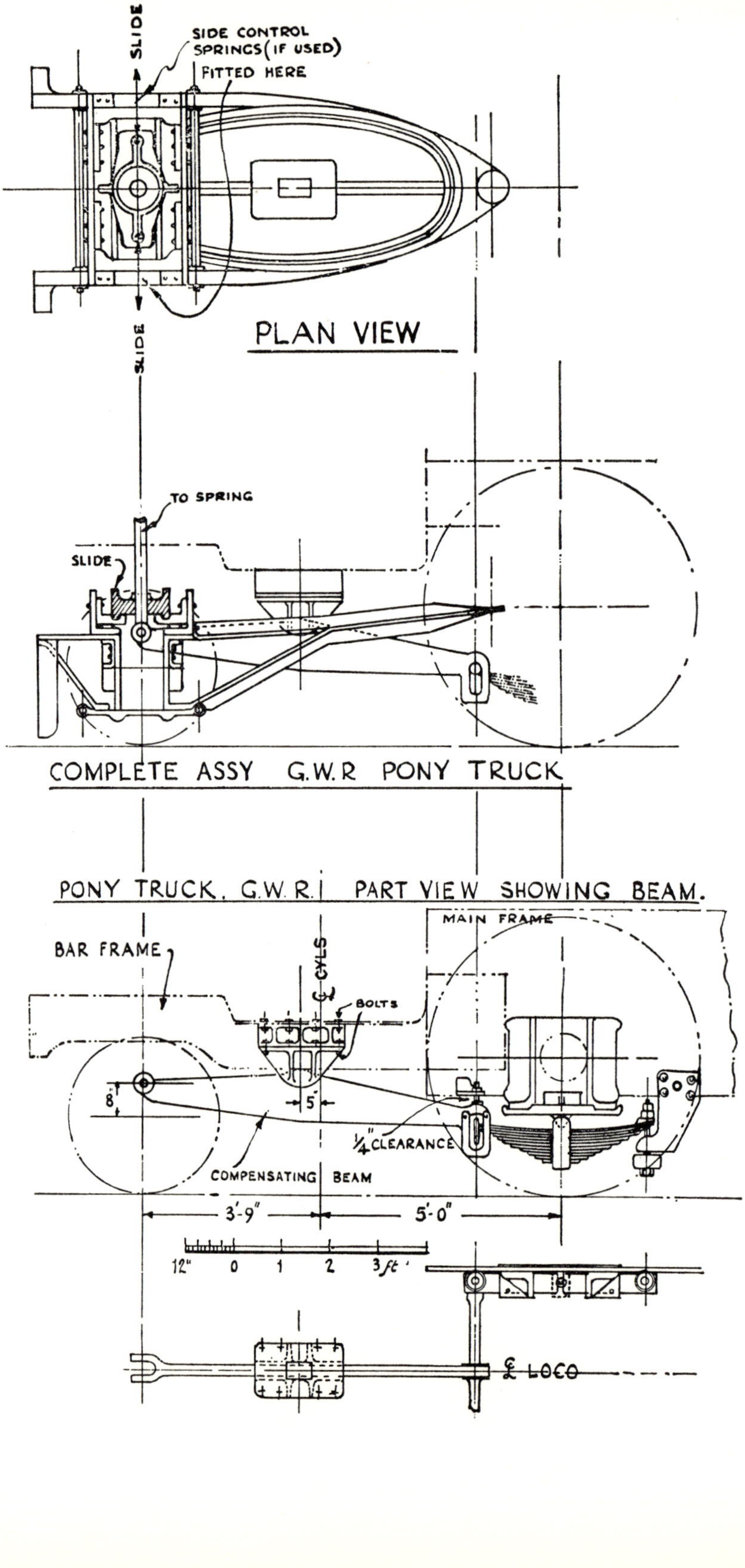

87 GWR pony truck

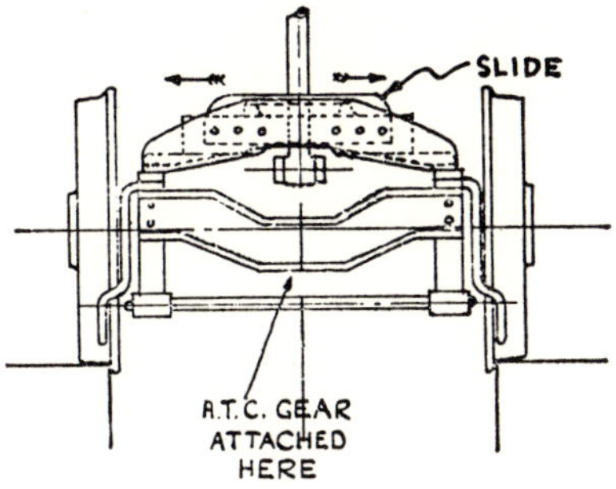

88 FRONT VIEW. G.W.R. PONY

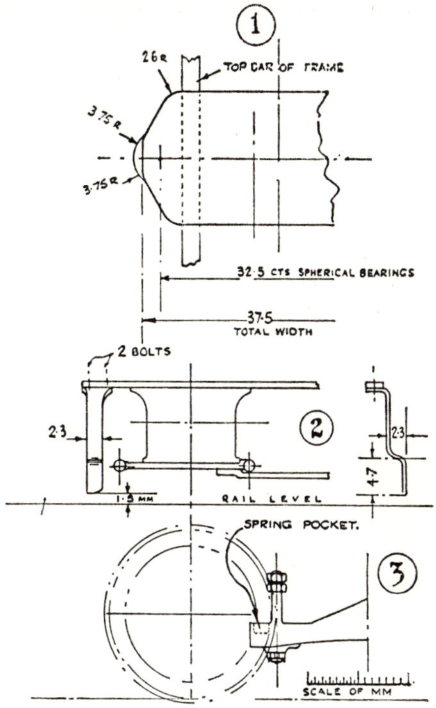

89 GWR 4-wheeled bogie bolster; modern pattern strengthened bogie; suggested modification to model spring

Hambleton, J. N. Maskelyne and others in our contemporaries and in books. The fact that these locos are not drawn to the scale the model maker wants them is no excuse whatever for not making. At the beginning of this book I gave instructions and diagrams how to redraw drawings to the chosen scale. Once again, I must stress, forget all about millimetres! Find an even measurement on the drawing from *Locomotives worth modelling* or any other journal and divide it into feet and inches. It only means dividing a certain space whatever it is into 12 equal parts. To anyone who is interested in the American 12 base arithmetic this should be simple.

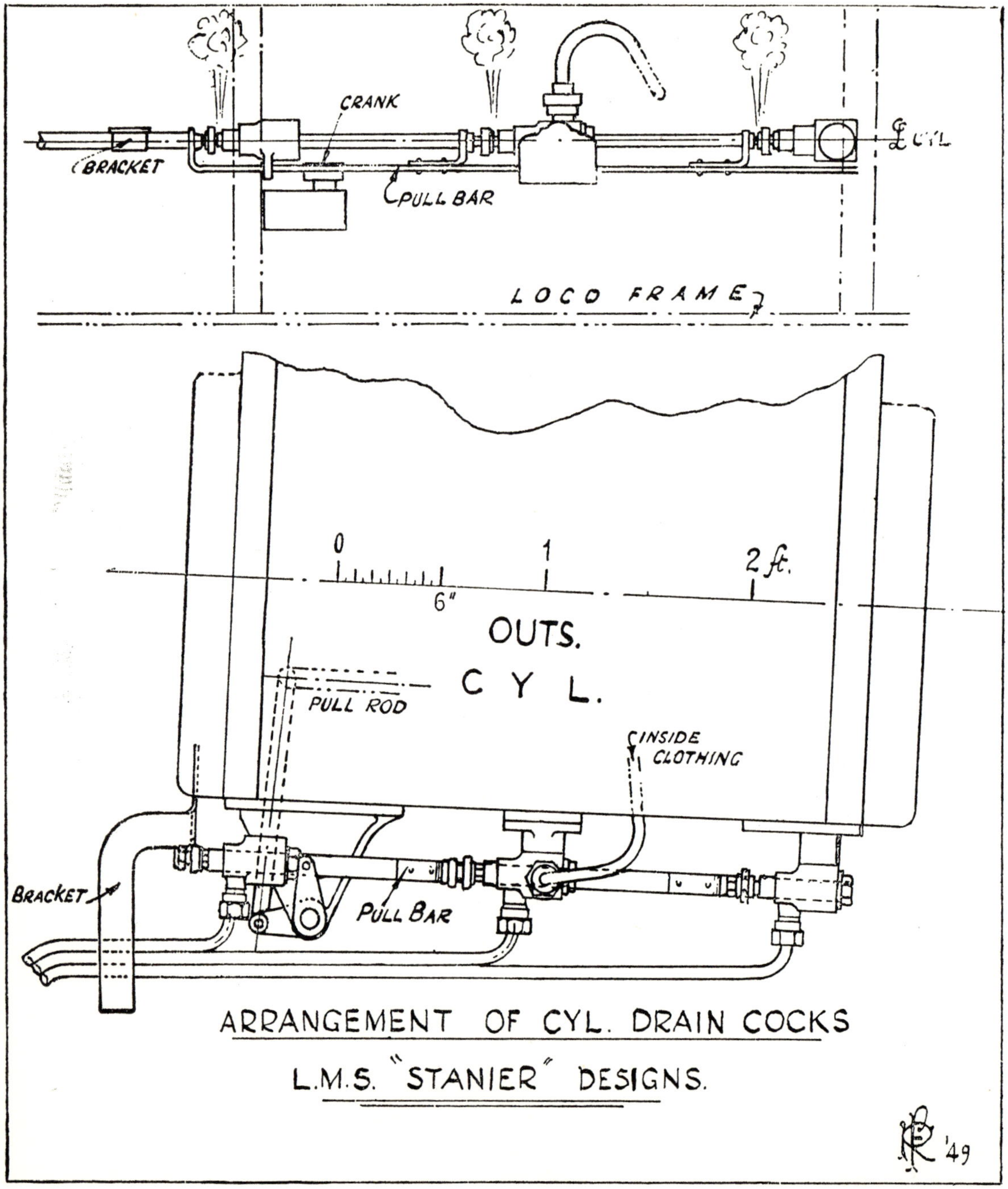
CRANK
BRACKET
PULL BAR
℄ CYL
LOCO FRAME
0
1
2 ft.
6"
OUTS.
CYL.
PULL ROD
INSIDE CLOTHING
BRACKET
PULL BAR
ARRANGEMENT OF CYL. DRAIN COCKS
L.M.S. "STANIER" DESIGNS.
'49

90

In the sketch will be seen the writer's usual method of making up a pair of outside cylinders. All the detail necessary for fixing the slide bars, the piston rod gland, etc., should be incorporated on the back cover before it is soldered in position. A small plate is attached to the underside, on which is built up all the necessary detail for drain cocks, operating rods, etc., and on the back of the completed cylinder is seen a square plate about $\frac{1}{8}$ in. thick drilled and tapped for fixing screws. The front cover should have incorporated on it the relief valve and any nuts if fitted, such as are found on early type locomotives. In the bottom sketch will be found a simpler method of making up a pair of cylinders for a OO gauge loco. The cylinder and piston valve is turned in one piece, and a wrapper plate made to go round the recessed part of the cylinder and valve and the whole sweated together. The cylinder itself should be drilled to take the slide bars before it is soldered in place. Complete cylinders cast in white metal are obtainable from the trade, and these can often be filed up and adapted for other types of locos, other than that for which they are supplied. Their only disadvantage is their weight. The method shown for making O gauge cylinders can be used for OO also; the

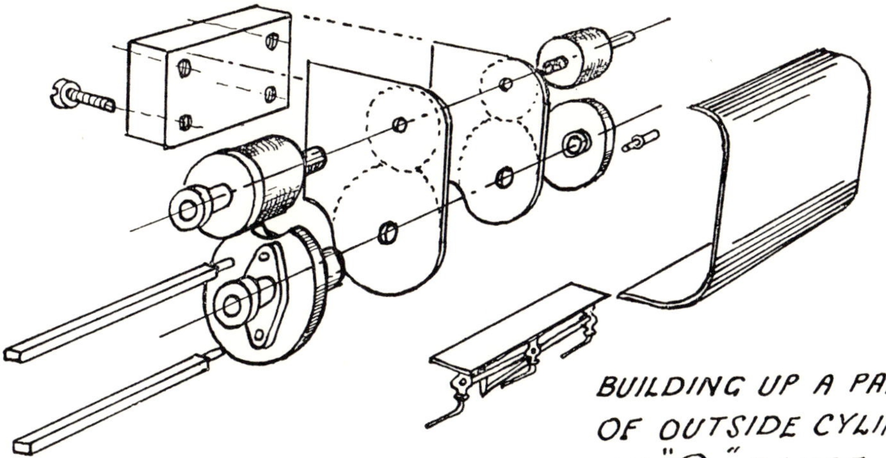

91

BUILDING UP A PAIR OF OUTSIDE CYLINDERS IN "O" GAUGE

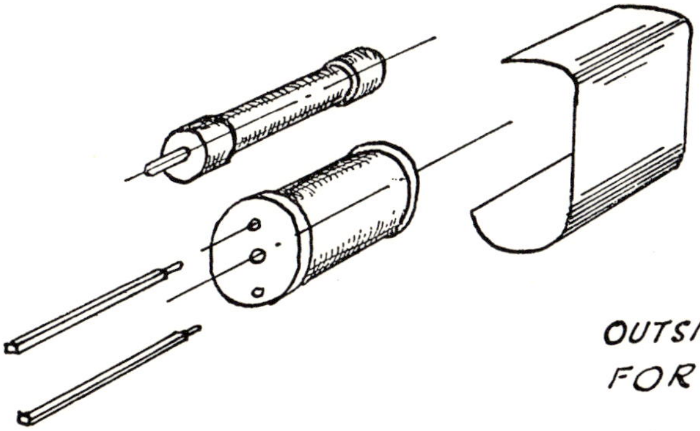

OUTSIDE CYLINDER FOR "OO" GAUGE

writer used this for OO gauge and also $3\frac{1}{2}$ mm. scale. The method shown for making OO gauge cylinders can also be used for O gauge where there is only the cylinder to deal with, and no piston valves, such as in the GNR Atlantic, Midland compounds and other types of this sort.

We now come to the all important subject of the valve gear. It is proposed to treat this subject at some length as the writer has recently been looking at photographs of model locomotives in books and the model journals and has come to the conclusion that not very many modellers, the trade not even excepted, know very much about Walschaert's valve gear and its functions. They seem to forget that we are discussing a model of a steam locomotive, and although it is electrically driven, the outside valve gear should be correct and function correctly. At exhibitions sometimes a modeller will be surprised that perhaps his own, or perhaps his friend's model gets no mention, while another perhaps not so nicely painted or finished gets an award. The judges are engineers themselves, perhaps full size railway engineers at that, and they look for details such as valve gear levers, pins, joints, etc., being correctly modelled. It is not enough to make a beautifully finished model, and then show the valve gear made up of a lot of bits of flat plate riveted together and called Walschaert's gear. There is a set of valve gear marketed of this type that is absolutely wrong, not one of the parts is correct either in its shape or its functions. Well a beginner might put this on his model, and wonder why it is found fault with by his more enlightened brethren. We have all got to learn and these articles are meant chiefly for the beginner, and it is hoped that he will find food for thought in the various drawings and sketches of Walschaert's valve gear. It is hoped that the trade will as well, especially those catering for OO gauge as if this valve gear is put on the market it will be a great help to those who have no workshop facilities, and little knowledge of valve gears. It is also hoped that the more advanced modeller will find useful tips for assembling this gear.

It is rather a fascinating gear to watch in motion if it is modelled properly, and the English version of it is very symmetrical being arranged as it is on the inclined principle as opposed to the American system of all square connections (see sketches C and D in fig. 92).

I have already mentioned the difference between inside and outside admission valves, and their relative effect on the positioning of the combining lever, and return or eccentric crank. This is only one of the many pitfalls of the novice in making this gear. There are many others as will be found on perusal of the succeeding remarks and drawings.

In fig. 93 will be found the layout of the gear giving the names of all the parts and throughout all the sketches of the gear these designations will be used. This sketch shows the gear aranged for inside admission piston valve engines such as the LMS Scots, Pacifics, Jubilees, etc.

We will take this sketch as a basis, and proceed to take the gear to pieces, and describing each part in detail, starting with the combining lever.

In fig. 94 will be seen the arrangement of the top joint. It will be noted on reference to this sketch that the top of the lever is forked. This can be done in a small model by making the lever of flat plate, and soldering another small plate on the back, with a distance piece between, thus producing a forked joint having two bearings for the valve rod, enabling it to move in a fore and aft direction without any lateral shake. The valve spindle travelling its valve will also assist in this direction. It is also usual to arrange for the valve spindle to travel in a guide.

This is nearly always left out on a model. (See general arrangement of the gear, and the sketch, fig. 94 lower, showing the LMS arrangement.) This sketch is, of course, simplified for an electrically driven model, because as long as it looks right from the outside, and functions properly, it will pass the critical eye. We are not concerned with lap and lead in dummy steam locos.

At the bottom of the combining lever is attached the anchor link or as it is

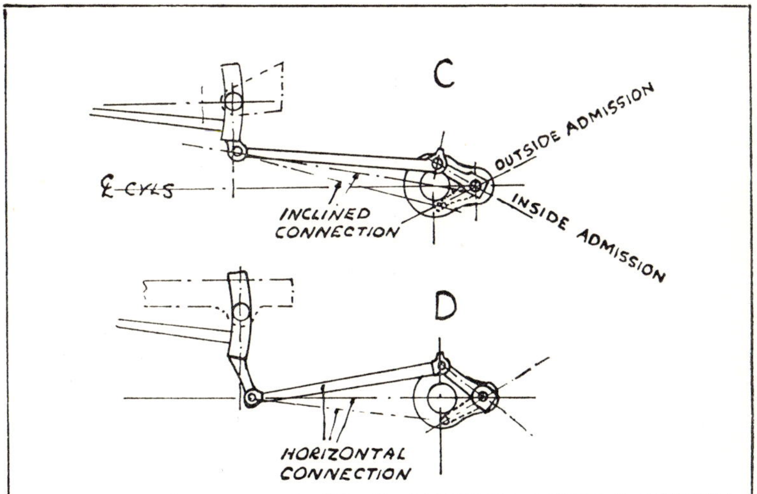

92 RELATIVE POSIT'ONS OF EXPANSION LINKS & RETURN. CRANKS:- "C" ENGLISH. "D" AMERICAN & CONTINENTAL.

93

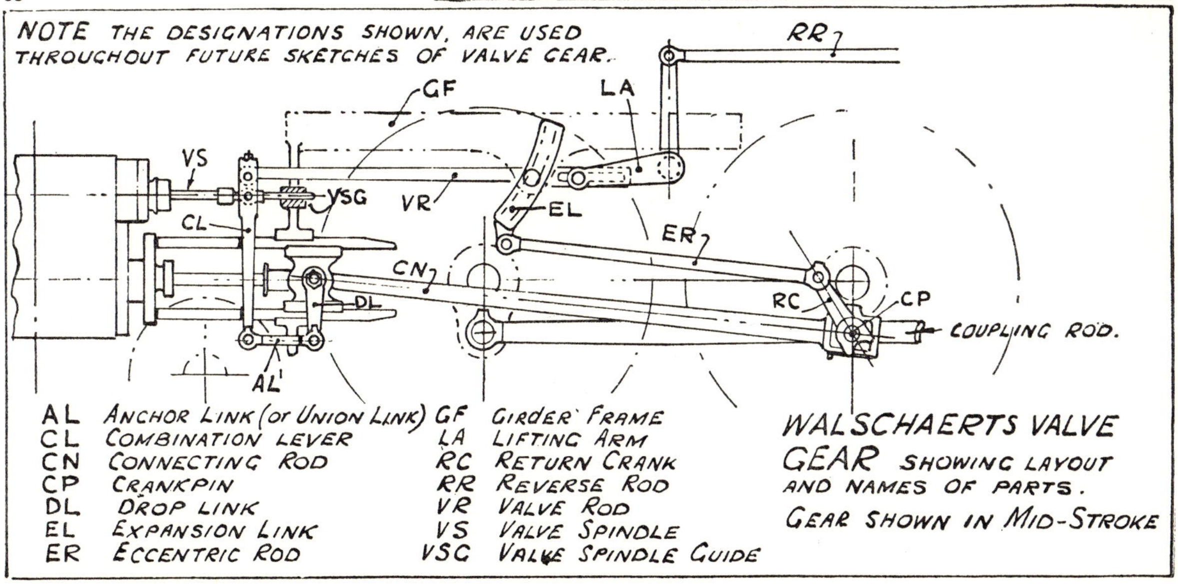

sometimes known, the union link. In small models this is almost always represented by a flat bar, rivetted to the combining lever. This is definitely wrong as it soon begins to wear and flop about in a lateral direction, eventually catching up somewhere on the rear bogie wheel. This little link should always be forked at both ends, or at least run in a forked end on both the combining lever and drop link on the crosshead. A dimensioned sketch (fig. 96) is given of the LMS arrangement of this link, anchor link, and two supplementary sketches (fig. 97) show other arrangements. If forked ends

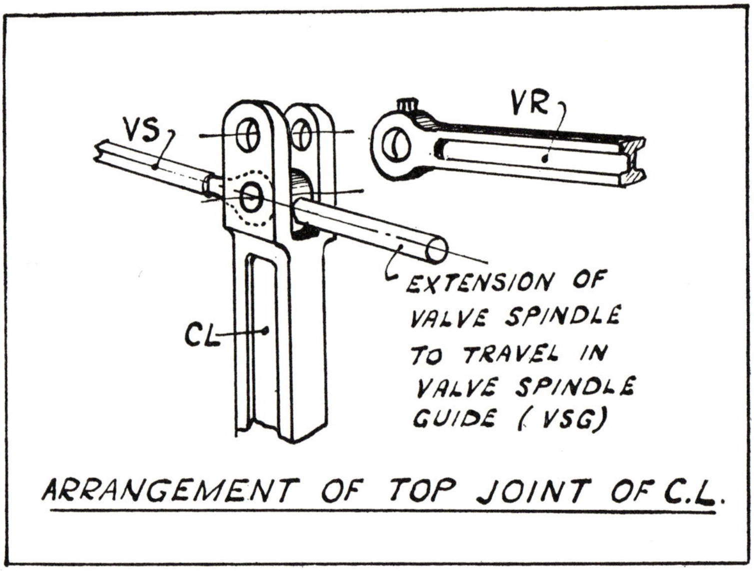

94

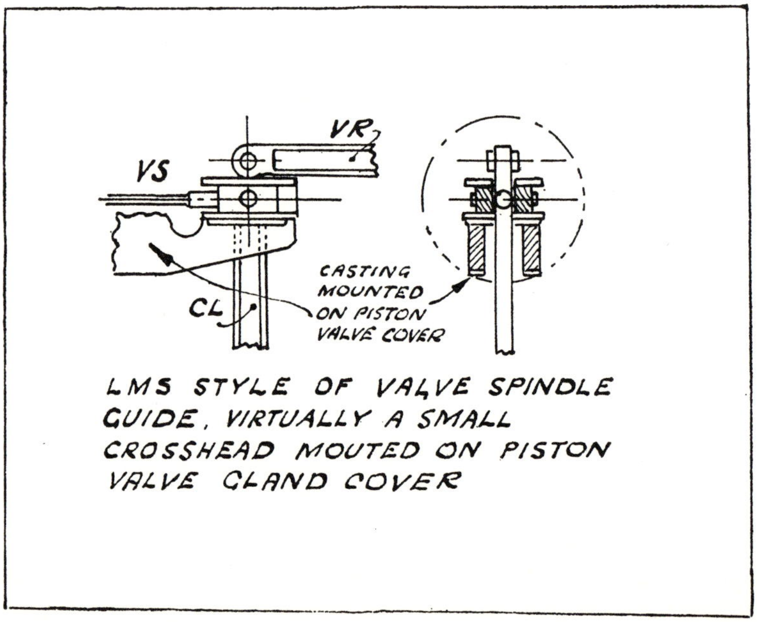

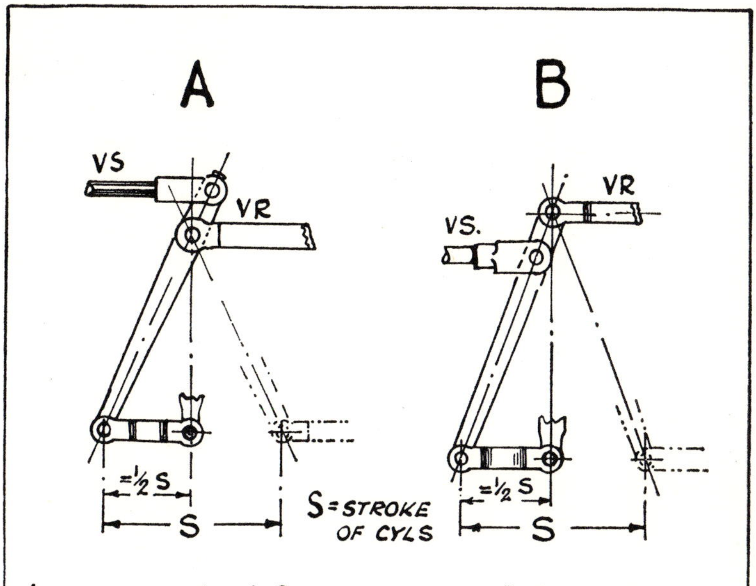

95 Arrangment of Connections of Valve Rod and Valve Spindles for; "A" OUTSIDE ADMISSION & "B" INSIDE ADMISSION.

96

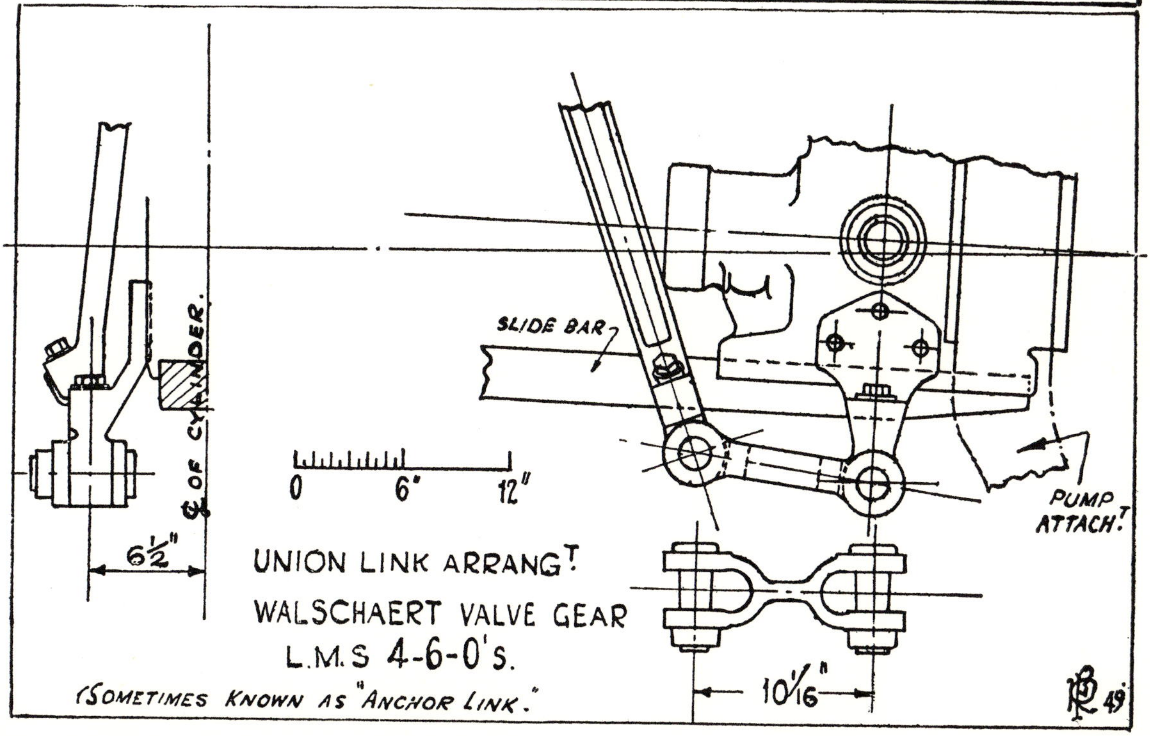

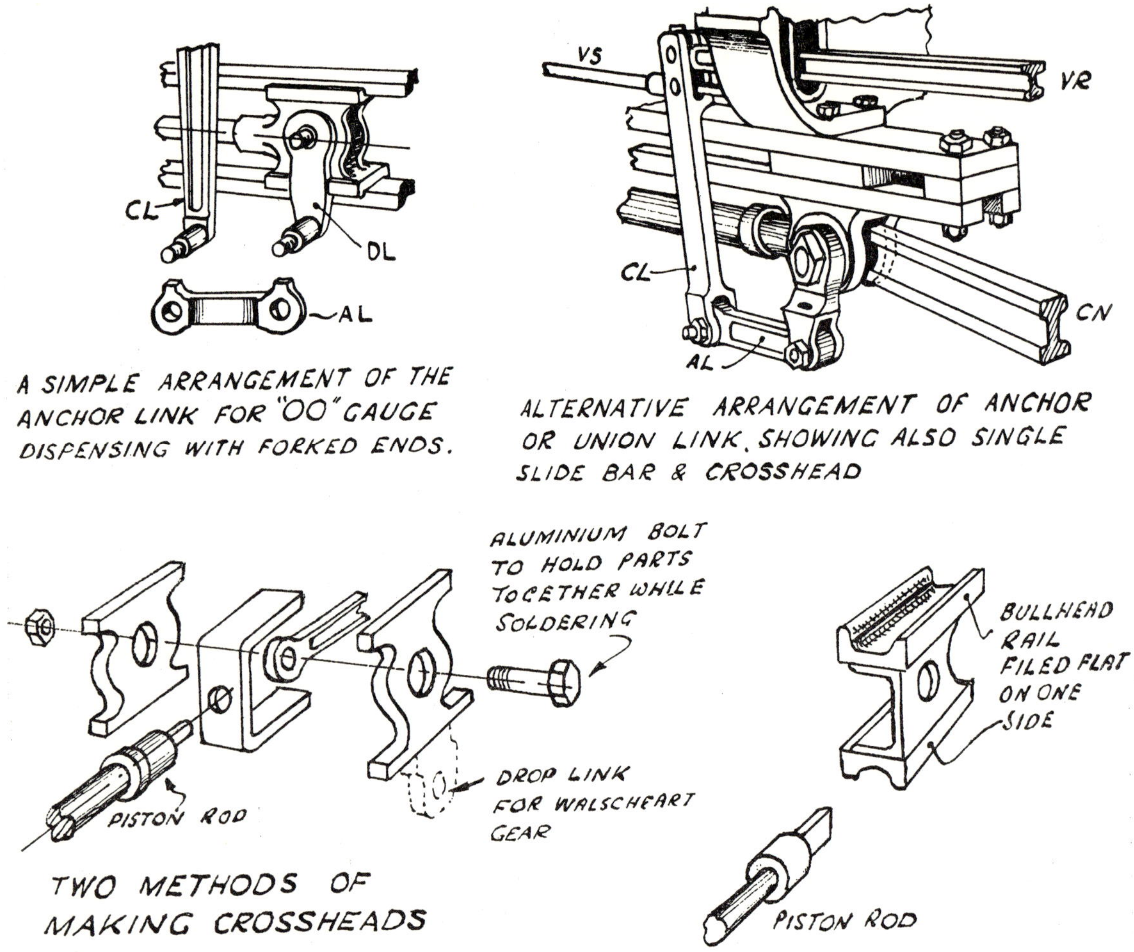

97 Anchor links (top) and making crossheads

are dispensed with, then the link must be made over scale in thickness at the eyes, in order that it travels in fore and aft direction only. It must also be made a good running fit on the pins of the crosshead and combining lever, but as previously stated it should be a forked link to be strictly correct.

The writer does not think any difficulty will be experienced in making forked ends in OO gauge as he has himself made them in HO gauge from $\frac{1}{16}$ in. square bar. In making forked ends, the bar must be cut to length, then drilled at each end. A saw cut is then made at each end sufficiently long enough to take the rods with which it engages, and then the link is filed to shape. Do not attempt to make it the other way round, i.e. shaping it first, and then drilling it. It will be found that the drill will wander when it breaks through the first half of the fork, and this will result in the link running crookedly. In O gauge models the links and pins of Walschaert gear should be made from steel, stainless preferably, and the links and pins should be case hardened. They will then run indefinitely without any trace of wear.

OO gaugers who are also watchmakers can likewise make them for hardening: it is quite possible as many parts of clocks and watches are hardened.

The next item to tackle is the crosshead, and the drop link. The sketches (fig. 97) shows two methods of making crossheads. The drop link can be made as part of one side of the crosshead and it will be immensely strong. It can also be made as a separate unit, and soldered or silvered soldered to the crosshead according to the size of the model. If it is made as a separate unit, the crosshead can be recessed on the bottom slide to take the link, and it will then be quite rigid, as shown in the sketch of the crosshead, drop link, combining lever, and anchor link. This sketch (top left) also shows a single bar type of slide bar and crosshead.

When we have made our crosshead we can insert the pin on which the anchor link runs and rivet it flush on the back of the drop link, taking care that the riveted portion of the pin does not foul the slide bar. Attach the anchor link and combining lever at the other end, insert the whole into the slide bars, at the same time inserting the piston rod and valve spindle into their respective positions, and mark off the position of the hole for attaching the valve rod. Referring to sketches A and B (fig. 95) the position of this hole denotes whether the engine is outside or inside admission. If the top of the combining lever is forked, insert a piece of plate between the forks, and treat it as if it were a solid piece of metal, centre pop and drill for the valve rod. Experienced modellers would no doubt have done this already, when making the combining lever from the drawing of the loco being modelled.

The Valve Rod and Link

There now is the task of making the valve rod itself. In some locos this rod is fluted, and a scheme of fluting is given for small models (fig. 98). The rod is made in the ordinary way, then bent to a half circle, held in the vice, and a square rat tail file run round it to produce the flute. Also shown is a built up method of fluting. The writer has used both methods with success. Those who have a completely equipped workshop will of course flute their rods with a milling attachment or fly cutter.

In making the valve rod due regard must be paid as to whether the rod is moved up and down in the link in front, or behind the latter. See sketches (fig. 100) of the Southern and LMS styles, which show both methods. Somewhere along the length of the valve rod, after or before the hole for the lifting arm, the hole for die block must be drilled. This will be found on reference to the drawing of the loco. The die block is the little block which runs up and down in the link to reverse the engine. In small electrically driven models it is usual to make Walschaert's gear in mid gear in order that the rod does not have to run up and down in the link at all, but strictly speaking this position does not impart any, or very little movement to the rod itself, and one of the functions of the gear is lost. If it is modelled in the bottom of the link or at the top, a certain amount of movement is imparted, which looks very well when the engine is in motion. As a model of an express loco spends most of its time running forward, the rod should be made to travel at the bottom of the link. In the case of tank locos of modern type, they run equally in either direction, and the valve rod should be made to

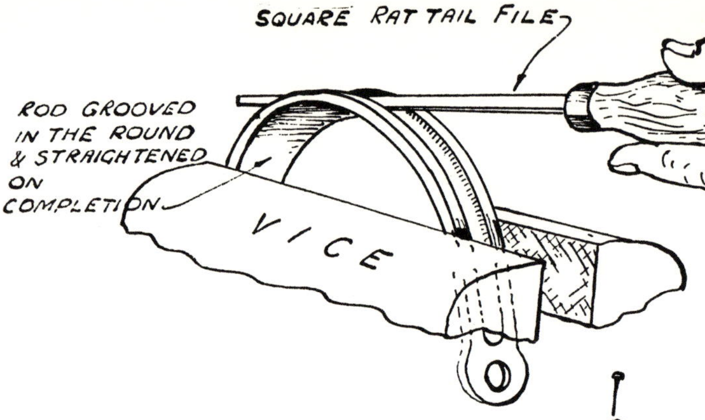

FLUTING "OO" GAUGE RODS & SMALL RODS OF VALVE GEAR FOR "O" GAUGE

98

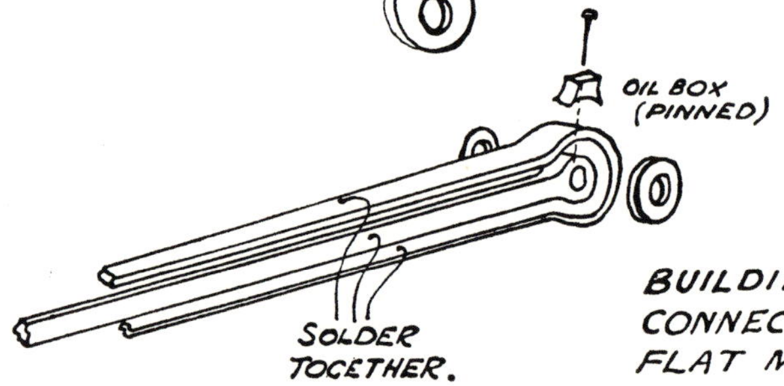

BUILDING UP A FLUTED CONNECTING ROD FROM FLAT MATERIAL

99

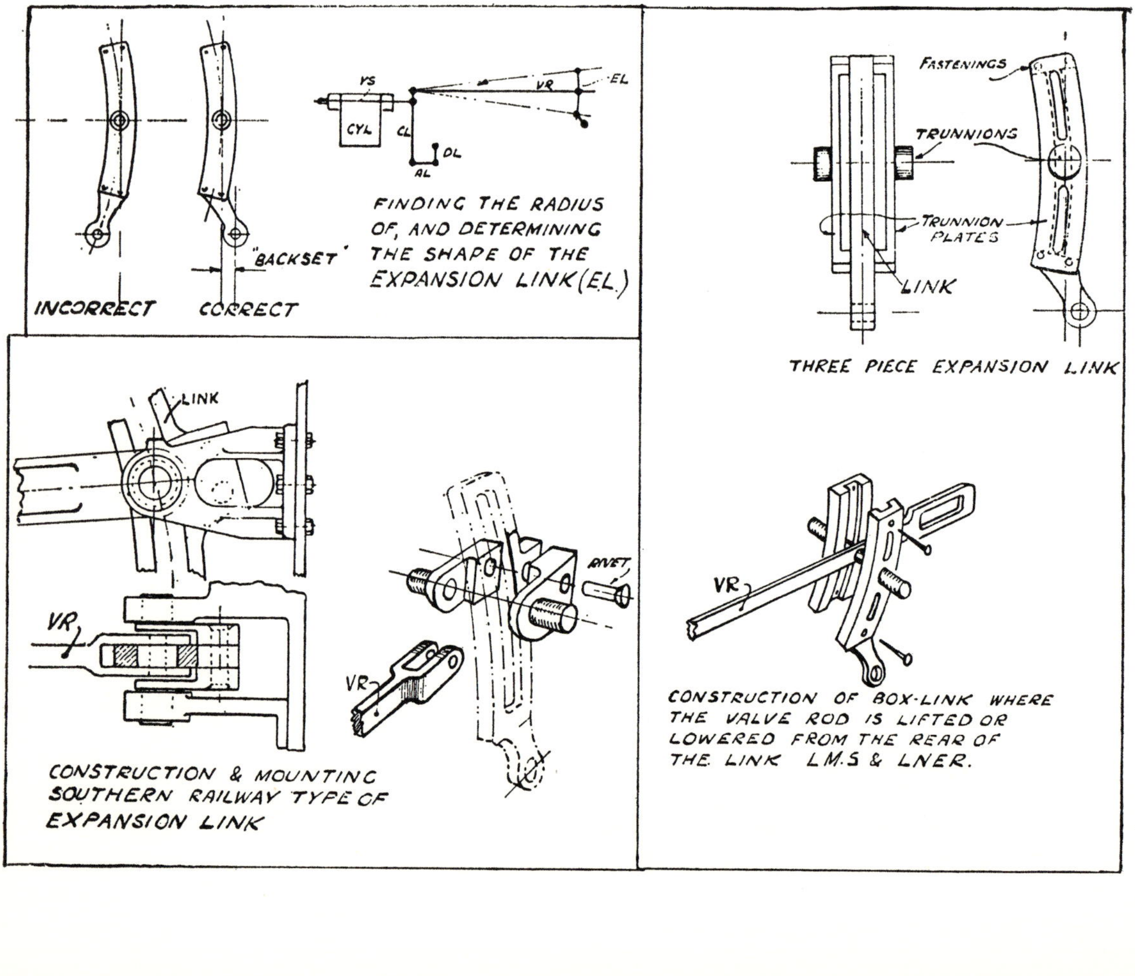

function properly, and travel up or down in the link. This will give rise no doubt to a lot of guilty consciences, as many run a 2–6–4 tank backwards, with the valve gear in forward gear, which of course would be impossible. Equally impossible of course is every engine on the model railway with valve gear in mid gear. The engine should not run either way in this state except light; it would not pull a train. These facts are mentioned as a matter of correct procedure, but as nine out of ten electrically-driven models are made by folk who have little or no knowledge of the function of a steam locomotive, there is ample excuse. But there is no excuse for those who do know how a steam loco works, and there are many who have gone in for OO gauge, who have previously made and run live steam locos, having given it up for lack of space, or a garden, but as a rule these modellers make their valve gear properly, inside as well as outside.

When we have made our valve rod, we must tackle the link itself. The radius of this is struck from the top of the combining lever, and there are two types, the single flat link, and the box link. The Southern Railway used the flat link, and it entails a special form of bracket to house it. The rear end of the valve rod is forked to travel in it, as shown in the drawing (fig. 99). The link itself is often modelled incorrectly, and in the sketch will be shown the right and wrong way of making it. The back set of the hole for attaching the eccentric rod is always there, although in some designs it is not always apparent, but it can easily be proved by drawing instruments on the drawing of the loco being modelled. The thing to aim at is to fit the correct type of

100 Lifting valve rods

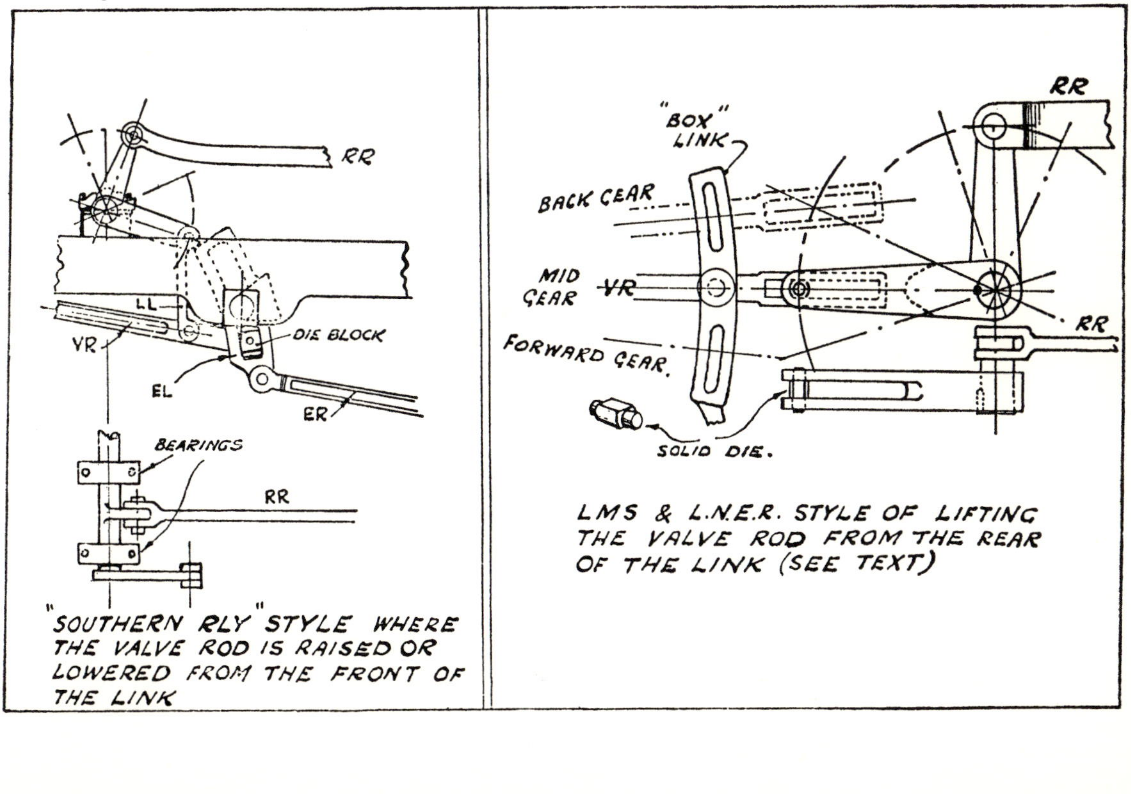

link for the loco being modelled. The LMS always uses the box link, and a method of making this is shown in the drawings. There are two little studs on the valve rod which engage in slides in the link itself, and on the outside of the link are two further studs which engage in the link bracket or girder frame, the two halves of the link being bolted or pinned together at the top and bottom. The author's HO gauge *Royal Scot* had a link made in this way. The link was made straight and bent to a curve afterwards. This will be found the simplest way to make it for those who have no lathe. The studs on the link which run in the girder frame are called trunnions. The drawing also details another way to make a link. This shows a plain flat link to which are attached trunnion plates. This gives the appearance of a box link when completed. In this case the valve rod, if it is to be lifted from behind the link, must have an eye in it to engage in the slot of the link, at right angles to the eye at the rear end of the link.

When the link is made it should be inserted on the valve rod and the rod worked up and down to see that it works freely. If the valve rod has been made to reverse behind the link, there will be a long slotted eye in the end, which engages in the lifting arm (see fig. 100), which is attached to the reverse rod. This arm is made from square bar and slotted for a portion of its length as shown in the plan view. The slotted portion should be long enough to cover entirely the slotted portion of the valve rod when the gear is in mid position. Attached to the forward end of the lifting arm is a little die block engaging in the slot without any shake. As this arm is lifted or lowered from the cab the die block works in the slot and so lifts or depresses the valve rod for forward and backward gear, as shown. The upright portion of the arm is always at right angles to the arm, and at the top end is attached the reverse rod. There are exceptions to this as a study of the loco being modelled will reveal, particularly in the LMS Pacifics where the reverse rod is underneath the footplate, but the function is the same in every case. The reverse rod should be made next, and the end of this is almost always forked, and should be made thus as it is seen above the footplate. Examples have been given already of types of reversing gear in the cab when dealing with cab fittings, and the other end of the reversing rod should be attached to this gear, usually of the screw type. Walschaert's gear is never reversed by means of the lever and latch type of gear.

The Return Crank

Having proceeded thus far we now have to provide means of rocking the link to impart motion to the valve. This is done by means of an eccentric crank, or return crank as it is usually called, through the medium of the eccentric rod.

When a "live" steam loco is being made, this rod is usually the last to be made as its length cannot be arrived at precisely except by trial and error during the timing of the gear, but as we are dealing with an electrically driven model of a prototype, the length can be found by reference to the drawing of the loco being modelled, if it is a definite prototype, but if free-lance, then it should be left to the last and the eccentric crank next made.

We will deal with the eccentric rod at this juncture. This rod has a plain eye at each end, and is usually fluted. It can be thus finished as already described for the valve rod. Do not forget at the rear end there is an oiling box similar to those on the connecting rod and coupling rods.

101 METHODS OF FIXING RETURN CRANKS.

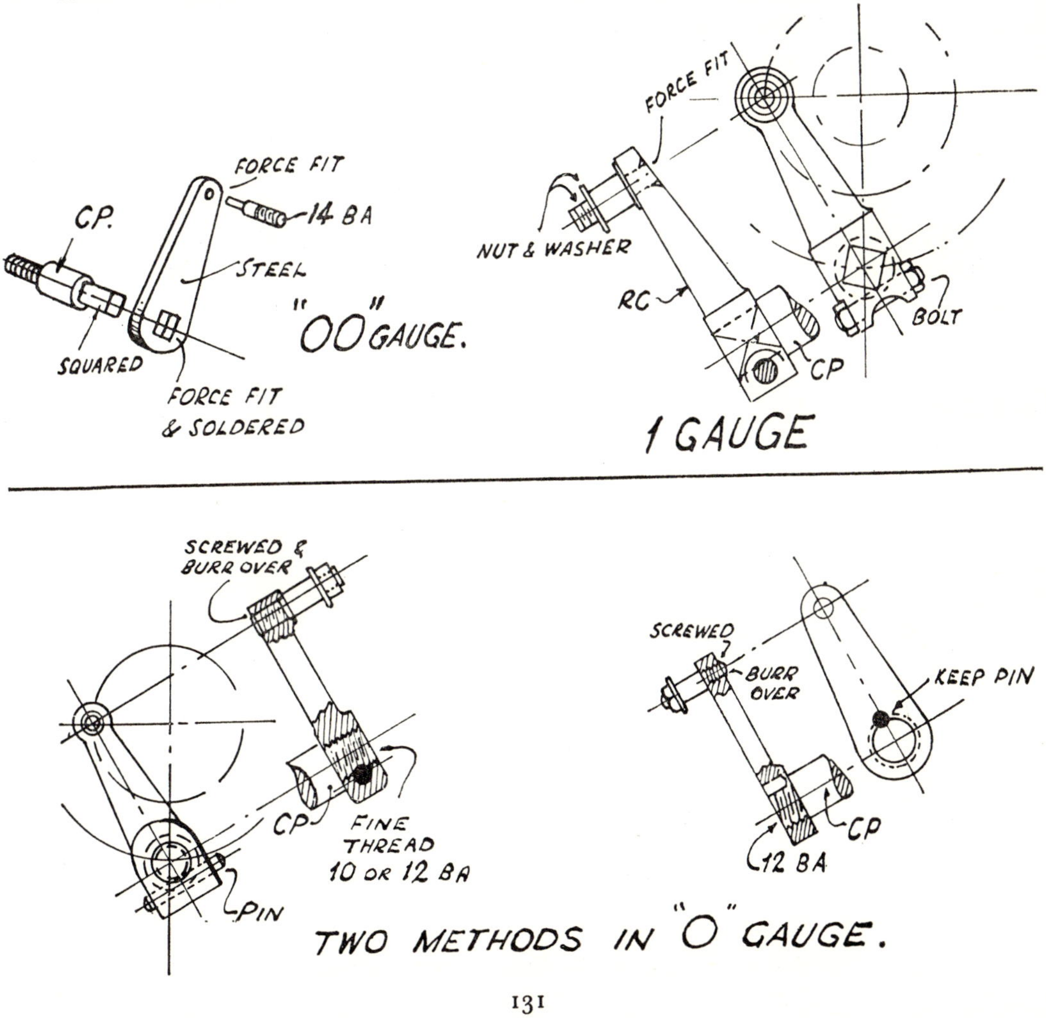

We now have the return crank to consider. This should be made with due regard to the size of the model whether it is OO gauge or larger. We have all at some time or another had the annoying accident of the return crank coming loose and revolving round its pin and jumping the gear. This will always happen if the crank is merely stuck on a pin and soldered. There is a great strain on this crank and it should be made to withstand it. The sketches show the various methods of fixing these cranks. It should always be pinned or secured on a squared pin. The pin on which the eccentric rod works should be made part of the crank, and the rod retained by a nut and washer much the same way as a coupling rod. When positioning the return crank, the drawings should be studied to ascertain whether the engine is outside or inside admission, and the crank position depends upon this, see sketches E and F. The length of the return crank is such that when it is in its correct position it should be equal to the length of the distance between the centre of the driving wheel, and the centre of the crank pin, i.e., half the stroke of the cylinders. Do not measure this off from the driving wheel, otherwise when the crank is in its correct position it will be too short.

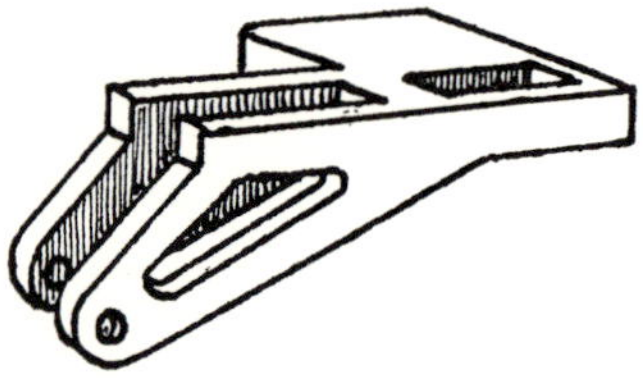

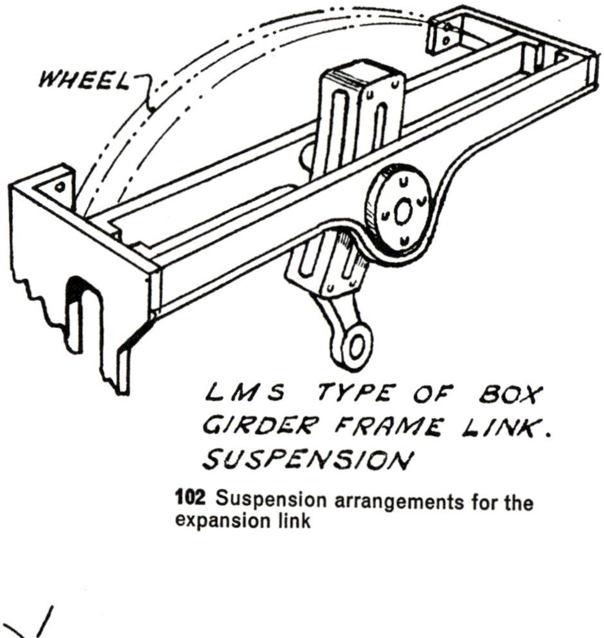

102 Suspension arrangements for the expansion link

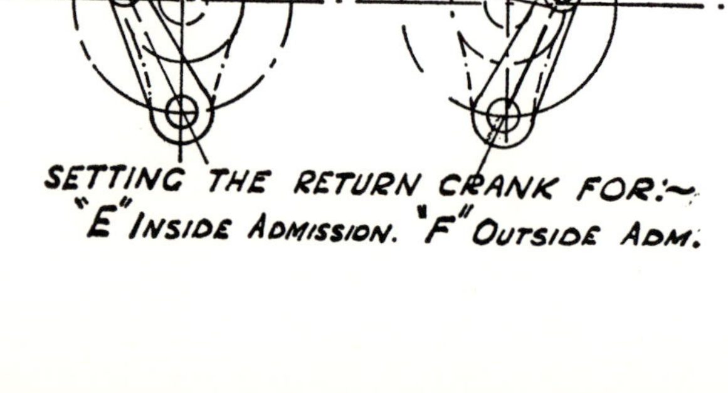

103 Crank setting

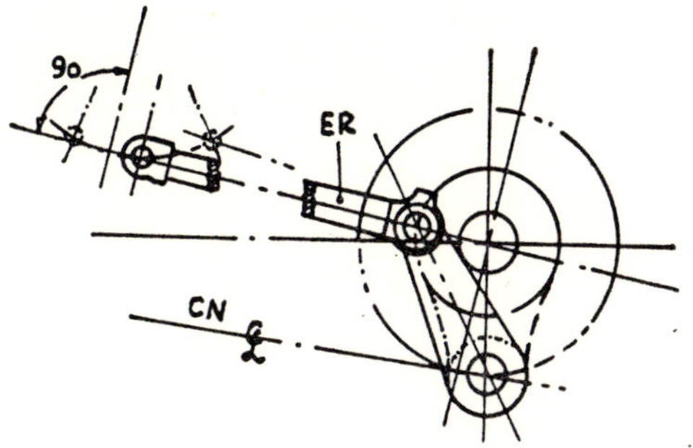

SETTING OUT THE RETURN (OR ECCENTRIC) CRANK ON THE MAIN CRANKPIN. 104
. INSIDE ADMISSION (PISTON VALVE) CYLINDERS.

Reference to the sketches will make this clear. Do not have any projecting portion of the main crank pin protruding from the crank, as the eccentric rod has to pass over the crank once in every revolution, and its way should be clear, by the thickness of the washer previously mentioned.

Having made our return crank, we can now attach the eccentric rod, one end to the link and the other (oil box) end to the return crank. If the rod in its running position is inclined inwards to the main motion do not worry this is quite usual in British engines, owing to our restricted loading gauge regarding width. The other thing to remember is that the link in its girder frame must clear the connecting rod on top dead centre, and the connecting rod must clear the coupling rod front pin. No mention has yet been made of the girder frame, these vary so much in their general design, but their function is always the same, i.e., to act as suspension for the expansion link. Two styles are shown, both very common in this country. One is made to embrace the driving wheel entirely (LMS) and the other to fit between the wheels (LNER). The Southern type of bracket also fits between the wheels. The method of making them is self-explanatory in the sketches and they are bolted to the main frame of the loco. The LNER type of bracket should be made from the solid, with hacksaw and files, but the LMS type can be built up.

Connecting and Coupling Rods

There only remains the connecting rod and coupling rod to complete our gear. In modern locos, the big end of the connecting rod, i.e., the end which goes on the crank pin, is usually of the plain eye type, but in older locos, the big end was usually very elaborate and if modelled properly, they look very engineering like.

The GNR Atlantics, both Walschaert fitted and with Stephenson gear, had the type of big end shown in the drawing. This type of end was very common about the 1900-1911 period, most of the outside cylinder engines being fitted with it, except the GWR who always went in for the plain eye type. Fluting of the connecting rod is fairly common, and should always be carried out on a model, as already shown. The little end, the end which fits in the crosshead, is a plain eye.

The coupling rod, if the loco is sprung, should be jointed just behind the middle driving wheel. If it is not, then the value of the springing would be lost. A method of doing this is shown in the sketch. The joint should be of the forked type. With the making of the coupling rod our Walschaert gear should be complete, and it is hoped that if the gear is being made for the first time the modeller will have learnt a considerable amount about steam locomotives. Taking into consideration that the various parts of the gear have had to be made properly it is just as well to make them work, and the various rods and levers can be reversed from the cab in a proper manner

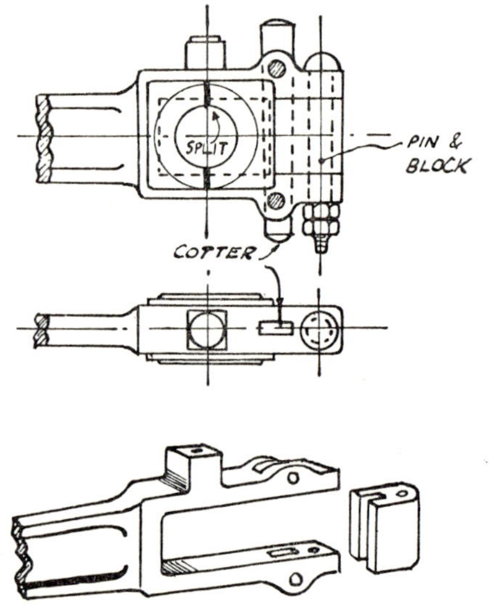

105 L.N.E.R (EX GNR) TYPE OF CONNECTING ROD BIG END.

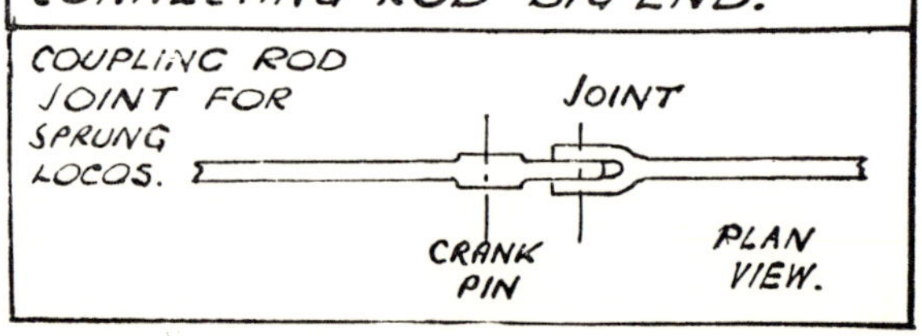

instead of fixing the gear in the inevitable mid-position. Some purists object to the human hand encroaching on the railway, but this is an extreme seldom capable of being carried out unless everything is electrical or mechanical including couplings on the wagons. Some one has yet to invent a really automatic coupler, and the human hand has usually to be brought into play to uncouple a wagon: why not to reverse a loco? It is all part of the fun and until we have real steam and real railway noises we must do a bit of make believe.

So far nothing has been said of Walschaert's gear fitted inside the frames such as in the GWR 4-cylinder locos, and some Continental compounds. When the gear is fitted inside the loco, it is exactly the same, with the exception that the return crank is replaced by an eccentric on the driving cranked axle, one for each cylinder. A drawing is given of one side of the motion of a GWR 4-cylinder loco. The valve rod has an extremely long forked end to clear the valve spindle guide mounted on the slide bars, and in front of this the combining lever is attached to a casting on the valve spindle, to which is fastened the rocker operating the valve spindles of the outside cylinders. If it is desired to operate the rockers on an electrically driven model of a GWR engine, the whole of the gear can be made as in the writer's models of the King and Castle class engines, or a simpler method can be used by attaching the eccentric direct to the rocker, dispensing with the link and valve rod, leaving only the valve spindle guide on the slide bars.

The eccentric rod will then be a long rod with a forked end as shown for the valve rod. If the gear is modelled properly, the frame carrying the links is a huge casting going right across the frames, and acting as a frame stretcher. It is made in two halves and bolted down the middle on the longitudinal centre line of the loco, after the links have been inserted. It is partly shown in the drawing.

Finally, before leaving the subject of valve gears, it is well to mention at this stage that all pins running in holes in the various rods, should be running fits, just that and no more or no less. A valve gear put together with a lot of brass pins riveted over sloppy holes will not last the proverbial five minutes. Unfortunately this method of making Walschaerts gear in OO gauge is far too common. A useful guide in OO gauge is to remember that a No. 62 drill is a running fit on 20 swg piano wire (treble strings). The writer has used old drills as pins in valve gear in HO and OO gauges. Always use steel pins, and as far as possible steel strip, stainless if obtainable, and of at least $\frac{1}{16}$ in. in thickness. It can always be filed a little thinner between the eyes and holes. Those working to 16.5 gauge have plenty of room without coming outside the extreme width of the loco, one of the advantages of this gauge. If the eyes are properly made, there is no need for washers to obtain clearance, as the thinning of the rod between the extremities provide the necessary clearance.

In O gauge the pins can be made properly with shouldered ends and screwed extremities, the rods being retained by 14 and 16 BA nuts. All the gear should be made of steel, nothing looks worse then German silver and tinned brass; these methods were used 20 years ago. If the motion is well lubricated, the rust problem should not occur, and if stainless steel is used, of course it will not rust at all. At this stage it can be mentioned that driving

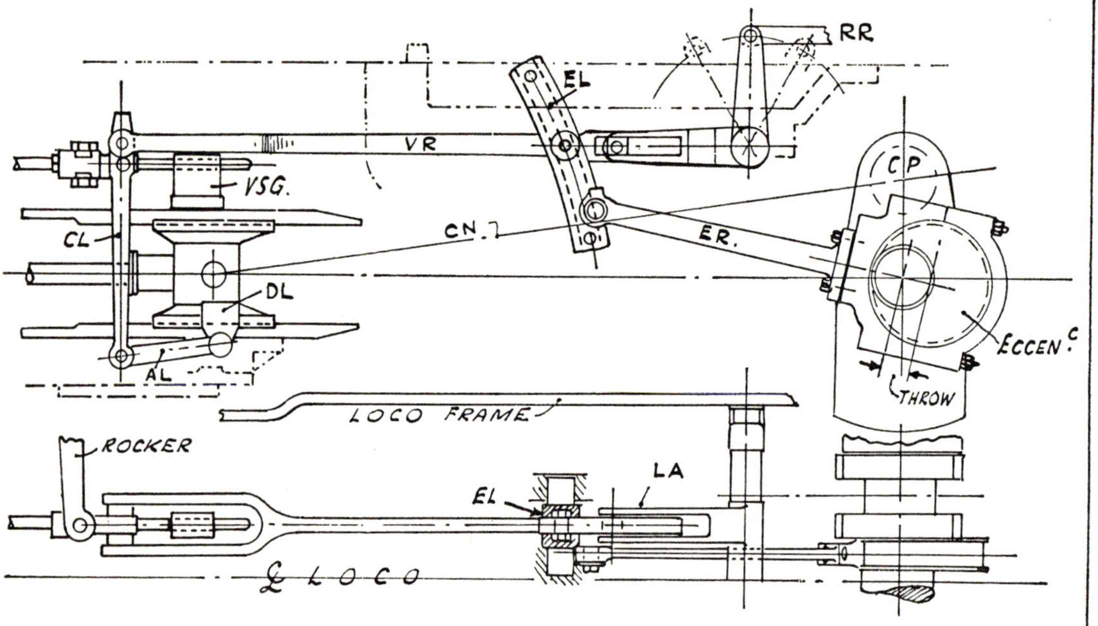

106 WALSCHAERTS VALVE GEAR ARRANGED FOR INSIDE CYLS.
AS ON G.W.R. "STAR", "CASTLE" & "KING" CLASSES

wheels should be painted with cellulose paint, oil will have no effect on this, as it will on ordinary paint.

The next type of valve gear to describe is the Stephenson gear. There are still many locos running today fitted with this gear, and it is mostly found on outside cylinder locos. This requires 4 eccentrics and a cranked axle. There are two eccentrics to each link called the forward gear eccentric, and back gear eccentric. It is an eminently suitable gear for use where the motion is transferred from the centre line.

Walschaert's Valve Gear

We have covered most of the details of Walschaerts gear as fitted to two-cylinder locos, and we will now pass to the 4 cyl. Loco as built by the GWR, where this valve gear is placed inside the frames and eccentrics are used in place of return cranks. In the drawing will be seen a layout of the gear as fitted to the GWR 4 cyl. express locos of the Star, Castle and King classes, (fig. 109).

The links are suspended in a large cast gear frame going right across the frame of the loco and acting as a frame stretcher. The drawing by Col. Templer shows this frame (fig. 107), a section through the centre longitudinally and part section viewed from the front of the loco and a plan of the whole

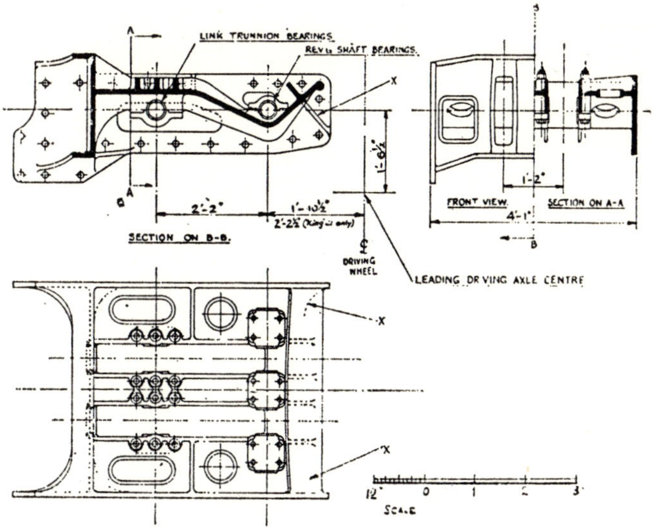

107 Inside gear frame of GWR 4-cylinder locomotives (actual size in 7mm scale)

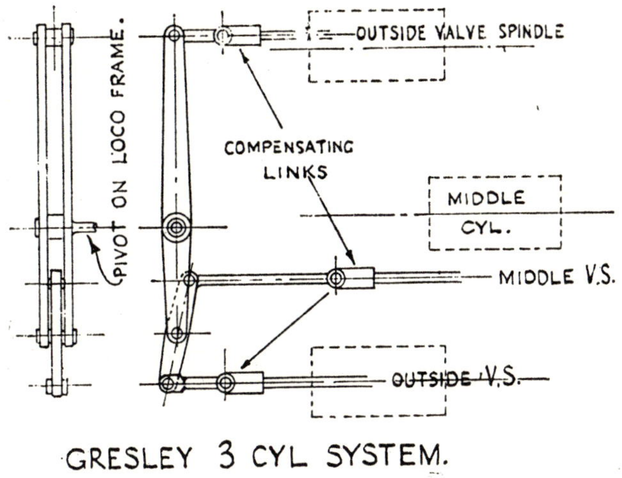

108 Gresley 3-cylinder locomotive gear system

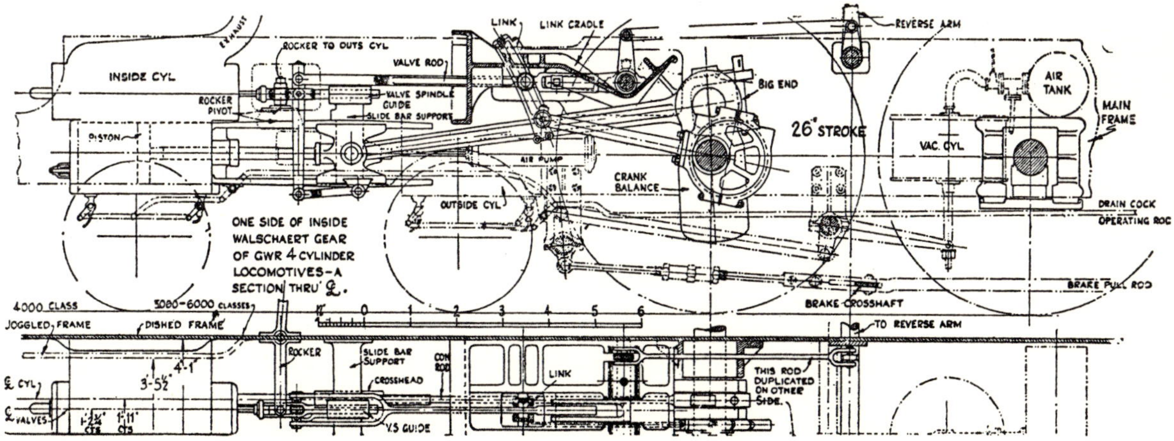

109 Walschaert's valve gear inside GWR 4-cylinder locos

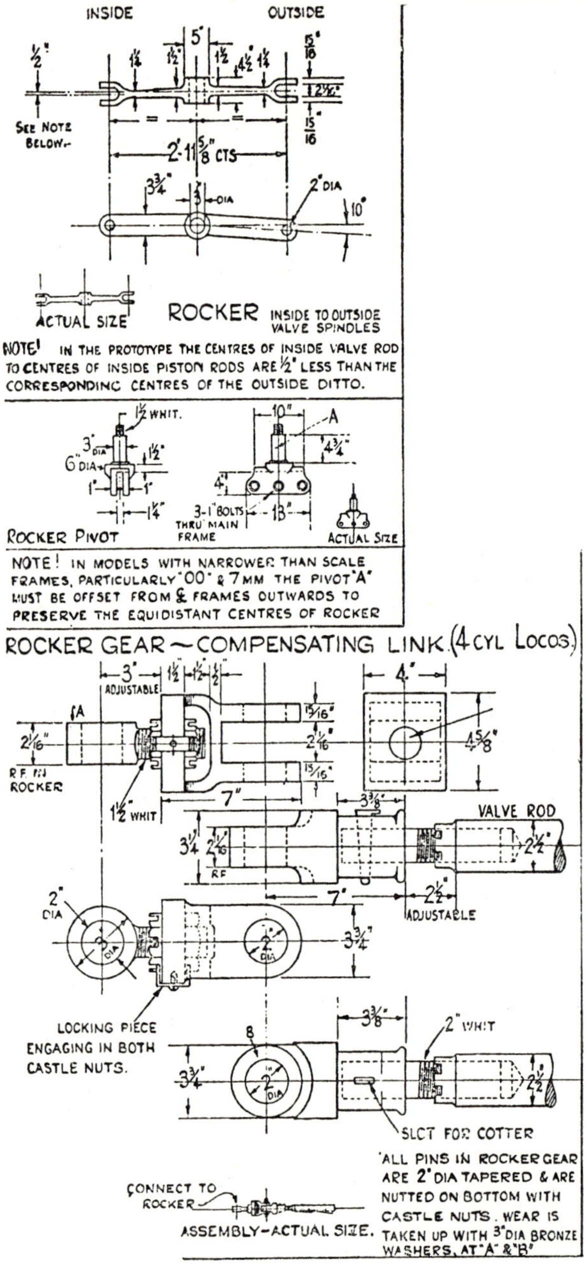

110

assembly. The drawing is self explanatory. There are six bearings, three for the links, and three for the reversing shaft. The links are fitted from underneath, and the reversing shaft from the top. Split bearings are used in all cases. There are one or two points which need comment. The web marked "X" is not shown on the GA of the loco, probably omitted for clearness no doubt and the curved profile shown dotted is put in from observation of the actual locos. The large openings in the side members of the casting are probably machining access holes, as is also the smaller one near the reversing shaft bearings; these also probably serve as lightening holes.

One further note: this gear frame is pitched 4 in. further forward on the King class locos, from the leading driving axle. This frame can be modelled quite accurately, with the exception of the width of 4 ft. 1 in. which of course will have to be modified to suit the width of the model frames.

As for the GWR valve gear itself, the links and pins follow the contours as previously described for the outside gear, with the exception of the valve rod, which has a very long forked end to clear the valve spindle guide. The place taken in the scheme of things by the large cast gear frame can be clearly seen in the layout of the gear. Part of the brake gear can also be seen, Attached below the pin for the valve rod on the combination lever is the connection for the rocker arm to the outside cylinders. Whatever method is used to attach this arm to the inside gear, the outside attachments must be modelled properly, as they are clearly seen under the footplate at the front end of the model. In a previous series of mine I pointed out that it is not possible to attach this rocker direct to the outside valve spindle as is often done in models. Anyone with the most elementary knowledge of mechanics should know that it is impossible to attach a rod moving in a fore and aft direction, to a member travelling in an arc, one or the other will set up a bending stress. In the GWR gear there is a compensating link attached at both ends of the rocker, and I give drawings of this compensating link, dimensioned off the full size engine, so that it can be used for any scale. The small sketch at the bottom shows the actual size for a OO gauge loco. It's a proper watchmaking job, but worth it. Next in order of importance is the rocker itself. It will be seen that the inside end is $\frac{1}{2}$ in. lower than the outside end, as the inside piston valves are this much lower in the frames. The outside end is also bent to 110 deg. in the horizontal plane, in a rearward direction i.e. towards the outside cylinder. Dimensions are again taken from the full size loco, and the small sketch shows actual size for 4 mm. scale. This rocker should be made, in OO, from $\frac{1}{16}$in sq. steel bar and in O gauge from $\frac{1}{8}$ in. sq. steel bar.

We next come to the rocker pivot which is mounted on the main frame in a rectangular hole provided for the purpose. Here we come up against the narrower than scale frames again, and the actual pins upon which the rockers work must be offset outwards so that they are approximately 4 ft. 2 in. centre to centre across the locomotive. In standard OO gauge this offset is considerable, as the engine is really running on 4 ft. gauge instead of 4 ft. $8\frac{1}{2}$ in., and the loco superstructure is built to the scale equivalent of 4 ft. $8\frac{1}{2}$ in. To make this the author usually turns the whole of pivot and the bracket in one piece, filing and sawing the actual frame bracket to shape, afterwards incorporating the necessary offset.

There is one other variation of Walschaert's gear used in these Islands, and that is a 3-cylinder variant in which three sets of gear are used, one for each cylinder. This was used to a large extent on LNER locomotives, but Sir Nigel Gresley invented a valve gear using only 2 sets of motion placed outside driving a third cylinder by means of levers.

In the Gresley version proper (fig. 109), there were only two sets of gears, operating the outside cylinders, the middle or third cylinder being operated by a floating lever, the extremities of which worked in little sets of slide bars in front of the outside piston valves; a sketch is given of this arrangement. Here again a compensating link was incorporated similar to the GWR arrangement, allowing the clevis or forked ends of the combining levers attached to the floating lever to be relieved of strain when working the outside valve spindles. I do not think any additional notes are required as the sketch explains itself, except to say that the outside valve spindles drive the middle one, not the other way round. The long lever is pivoted to a fixed point so that its arms are of unequal length, i.e. in the ratio of 2 to 1. The long end is jointed to the right-hand valve spindle extension and the short end to the centre of the floating lever. Due to the combined action of the levers the motion of the centre valve is 120 deg. out of phase with the outside ones. With regard to the uneven beat of the three cylinder engines, any defect in the distribution of steam in the middle cylinder would result in two uneven beats per revolution. This usually occured when the Gresley Pacifics were in full gear, and it was a little less apparent when the engines were notched up. To overcome this Mr. Gresley reduced the lead of the middle cylinder piston valve by $\frac{1}{16}$ in., and the beats of the three cylinders were more or less equalised. As is well known this gear was ideal providing it was properly maintained; in fact the world's record speed for a steam loco was attained by a locomotive using this gear. Unfortunately the war caused maintenance to get in arrears, and undue wear in the links and pins of the gear caused the Gresley arrangement to be shelved in favour of three separate sets of gear for the three cylinders, which arrangement was standard on the LNER. The inside set of gear was operated by an eccentric as in the GWR version.

Stephenson's Valve Gear

We will now deal with the Stephenson gear (fig. 111) which, up to quite recent times, was the commonest valve gear used on British locomotives both with inside and outside cylinders, and is still almost universally used with the former. It was first adopted by the Stephensons in 1843 and was never strictly speaking invented, for it grew, so to speak, from the old gab motion by connecting the ends of the eccentrics by a curved link. The gear has very rarely been placed outside in British practice, but this was quite a favourite position for it on early Continental locos, and the celebrated Thomas Crampton so employed it. But history has a curious way of repeating itself, some LMS Class 5 4–6–0s were built with this gear fitted outside in place of the standard Walschaert's arrangement.

Reference to fig. 111 will show that the gear is operated by two eccentrics to each valve, connected by a curved link. This link is slotted to receive a die-block which in turn is pinned to a forked extension of the valve rod, the valves in this instance being between the cylinders, in which position they allow of the most straightforward application of this gear. The expansion link, as it is generally termed, is supported on a pair of suspension links through the medium of a bracket secured to the link at about its centre, the other ends of the suspension links being pinned to an arm fixed on the weigh-shaft; another arm fixed on one end of the weigh-shaft is connected to the reversing rod and reference to the drawing will show that the two

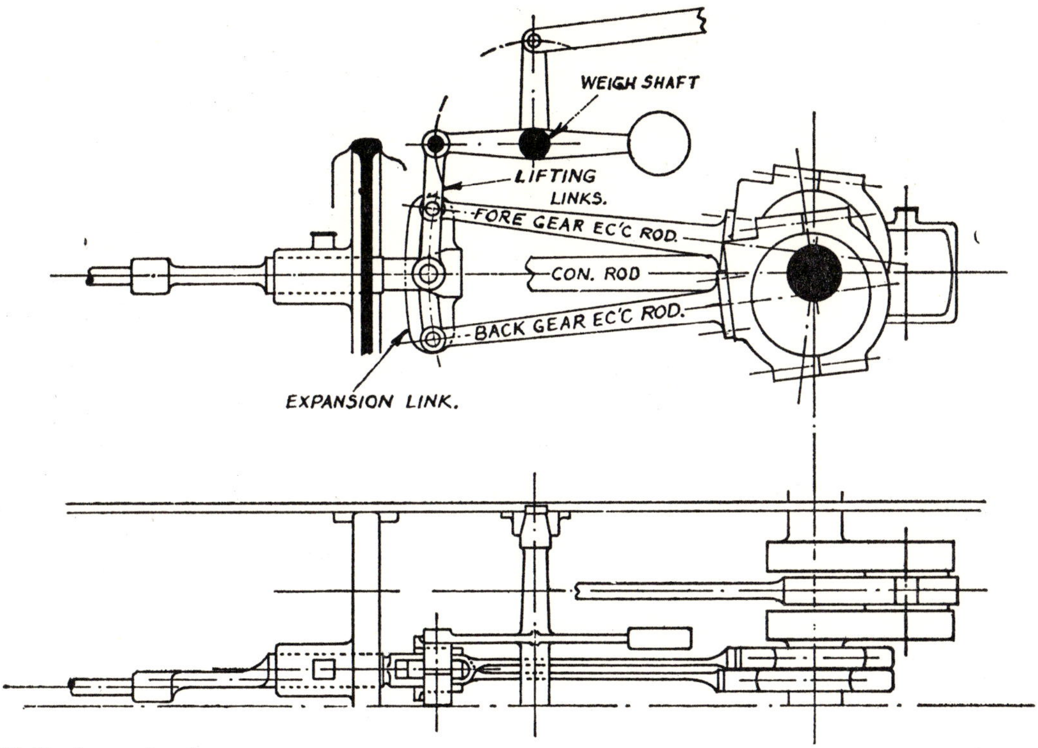

111 Stephenson's valve gear

arms act as a bell crank so that when the reversing rod is moved forward or backward the expansion link is raised or lowered so bringing the valve rod under the influence of either the forward or the backward eccentric. In the normal arrangement of this gear the eccentric coupled to the upper end of the link is always the fore gear eccentric and is generally the one adjacent to the crank web. A disadvantage of this gear is the weight of the parts which have to be moved when the engine is notched up or reversed and to overcome this the weigh-shaft arms are often extended and fitted with balance weights as shown, alternatively, some designers fit a balancing spring.

The Stephenson gear is an extremely adaptable mechanism. Valves above or below the cylinders can be driven by it direct if they are suitably inclined, or, if the valves are of the piston type on top of the cylinders as in most modern designs, the motion can be transferred to them by means of rocking levers and this is the normal arrangement in such cases. Again, the cylinders may be outside with the valves between the frames, in which case the gear drives them direct, or valves and cylinders may both be outside in which case the drive is taken through a rocking shaft as in standard GWR practice. The drawing (fig. 111) shows the arrangement of the gear in the GWR Hall class; it was designed originally by the late Mr. Churchward for his standard engines and all GWR outside cylinder classes use this gear—except of

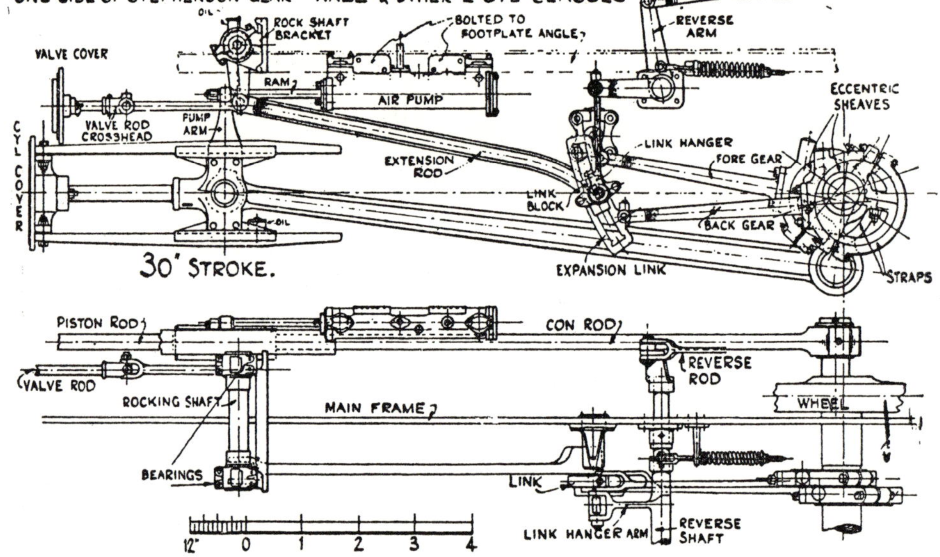

112 ONE SIDE OF STEPHENSON GEAR - "HALL" & OTHER 2 CYL CLASSES

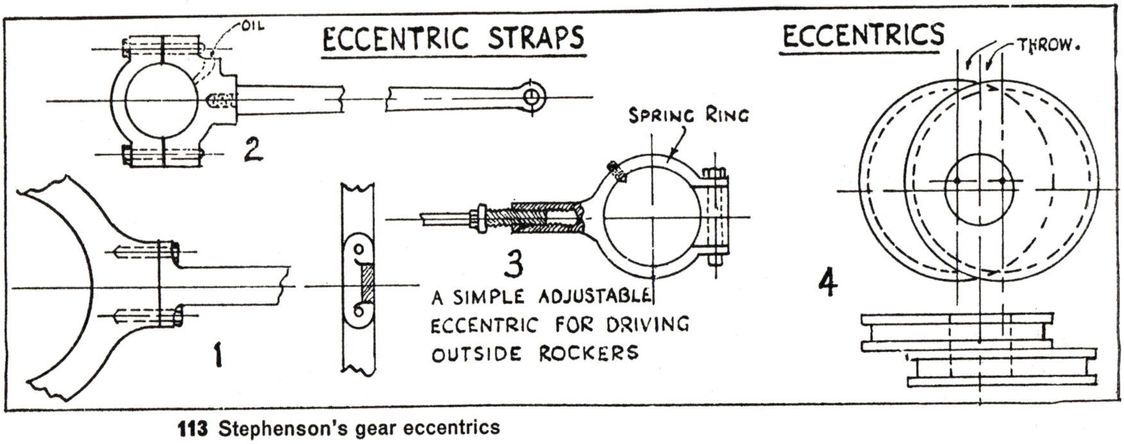

113 Stephenson's gear eccentrics

course the 4-cylinder engines—it being adaptable to the different classes simply by altering the length of the extension rod and in one case the eccentric rods. Students of the locomotive should note the very short eccentrics and the marine type link in which the eccentrics are coupled to the link in such a place that the full throw of the eccentric is imparted to the valve in full gear.

To revert to the LMS class 5 loco already mentioned, the eccentrics are replaced by a double return crank mounted on the driving crank, and the layout of the remainder of the gear follows the standard GWR arrangement described above, a pendulum lever taking the place of the rockers and forming a means of connecting and supporting the extension rod and valve rod.

It is impossible in the space at our disposal to describe in greater detail the numerous different arrangements of this gear and what has been said must suffice; readers seeking for information of the arrangement applied to a particular loco should study the drawings published in such papers as the *Engineer*, the *Railway Gazette* etc., or the records of the Patent Office Library.

If this gear is to be fitted to a small scale loco, great care must be taken in the making of the various parts and particularly to the fit of the pins in the holes, for otherwise the gear when assembled will be sloppy and jerky in movement and be a disappointment. Eccentric rods and other parts should have proper forked ends, about the making of which notes have already been given in this book and the mating parts should be carefully fitted to them. Probably the cranked axle will offer the greatest difficulty to the amateur, for in O gauge there is only about an inch in which to accommodate two cranks of adequate strength and four eccentrics. Some sketches showing methods of making cranked axles have already been given, and if the operator has access to silver soldering or brazing facilities it is better to silver solder or braze the complete assembly and then finish turning it in the lathe. Alternatively, the eccentric sheaves may be made in two halves and pinned to the shaft, the straps hiding the pins when the gear is erected; this method makes for a stonger cranked axle.

Regarding the eccentric straps and rods, the former should be made from brass bar or gunmetal and the lugs should be long so that the securing bolts may lie close to the sheave. In fig. 113 various methods of coupling the straps to the sheaves are shown; correct practice is to make the strap and rod separately as at 1, and a simplified version of this for small models is shown at 2. Or the rod and strap may be made in one, but great care will be necessary to ensure that the length is correct and a method of making an adjustable rod is shown at 3—it is hardly necessary to point out that this is not full size practice. If the rod and strap are made in one piece, it is better not to drill the hole in the rod for the attachment of the link until the strap has been fitted to the sheave; this hole can then be marked off, the rod dismounted, the hole drilled and the eye finished, and in the case of the Stephenson gear the two rods to each link can be marked off together.

A pair of eccentrics is shown at fig. 113/4, and it will be noticed that they are grooved to mate with a ridge formed inside the strap, so that when the

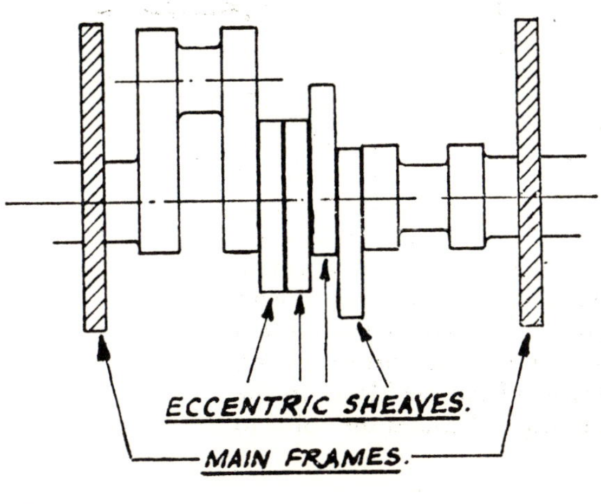

114 Stephenson's gear eccentric sheaves

strap and sheave are assembled, their outside faces are flush with one another, the groove and ridge preventing the strap moving sideways off the sheave. Machining the groove and ridge in the very small parts of an O gauge model may prove a difficulty; an alternative is to turn just a shallow groove in the sheave to take the point of a grub screw in the strap (see fig. 113/3). But if the whole of the axle between the inner crank webs is occupied with eccentric sheaves, these and the straps may be quite plain, for when all four straps are assembled, each will lie snug against its neighbour and the outer ones against the crank webs, so that movement off the sheaves will be impossible.

In the case of electrically driven models of GWR locomotives, the model maker may not wish to go to the length of reproducing the whole of the motion; in that case there is no reason why a single eccentric should not be fitted coupled direct to the inside rocker. One point in connection with inside motion should perhaps be stressed, and that is that the use of a cranked axle obviously entails some form of split bearing to enable it to be fitted in the frames whether the model is sprung or not.

Before taking leave of the Stephenson gear we must mention that the eccentric leads the crank by a right angle plus the angular equivalent of the lap and lead of the valve in the case of slide valves and outside admission piston valves, and follows the crank by a right angle minus the angular equivalent in the case of inside admission piston valves. In an electrically driven model, the correct positioning of the eccentrics in relation to their crank does not of course matter in the slightest; it just imparts that life-like impression of the gear when it is motion.

Joy's Valve Gear

An entirely different form of valve gear which achieved considerable popularity during the last century is that invented by David Joy; it was originally designed by him for marine engines and was first used in this country on the Furness Railway. But Francis Webb of the LNWR took it up with tremendous enthusiasm, and it remained the standard valve gear on that railway up to the Grouping. The great advantage claimed for it was that by dispensing with eccentrics it greatly simplified the cranked axle, and Webb exploited this by fitting a central bearing on many of his locos. The usual arrangement of the gear is shown in fig. 115 from which it will be seen that the motion is taken from a point about $\frac{1}{3}$ along the connecting rod where a link called the correcting link, or jack link, is attached. The other end of the jack link is attached to the anchor link, which is in turn pinned to a fixed point on the engine frame. At a point about $\frac{1}{3}$ along the jack link a pair of vibrating links are coupled to it the other ends of which are coupled to the radius link. Adjacent to this latter connection each vibrating link carries a die-block which runs in a curved guide formed integral with the reversing shaft to which the reversing rod is coupled in the normal manner. The operation of reversing the loco moves these curved guides, with the result that the up and down movement of the die-blocks in the guides imparted by the linkage from the connecting rod causes the valve to move to and fro.

It will be seen from fig. 115 that the simplest application of this gear is to a locomotive having the valves either above or below the cylinders and in his 6-wheeled 3-cylinder compounds, Webb adopted the latter arrangement. He drove the valves of the outside high pressure cylinders by Joy's gear turned upside down, and these old engines make such lovely models that we hope the drawing showing the gear as fitted by Webb to his Teutonic class, fig. 117, will prove of interest. No dimensions have been given, as it is thought that modellers will prefer to use the drawing as a guide, since the various classes of engines to which this gear was fitted differed dimensionally as regards wheel diameter, wheel-base, etc. In this arrangement of Webb's, the curved guides were mounted on a circular plate carried in a bracket fixed under the lower slide bars; an arm extended downwards from the guide plate to which was coupled the forward end of the reverse rod, this being, of course, on both sides of the engine, and the weigh-shaft proper under the footplate.

Joy's gear was also extensively used by T. W. Worsdell both on the GER and the NER, and fig. 115 shows the arrangement for his GER 2–4–0 locomotives, and this may be taken as typical for all inside cylinder applications of it, the L&Y also fitted many engines with it. So far as locomotives are concerned the gear suffered from two serious drawbacks; one was the severe weakening of the connecting rod at the hole taking the jack link connection and several connecting rod fractures occurred on the LNWR on this account, and the other is that the rise and fall of the driving axle under

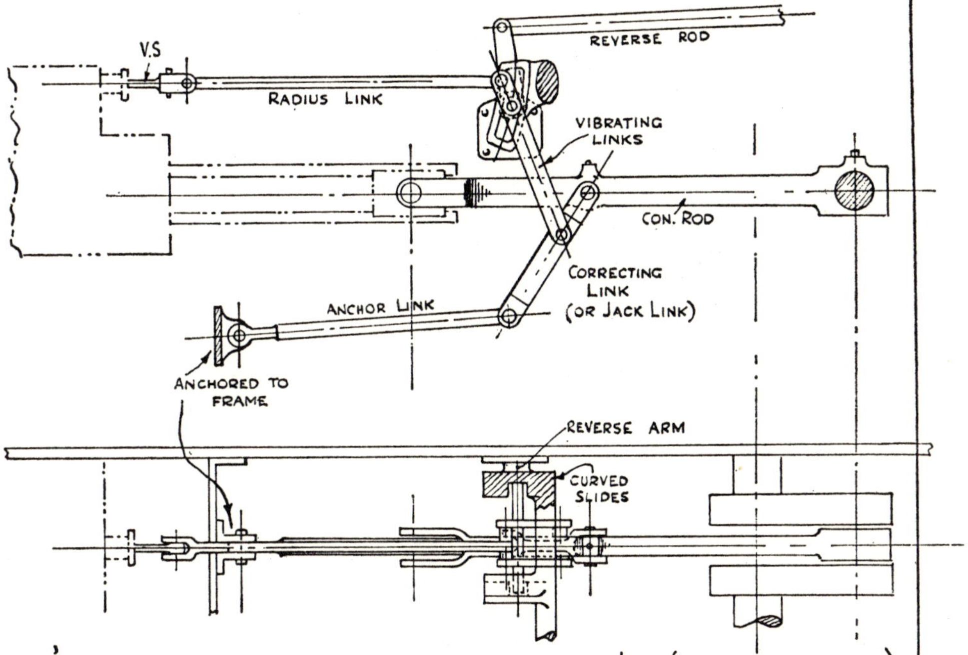

JOY'S VALVE GEAR AS FITTED TO G.E.R. 2-4-0 (WORSDELL 1882)

115

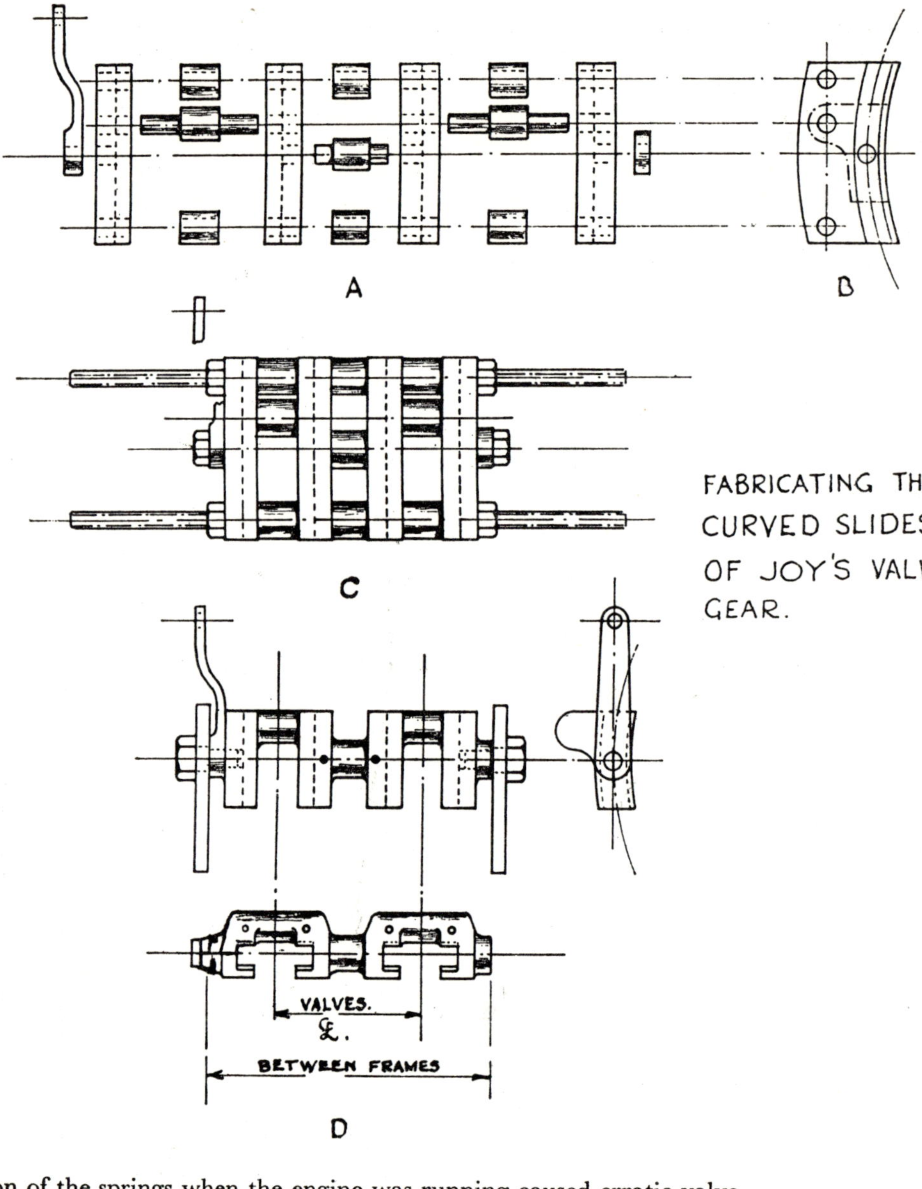

116

FABRICATING THE CURVED SLIDES OF JOY'S VALVE GEAR.

the action of the springs when the engine was running caused erratic valve events. In marine practice, the latter fault was, of course, entirely absent, and the former was not unduly felt because the engine speeds were so much lower and more constant.

With the exception of the reversing shaft, modelling this gear should not present any great difficulty; as with the Walschaert's and Stephenson's gears the great thing is care and the accurate fitting of the various parts together. We will, however, deal in some detail with the reversing shaft, not because we think that large numbers of modellers will fit inside Joy's motion, but because the method to be described is adaptable to other components, the parts of which must be accurately lined up and where, as in the case of O gauge and smaller models, machining from the solid is impossible. In fig. 116 A, is an exploded view of the various parts as seen from the cylinders looking towards the firebox; mild steel should be used throughout, except where stated otherwise, and the curved guides are best machined in the form of a complete ring from which segments to the contour of the full lines in B are cut off, soldered together, marked off and drilled as shown at B, and separated. (When soldering them together make sure that the grooved faces of each pair face one another.) The other parts required as shown at A are three pairs of distance tubes which may be of brass, three spacers having their ends reduced to suit the holes in the guides—the fit should be slightly slack—the reversing arm shown on the left and the washer on the right. The widths of the various parts must be such that when the job is put together the centre lines through the two pairs of guides coincide with the valve centres and the overall width will allow the shaft to fit between the frames as shown at D; these are matters for the Drawing Office. The next step is the assembly and A shows where the various parts fit together, the two outer spacers becoming the yoke pieces which unite the two guides of each pair, and the centre one forming the central portion of the shaft. Two long steel bolts are required which pass through the top and bottom holes in the guides and the three pairs of distance tubes, and the whole is secured with nuts on the ends of the bolts. It then appears as shown at C. Leave the nuts hand tight and clamp the end of the bolts, which have been left long for the purpose, to a flat plate with suitable packing pieces under the bolts to keep the work clear of the plate, and other pieces over them to take the clamps, which should be of the variety known as tool-makers' clamps. We advise using ground steel stock for the plate and packing pieces: it is obtainable from any reputable metal mechant in a large variety of stock sizes and a selection of these is invaluable in the home workshop; it is not expensive. We recommend using ordinary solder for joining the parts together because the much greater heat required for hard

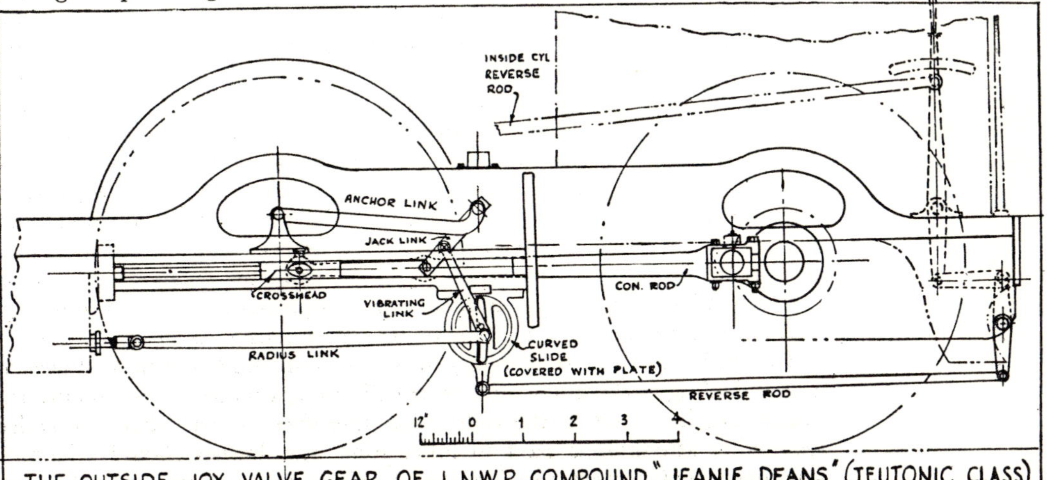

117 THE OUTSIDE JOY VALVE GEAR OF L.N.W.R COMPOUND "JEANIE DEANS" (TEUTONIC CLASS)

soldering or brazing is liable to cause distortion, and this cannot be rectified by subsequent machining. Using a fairly heavy iron, a generous fillet of solder should run in where each spacer joins a guide, and between the reversing arm and washer and the outer guides, these two components being held in position by suitable size bolts through the central holes in the outer guides, the nuts being on the inside. It will greatly assist in obtaining sound joints if the mating surfaces have been previously tinned, and this is why the ends of the spacers should not be too tight a fit in the holes in the guides—you want the solder to run right through the joint. Take care that the solder does not run where it is not wanted and unite the distance tubes to the guides, as this will make the final cleaning up to plan more difficult; a little graphite grease smeared on these parts should discourage the solder from taking to them. For additional strength it is advisable to pin the guides to the three spacers as shown at D, having done which the bolts and distance tubes can be removed. It remains now to clean up the four guides to the contour shown by the chain lines at B, when it will be seen that the top and bottom holes will disappear, and to put a chamfer on the back edges of the yokes as shown at D, which will add just that little touch of realism to the finished job. The reversing shaft is pivoted in the frames on two screws of suitable size, the frames being tapped to receive them. The ends of these screws are reduced in diameter to fit the central holes in the two outside guides, also passing through the reversing arm and washer as shown dotted in the upper drawing at D. Note that the ends of these pivot screws must not project into the grooves in the guides as they will foul the die-blocks; the same warning applies to the ends of the central spacer.

Connecting Rods, Cross-heads and Slide Bars

We now pass on to the remainder of the inside running gear, the first component claiming attention being the connecting rod. This has already been dealt with in so far as outside cylinders are concerned, but in amplification of the previous notes we show in fig. 118 two further types of big end. That at A is a simple imitation job quite suitable for a small scale model and easy to make, while that at B is a more elaborate arrangement including a screw wedge adjustment for taking up wear in the brasses, and ideal for a larger steam driven model. The big end of the inside connecting rod must obviously be in two halves bolted together, otherwise there would be no means of getting it on to the crank pin, and in fig. 119 are shown various types of inside big ends. The type shown at (a) is really a simplification of the marine big end; it should be made in hard brass or gun-metal, the two halves sawn apart and filed up true and square, then sweated together marked out and drilled for the crank pin and securing bolts, separated, placed round the crank pin and bolted up. There is no means of taking up wear in this type, and when it has worn to a sloppy fit a new bush must be fitted. However, we are dealing in the main with electrically-driven models where no driving stresses are imparted to the rods; wear therefore, is very slight, provided reasonable attention is paid to lubrication and bushes should seldom if ever need replacement provided—and this is really important—they are

118

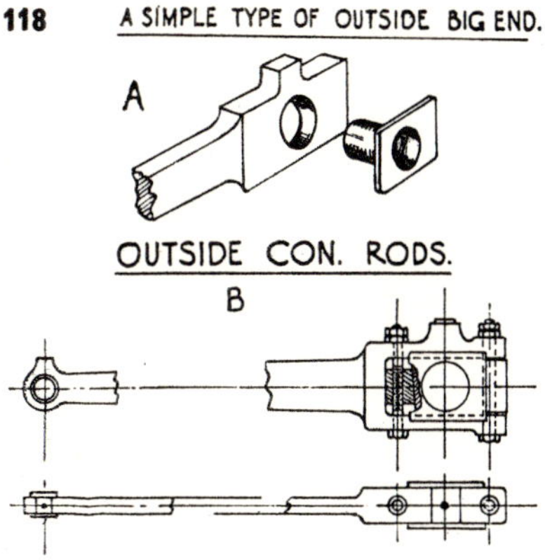

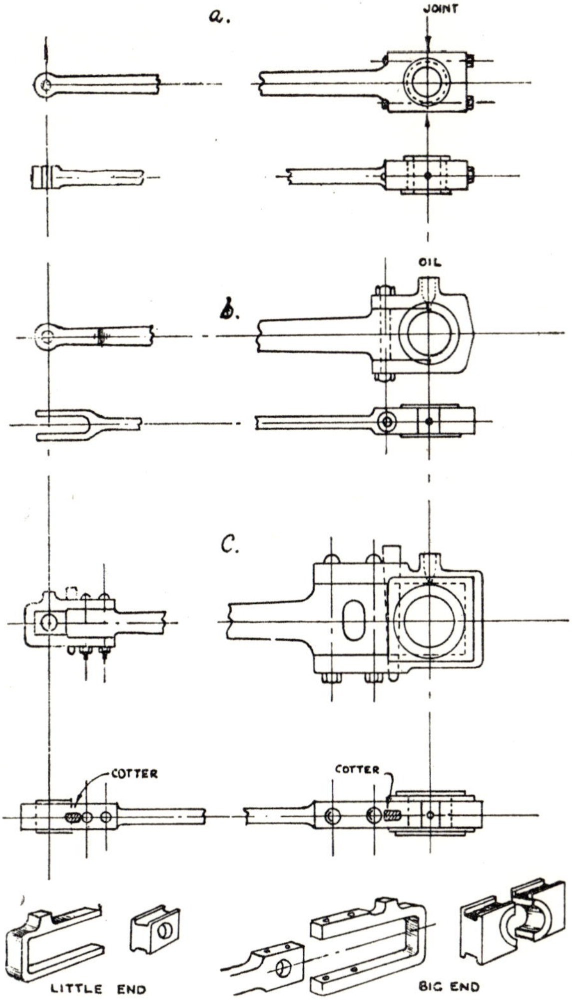

119 Inside connecting rods

made of phosphor- or manganese-bronze; for goodness' sake do not use ordinary common brass for bushes for they will not last the proverbial five minutes.

Having digressed slightly, we now turn to the type of big end shown at fig. 119 (b). This is a strap type of big end and the strap is fitted before boring the bearing. The sides of this big end are quite flat and it is fitted with renewable bushes or brasses to give them their correct title. Note that the little end of this rod is of the forked type, embracing the cross-head. (Any type of little end can, of course, be used with any type of big end). At fig. 119 (c) is shown the standard strap-ended British connecting rod; it is more elaborate than (b) and it will be noted that the strap is arranged to accommodate a cotter to take up wear in the brasses. A similar design is employed for the little end of this rod, but it is quite unnecessary to attempt to reproduce this in a small scale model.

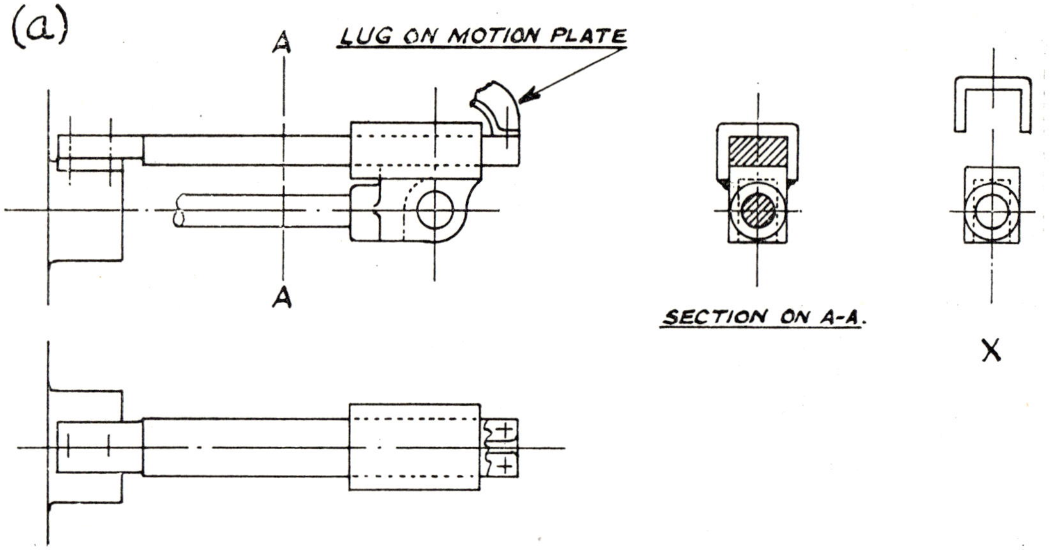

120 Inside cylinders' cross-heads and slide bars

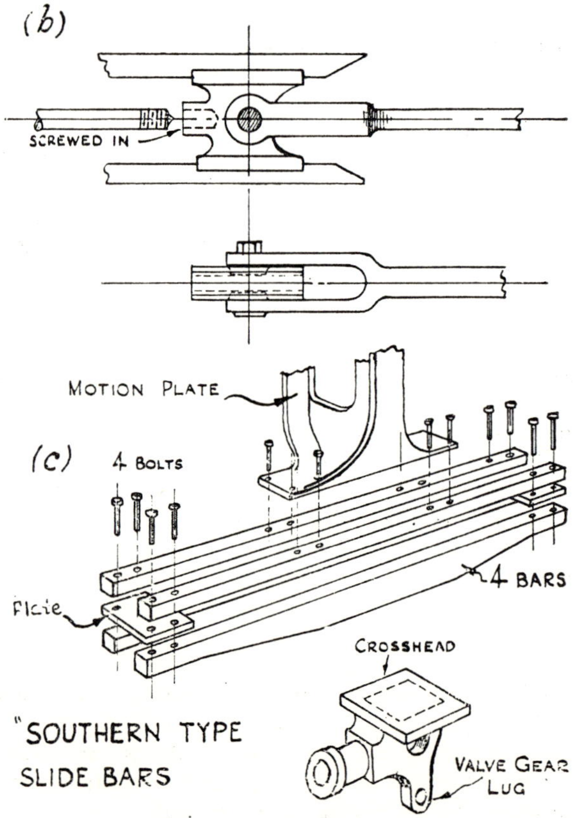

The next items to consider are crossheads and slidebars. The former are often troublesome items to make and a few suggestions for tackling them have already been given in this book with particular reference to those required for two-bar slide bars, but there are other types to suit one, three or four bar slide bars, fig. 120 (a) shows the type of single bar and cross-head as used for many years on the GER and other railways, simplified to suit a small scale model, and it presents no serious snags that we can see. The crosshead is in two parts, the lower part being prepared as usual to receive piston rod, gudgeon pin and the small end of the connecting rod, and the upper part being in the form of a channel which can be bent up from a piece of strip material. The two parts should be clamped together with a piece of the same stock as is to be used for the slide bar between them and soldered along the joints, preferably with silver solder. In larger models the crosshead may be made as in full size practice with the top plate bolted to the lower portion. If a fork ended connecting rod is used, the crosshead is simpler to make as it does not require to be slotted to take the small end; in this case the part taking the fork should be reduced in thickness. At (b) is shown a two-bar system with a crosshead arranged to take a forked small end, and requires no further comment. At (c) is shown a model form of the four bar type of slide bar and crosshead used by the SR on their Schools and Nelson and Pacific classes, while a similar design but using a single wide top bar instead of two, forming the three bar type was introduced by Gresley many years ago and remained the standard on the E&NE Regions of BR. One other form of slide bar and crosshead is worth noting as it was used on many of the older inside cylinder designs; there were four parallel bars quite close together; the cross head consisted of two slipper blocks each running in a pair of bars with the little end of the connecting rod pinned between them. The space between the two pairs of bars gave clearance for the angular movement of the connecting rod. The only extensive application of this arrangement to outside cylinders known to the authors is that by Webb, who used it on his Compounds, and if readers will refer to fig. 117 they will find it illustrated.

Slide Bars, Motion Plates and Brackets

Slide bars, whatever their type, are normally secured with bolts to bolting faces machined on lugs on the back cylinder cover. Although in a small model it will not be possible to adhere strictly to full-size practice, it is important that the bars should be firmly anchored to the cylinder cover and the use of a plain soldered joint with the bars merely butting against the cover is unlikely to stand up for long. A good plan is to make the dummy stuffing box integral with the lugs and to secure the bars to the latter by means of a countersunk screw, the slot of which can be filled with solder and dressed flush afterwards. The back of the stuffing box should have a spigot turned on it to fit a hole in the cover and so ensure proper centralisation. In some prototypes the lugs to which the slide bars are bolted do not protrude far enough through the cleading plate to permit the use of the above method if an accurate representation of the prototype is insisted on, and in such cases some other dodge must be adopted for securing the bars,

121 Securing slide bars

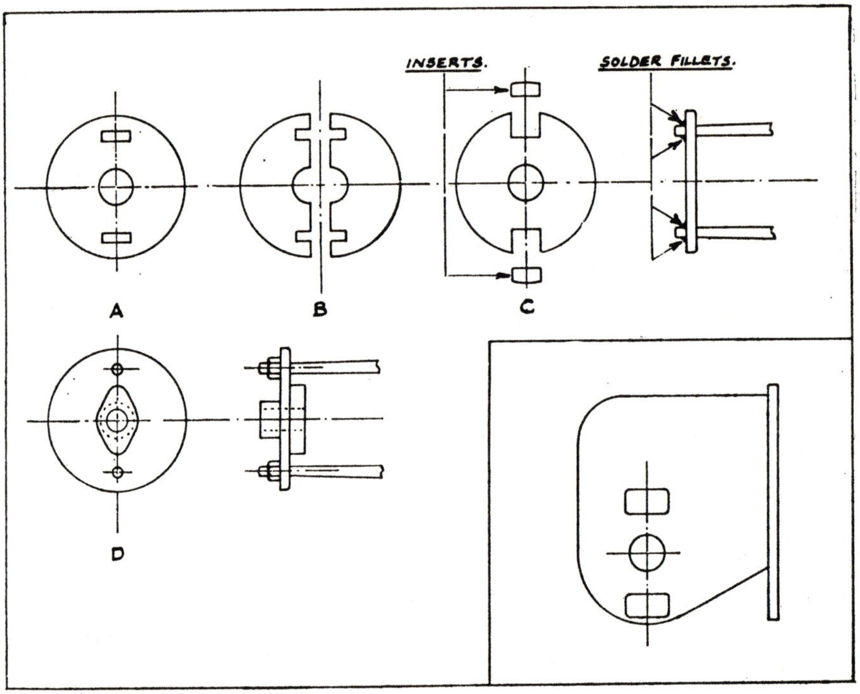

122 Slide bar clamp

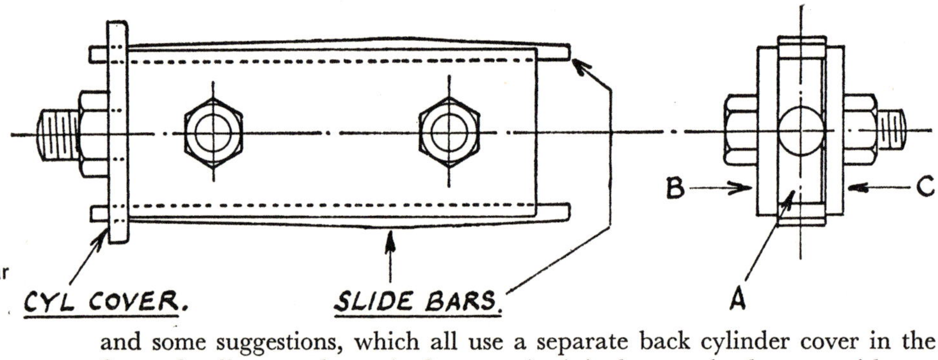

and some suggestions, which all use a separate back cylinder cover in the form of a disc, are shown in fig. 121. At A is shown a back cover with two slots to receive the ends of the bars. B and C are variations of this which avoid having to cut the slots as such: the cover at B is in two halves while that at C is cut away to receive the bars and little filling pieces are inserted after the bars have been fixed; in both cases the bars are soldered to the back of the cover as shown on the right. D shows a cover with two holes to take spigots turned on the ends of the bars; the spigots may be tapped and the bars secured to the cover with nuts at the back. It is intended that a separate stuffing box as shown at D should be used with all these alternatives, its spigot passing through the central hole in the cover and the hole in the end plate of the cylinder itself, thus centralising the lot as before. Note that the end plate must have holes cut in it, as shown in the inset, to take the ends of the slide bars so that the cover may lie flush against the end plate.

When assembling slide bars of the two bar type, the clamp shown in fig. 121 will be found useful for ensuring that the bars are parallel in both planes which is important, for lack of parallelism can only be compensated by making the crosshead a sloppy fit which looks bad when the engine is running. The clamp can only be used with a separate cylinder cover since it is secured to this with a nut at the back while the bars are being fixed, and for this reason we recommend that a separate cover should always be used. The clamp may be made from three steel strips marked A, B and C in the end view of fig. 121. The central strip A has a spigot turned on one end and this is tapped to enable it to be secured with a nut against the cylinder cover through the central hole. The width of A to begin with must be exactly that of the slide bars, and as the diameter of the spigot cannot be more than the width of A, this determines the size of the hole in the cover. The depth of plate A must be exactly the distance between the slide bars. The outer plate B is permanently fixed to A by screws (if milling facilities are available, A and B can of course be of one piece of material, the rebate being milled), and the thickness of A is now reduced slightly by removing metal from its outer face so as to ensure that the clamping plate C will take

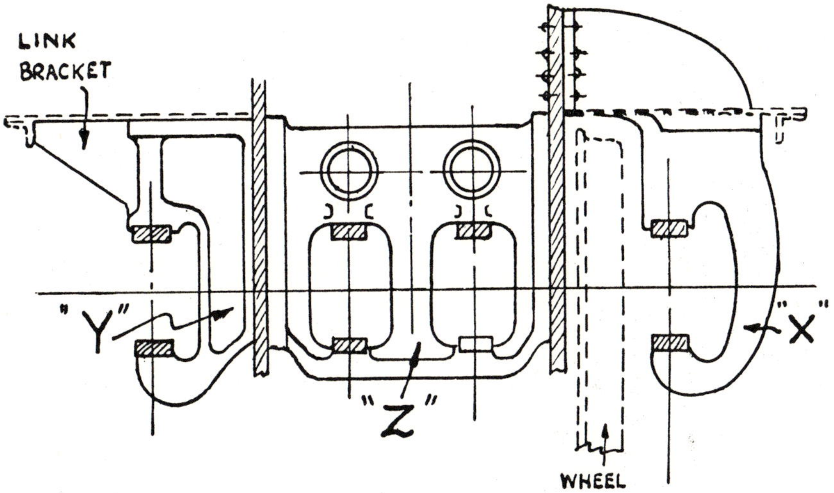

123 Motion plates

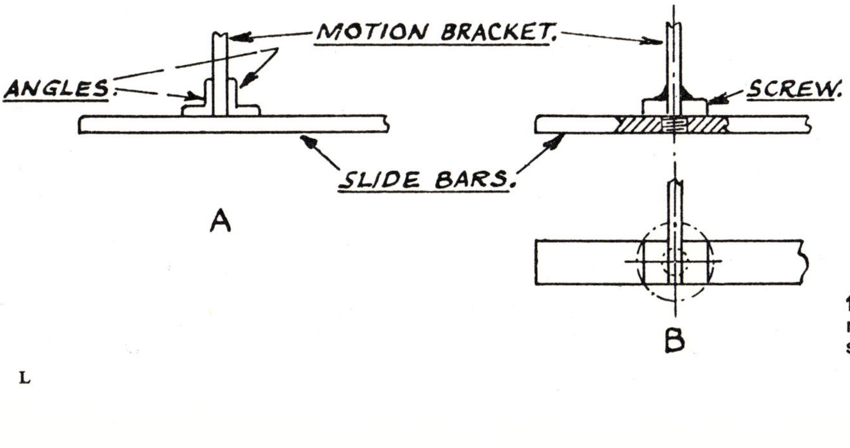

124 Angle re-inforcement at slide bar joint

a grip on the bars when they are loaded in the clamp and not on A leaving the bars loose. Two holes are now drilled through all three plates to take bolts of a suitable size and the clamp is ready for use. It will be seen from fig. 121 that the clamp will hold the bars at the correct distance apart and square with the cylinder cover while they are being secured to the latter. After this has been done, remove the nut from the back of the cylinder cover but leave the clamp in place; the reason for this will appear shortly.

The next component to claim our attention is the motion plate or motion bracket, the functions of which are to support the slide bars, provide bearings for the valve rods to work in, brackets on which rocking levers can be hung, brackets for carrying the expansion links of Walschaert's gear, if outside to support the running plate, and to act as a frame stay if inside. From the foregoing it will be evident that the design of motion plate or bracket depends upon not only whether the cylinders are inside or outside the frames —or both—but upon the general layout of the motion, the type of motion used, the location of the valves, and the type of slide bars. In the case of outside motion brackets bogie wheel clearance must be allowed for, and the special type of bracket shown at fig. 123 is suitable for a multicoupled loco where the leading coupled wheel is immediately behind the slide bars. Many modern prototypes with outside Walschaert's motion use a motion bracket which is typified by Y of fig. 123, in which lugs or bosses are incorporated at the top surface to carry the running plate and at the rear face similar provision is made for the attachment of the front end of the link bracket. Inside motion plates are of the general form shown at Z of fig. 123, which shows a plate designed for valves above the cylinders; it is something after the nature of a spectacle plate, and if the valves were between the cylinders or underneath, the holes for the valve rod guides would have to be positioned accordingly. In all cases surfaces are machined on the motion plate or bracket to which the slide bars are bolted, their number and location depending on the arrangement of the bars which we have dealt with above. These plates and brackets present no particular difficulty to the modeller for they are easily made up from plate and strip material; in larger models castings can be used if a pattern is available. As in the prototype, so in the model the slide bars should be firmly anchored to the motion bracket, and for this operation our clamp of fig. 121 should again be used to hold the slide bars in place while being secured to the motion bracket; this is why we advised leaving the clamp in place after it had been used when the bars were fixed to the cylinder cover. It is unsound to rely merely on a plain soldered joint between slide bars and bracket, and little angles should be made up and fitted to reinforce the joints. This is shown at A of fig. 124, while at B is shown another method; here holes are drilled and tapped in the slide bars on the centre line of the motion bracket to receive screws with large plain heads which will have to be made specially on the lathe. These are screwed into and sweated to the bars, after which their sides are dressed flush with the bars and their ends squared off as shown by the full lines in the plan view. Slots to receive the motion bracket are then cut in the heads of the screws, and the bracket soldered in. The advantage of this method, which may perhaps at first appear a little tedious, is that it provides a positive location for the motion bracket. If this method is used, the screws should of course be fitted to the bars before the latter are assembled to the cylinders.

The motion bracket should be secured to the frame by screws, so also should the cylinder, so that the whole is capable of being dismounted from the frame as a unit should this be necessary. In some designs it is possible to reinforce this assembly by means of a stay between the motion bracket and cylinder, concealed by the running-plate valance, the stay being made from a piece of plain strip material; in others it may be more convenient to build up the cylinder and motion bracket assembly on a short piece of plate which can be secured to the main frame by screws.

Coupling Rods and Brake Gear

Finally, to round off the running gear of the locomotive, we will amplify the very brief reference to coupling rods which was made earlier on page 134. Particular attention should be paid to the correct shape of these rods and whether they are fluted or plain in the prototype, for they are very characteristic details of any locomotive and a rod with incorrectly shaped eyes or of the wrong section will do as much to spoil the character of the model, however beautifully made, as the wrong shaped dome or chimney. The all too prevalent use of the obvious piece of bull-head rail, particularly in OO gauge, is not only incorrect but looks awful. This dodge is resorted to in order to obtain a fluted rod without trouble, but it is impossible to form the eyes correctly—in fact, there is no metal left from which to form them. An improvement would be to file up little washers to the contour of the eyes with an oil box incorporated and solder these over the holes in the rail; they would look the part from the front, but viewed from the end would not, and instead of going to the trouble that this would entail, why not go the whole hog and file up the rod out of strip metal, fluting it by the method already given on page 127, if milling facilities are not available? However, fluted rods are by no means always used on locomotives, and there is no excuse for a plain rod not being correctly modelled to the prototype.

In our previous notes on this subject, attention has already been drawn to the reason why multi-coupled engines require jointed coupling rods, but in an unsprung model the rods are better made in one piece and jig-drilled together with the frames; either can be used as a jig for the other, or a separate jig can be made from which both frames and rods can be drilled. Dummy joints can be filed up and fitted afterwards so as to give the correct appearance. Fig. 125 shows various types of rod; it is thought that the sketches should be self explanatory and require no further comment. Included in this figure are two more suggestions for securing the leading end of 6- or 8-coupled rods where clearance may be very small between the crank pin head and the motion. The figure also shows an arrangement which avoids the normal joint by placing one eye over the other on the same pin which is stronger and simpler than the jointed rod. There is a precedent for this in full-size practice, for the trailing rods of Webb's 8-coupled mineral engines on the LNWR were so fitted. In a sprung model, where the wheels are already in place, the centres of the coupling rods should be very carefully marked off from the centres of the wheels, and if the wheels have been properly finished off by skimming between centres in the lathe, the pop

125 Coupling rods and joints

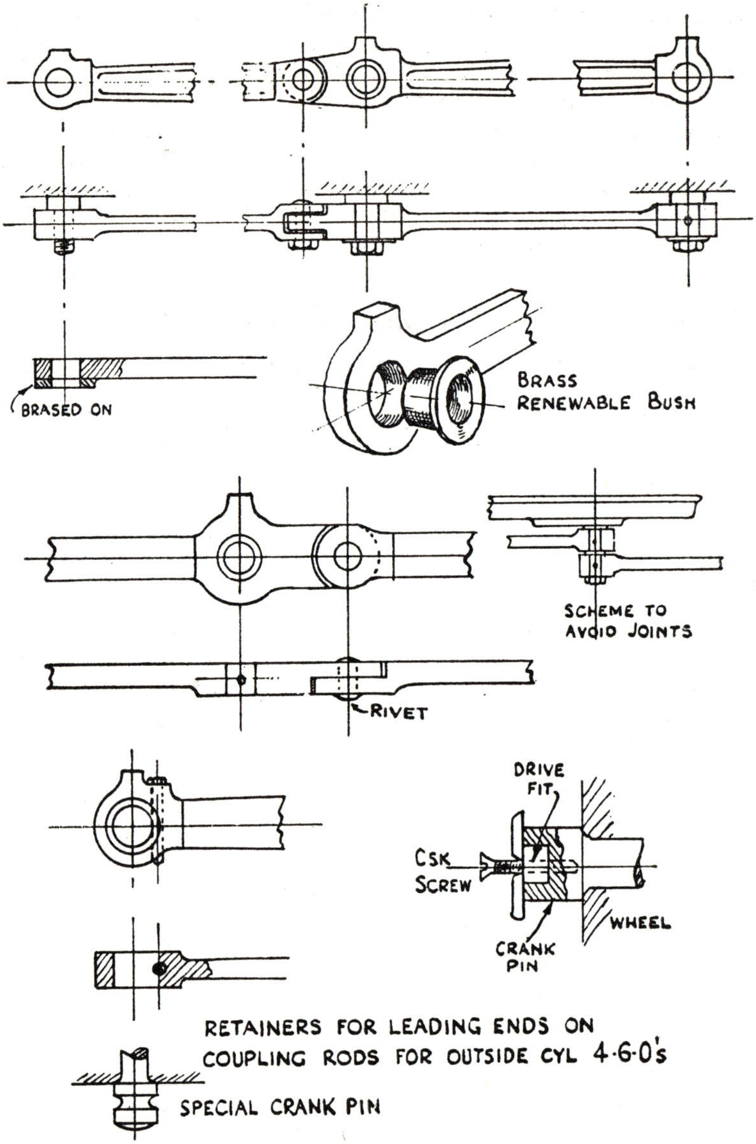

marks in the axle ends should be used as a guide. Each rod should be marked off separately and they should also be marked right hand and left hand in case any little inaccuracies have crept in while assembling the frames, wheels, axleboxes, etc. In the case of a jointed rod, the joint should be made first and bolted or lightly riveted together, and the whole rod then treated as a solid rod for marking out.

The brake gear is an essential portion of the locomotive, and no model that has any pretensions to an accurate representation of the prototype can be regarded as complete unless it is so fitted; moreover, brake shoes and

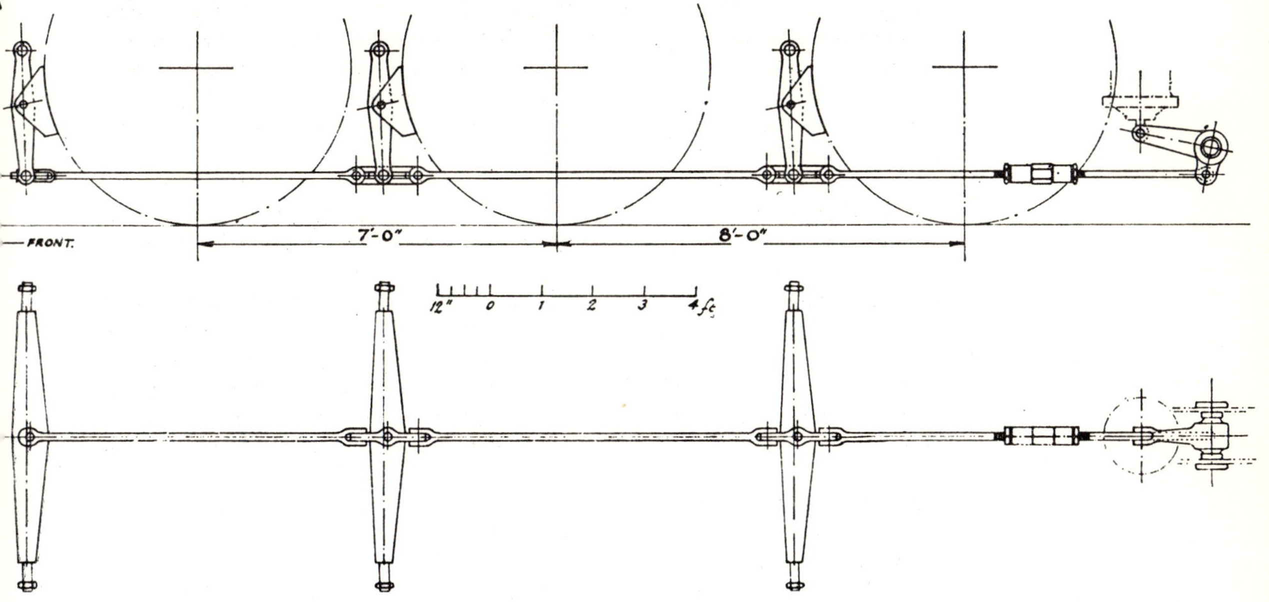

BRAKE ARRANGEMENT, L.M.S.R. CLASS 5 MT.

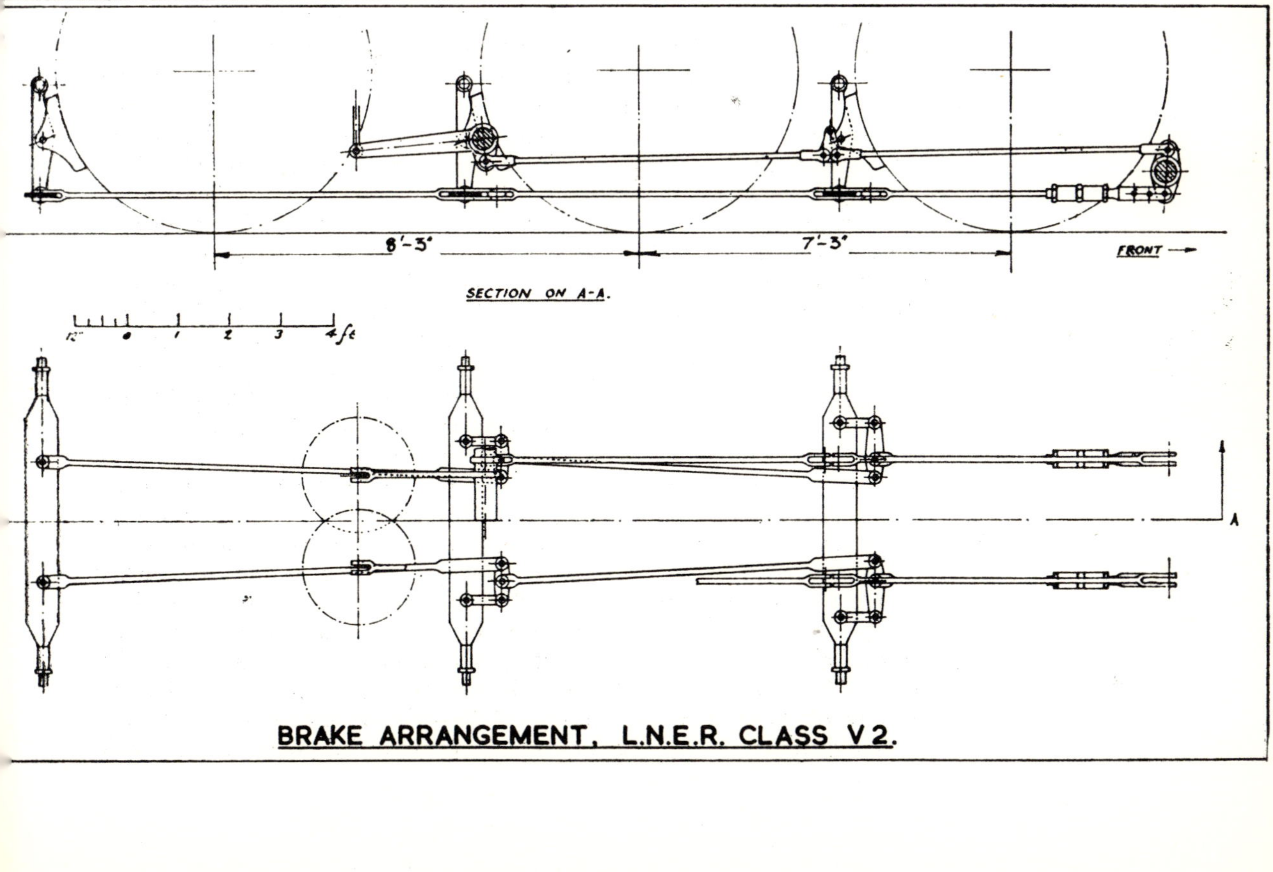

BRAKE ARRANGEMENT, L.N.E.R. CLASS V 2.

hangers are very characteristic details and care should be taken in trying to get their proportions correct. This is by no means always easy, because many prototype drawings do not show the brake gear and in such cases a careful study should be made of available photographs; a note-book and two foot rule taken on running shed visits also provide means of obtaining accurate data from life.

In the earliest days of railways, locomotives were not fitted with brakes at all; when it became evident that some sort of retarding force was necessary, hand-operated brakes were fitted to tenders only and in some cases to the carrying wheels of locomotives, but there was an opinion that to brake the driving wheels would throw objectionable stresses on the coupling rods and running gear and it was not until continuous brakes were adopted, which resulted in heavy stresses being thrown upon the drawgear in consequence of the locomotive not being efficiently braked, that the necessity for this evil was accepted. In the early days of brakes, the blocks were of timber and the hangers were of strip iron with the top and bottom ends forged to form eyes, the top eye being pivoted to the engine frame and the bottom one providing the connection for the pull rods. Towards the latter part of the last century, cast iron brake blocks superseded the timber ones and flat plate hangers took the place of the earlier pattern.

Brake rigging, by which we mean the pull rods which connect the source of power with the brake hangers, is of two general types, viz., compensated or uncompensated, and may be either outside or between the wheels. If the rigging is outside the wheels, the lower ends of the brake hangers are connected on opposite sides of the engine by rods over the outer ends of which the eyes of the pull rods are fitted and secured by nuts and split pins. If the rigging is between the wheels, the lower ends of the hangers are connected by transverse beams to which the forked ends of the pull rods are bolted. With internal rigging there may either be two sets, one on each side of the engine just clear of the springs, or there may be one set only disposed centrally. In the early days of brakes, the rigging was generally outside and uncompensated, but there was a gradual change to inside rigging and this is nowadays the standard arrangement, although some modern designs still have it fitted outside, as witness the GWR pannier tanks and the Southern Pacifics. Modern practice, however, favours inside rigging, usually but by no means always compensated, and in figs. 126 to 129 we show four representative arrangements. Fig. 126 shows that used on the LMSR Class 5 4–6–0s; it is a straightforward layout with central pull rods acting direct on the beams, the power cylinder being under the footplate. Fig. 127 shows the much more complex arrangement of the LNER Class V2 Green Arrow locos; a double set of pull rods is used acting through compensating levers, the power being taken from two 24 in. vacuum cylinders located between the middle and trailing coupled axles. Owing to their size, it is not possible to place the cylinders side by side, so they are staggered one above the other, and in consequence of their position in the frames an auxiliary brake shaft is provided at the front of the engine to reverse the motion in order that the pull rods may all be in tension when the brakes are applied. This dodge has frequently to be resorted to on account of the difficulty of finding room for the vacuum cylinder. At fig. 128 is shown the brake arrangement of the GWR

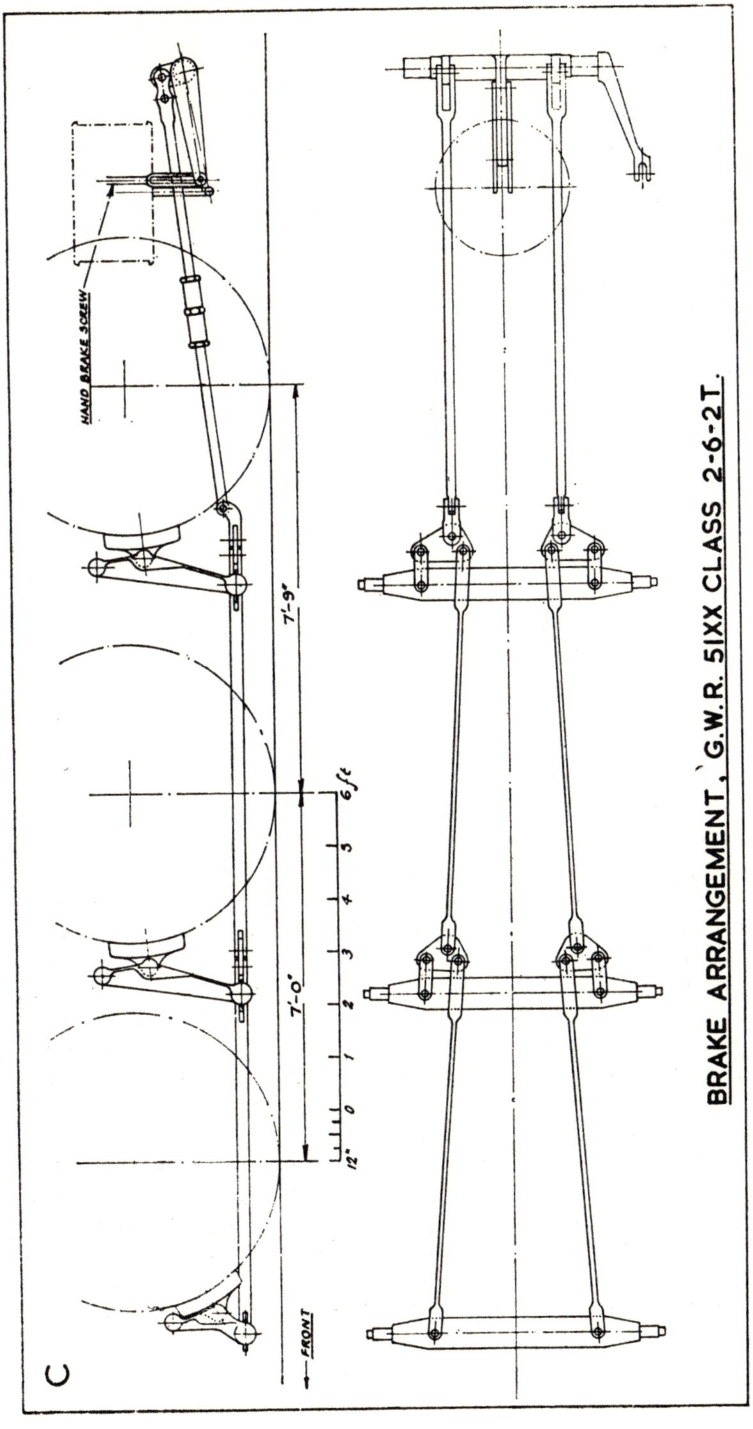
HAND BRAKE SCREW
7'-9"
7'-0"
12" 0 1 2 3 4 5 6 ft
FRONT
C
BRAKE ARRANGEMENT, G.W.R. 51XX CLASS 2-6-2T.

128

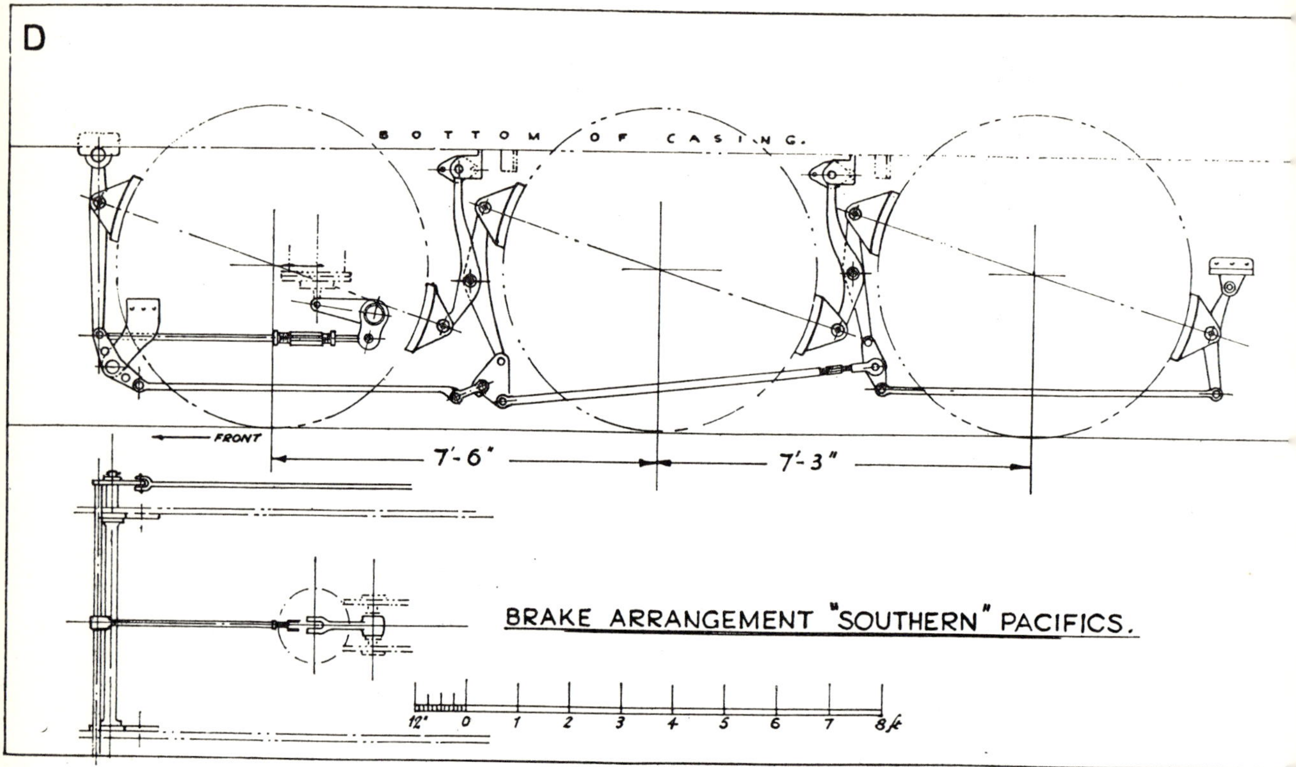

129

large 2–6–2T of the 51XX and similar classes; like that at fig. 127 it has a double set of compensated pull rods but the pull is direct from the vacuum cylinder in the normal position; we have selected this example because it shows the hand brake connection, some such arrangement being necessary on all tank engines and on tenders. These four drawings also show how the vertical movement of the piston in the power cylinder, or the hand brake screw, is imparted to the pull rods through the two levers on the brake shaft which virtually form a bell crank; note particularly that the longer lever is connected to the source of power and the shorter one to the rigging so that the force applied to the brakes is multiplied in proportion to the lengths of the levers, except in the case of the Southern Pacifics, shown at fig. 129, of which we shall have more to say anon.

The object of compensating the brake gear is to allow for unequal wear of the brake blocks, and a study of the drawings in figs. 127 and 128 will show how this is achieved by coupling the pull rods to the equalising levers. With uncompensated brake gear frequent adjustments are necessary, for brake blocks always wear unequally, with the result that those that do the most work wear the tyres more and this leads to obvious other troubles.

Brake Rigging

Certain other special brake arrangements deserve brief mention before we leave this historical sketch. On his early coupled LNWR locomotives, Webb used a pair of shoes between the wheels, one shoe operating on each tyre through the medium of a single hanger. On his 4-cylinder compounds, the shoes were disposed similarly, but each had its own hanger and the arrangement of levers by means of which the two beams were caused to move in opposite directions when the brakes were applied is shown diagrammatically and not to scale in fig. 130. It will be noted that the brakes were compensated but that one pair of rods was in compression when the brakes were applied. Another disadvantage of this disposition of brake blocks is that the application of the brakes causes the driving axles to be forced apart, and this throws considerable stresses on the coupling rods if the axleboxes and horns are worn.

Another and much to be preferred arrangement was favoured by several designers some years ago; this was the clasp brake in which each driving wheel was provided with two shoes, one on either side, the underlying advantage being that axleboxes and running gear were relieved of braking

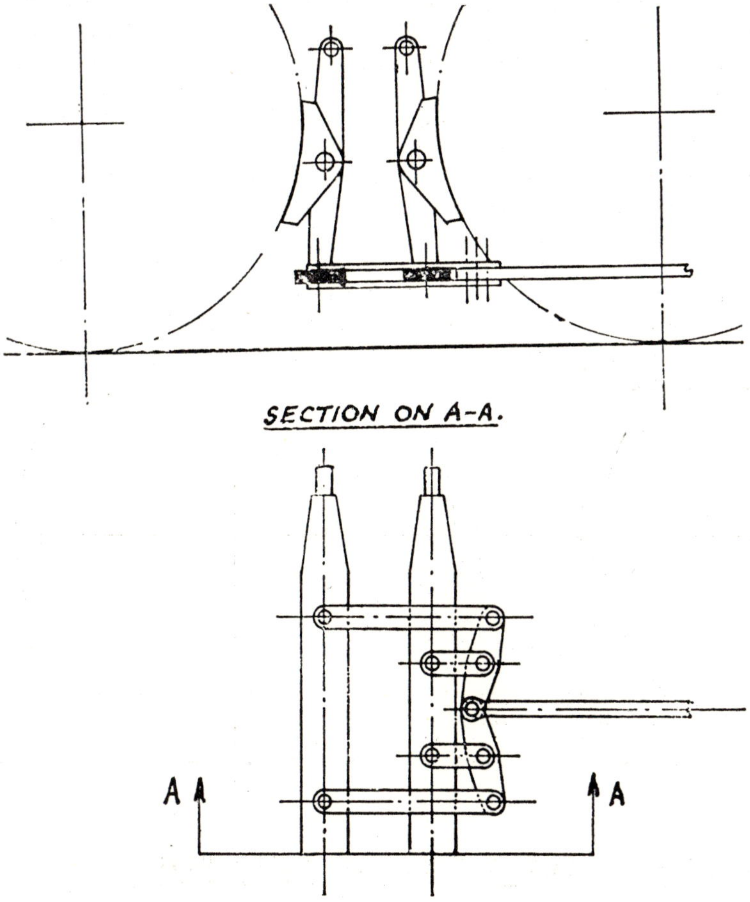

130 Brake rigging on early LNWR locomotives

stresses. Stroudley used this system on his singles and front coupled engines and Johnson on his Midland singles and compounds, and the later compounds designed by Deeley and Fowler also had it. The arrangement of the brakes on these engines is of more than a little interets and we give a drawing of it in fig. 131, the brakes were operated by a steam cylinder disposed centrally between the coupled wheels and acting directly in opposite directions on the two inner hangers from which the pull was transferred to the outer hangers by outside pull rods provided with adjusting warwicks. Incidentally, this drawing is a good example of our earlier remark that the brake gear is a characteristic detail; a model of one of these engines would hardly look the part if the brake gear were not fitted.

Gradually, however, the brake mechanism of British locomotives became more or less standardised in the form of one shoe to each wheel operated by internal compensated rigging. However, history has a curious habit of repeating itself, as we have mentioned before in these articles, and not the least interesting feature of those very interesting engines, the SR Pacifics, is the arrangement of the brake gear. This is shown in fig. 129 from which it will be seen that the brakes are of the clasp type operated by outside compensated rigging; the action of the gear should be clear from the drawing the brake cylinder being inserted in approximately, as this varies according to the class of engine, and the position of the oil bath of the valve gear.

The Continental practice of fitting brakes to locomotive bogies has never found favour in this country, although Churchward made it standard practice on his outside cylinder designs; but his successor rapidly removed it from about 1924. On the Midland, Fowler fitted bogie brakes to his rebuilds of Johnson's 7 ft. 0 in. 4-4-0s.

The brakes of tenders operate on exactly the same principle as those of locomotives and do not require any amplification of what has already been written; the only point to note is that, as tenders are fitted with a hand mechanism for operating brakes in addition to power, the brake shaft must be provided with the necessary connecting lever as we notice in the case of tank locomotives.

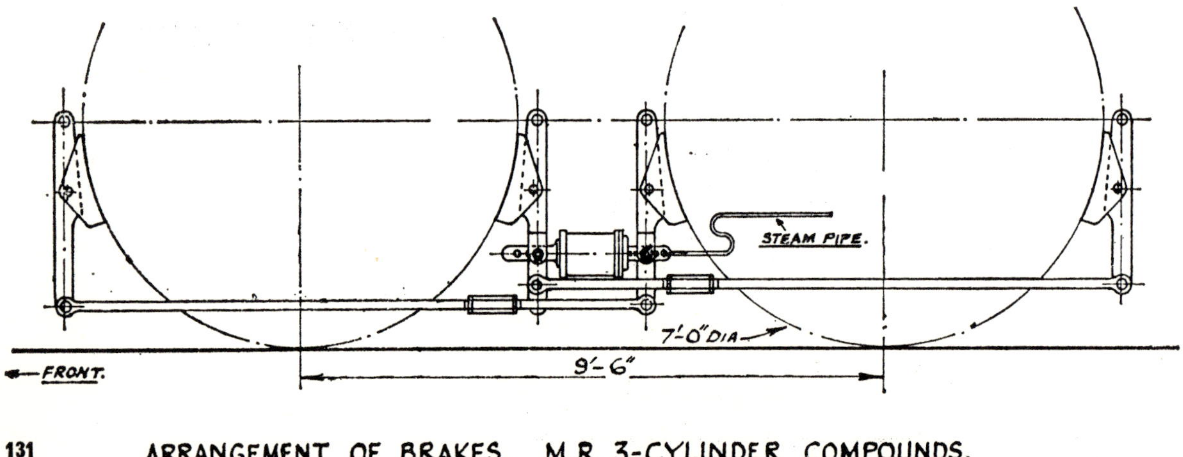

131 ARRANGEMENT OF BRAKES, M.R. 3-CYLINDER COMPOUNDS.

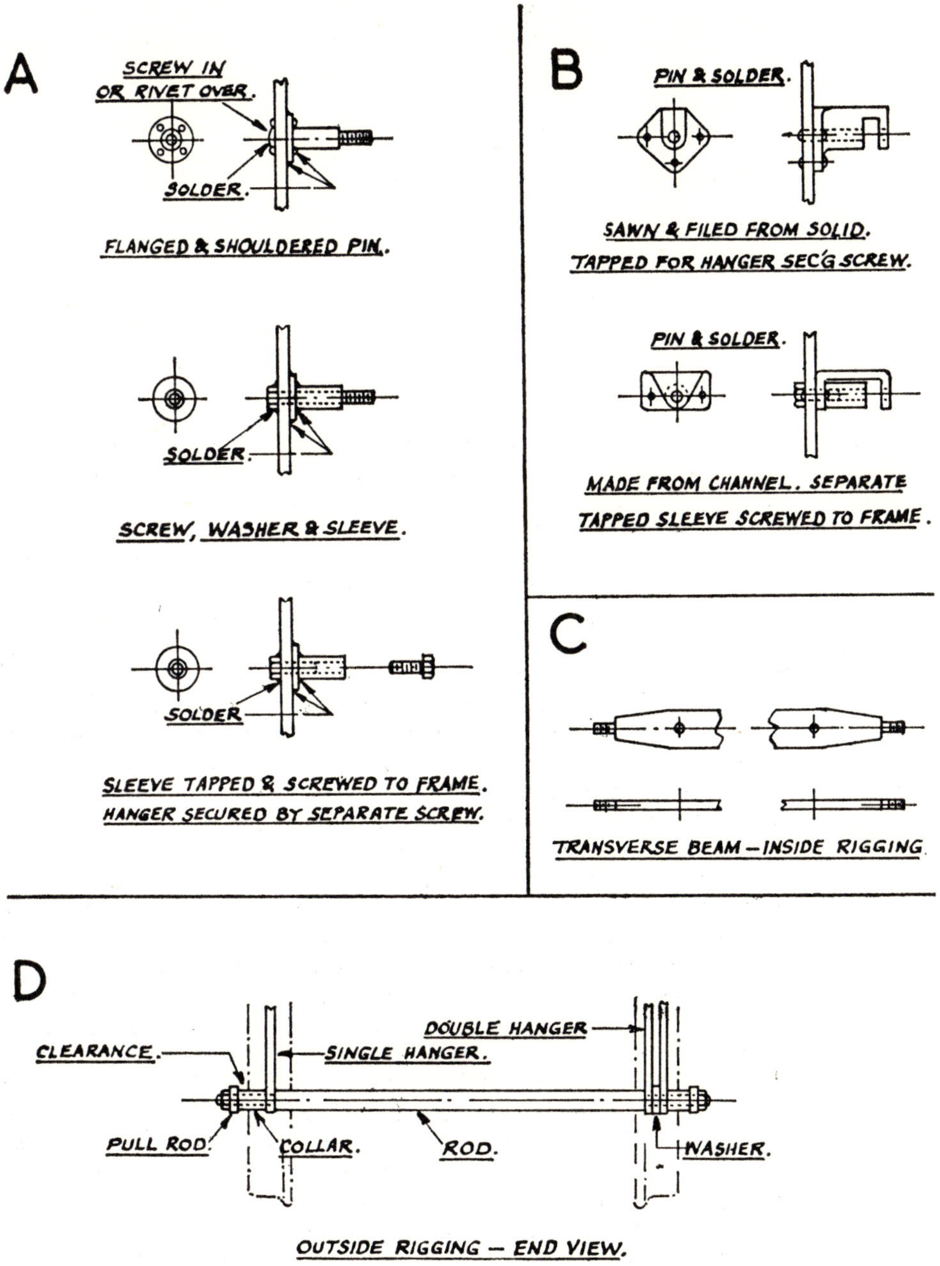

132 Single and double hanger brakes

We will now consider the making of the various parts of the brake gear beginning with the hanger brackets. These vary from what is simply a shouldered pin with a flange for riveting or bolting to the frame as used on the old GNR and other railways, to a quite elaborate casting. The former type is shown at A of fig. 132, with some suggestions for modelling it. This simple type of bracket will probably satisfy most modellers for, although it may not be true to prototype in all cases, when all is said and done the hanger is small and not very conspicuous and it may even be concealed behind running-plate valances, footsteps, etc. However, for those who desire greater accuracy some suggestions are given at B of fig. 132 for modelling the cast type of bracket. This type of bracket may be elaborated to any extent to which the individual modeller may feel disposed.

The brake hangers call for little comment as they will be made from strip material drilled and filed to contour. For O gauge, $\frac{1}{32}$ in. is about the right thickness, and several should be seated together marked out, drilled and filed as one and then separated. The modern GWR hanger is a most awkward job to model accurately being a ribbed forging with a thickened portion which is slotted to take the brake shoe. (See figure 128). This is another case where the individual must use his discretion, for short of a die-casting, the only way to model such hangers is to build them up—a tedious business which would certainly require an assembly jig to hold the parts while soldering them together.

The next item to claim attention is the brake block, and here are some suggestions for making it:

1. From the solid. Mark out as many as are needed on a strip of material of the correct thickness, drill, cut off and file to contour. Make a saw-cut for the hanger if single, and file away both sides of the part taking the hanger if the latter is double, so that the finished block appears as at A of fig. 132. Owing to the thickness of the material, unless you are very skilled with the file it is better to file them one by one.

2. From a length of bull-head rail bent into a ring the inner diameter of which matches that of the wheel tread. Remove outer web and finish as for 1 above. The resulting block is only suitable for double hangers. See fig. 133, left.

3. Turn a ring the inner diameter of which matches that of the wheel tread—an old cast iron wheel of suitable size makes a useful blank—and for single hangers turn a groove in the outer periphery of the ring, and for double hangers face back both sides of the ring leaving a central rib, as shown in fig. 133, right. Before dismounting from the lathe, scribe a line round the ring to mark the centre line of the holes. Then proceed as before.

4. Casting in type metal. Articles on casting small components have already appeared in the pages of the model press, and if a number of blocks is required this method is well worth consideration. It does not matter if blocks are required for wheels of several different diameters, for if the mould be made to suit the wheel of largest diameter, the castings from it can be filed to suit wheels of smaller diameters.

We ought perhaps to remind two-railers that their brake blocks must either be made of an insulating material such as ebonite, plastics, etc., or have the faces that may come in contact with the wheel covered with an insulating medium such as paint, durofix, paper shallac'd on, etc. We prefer

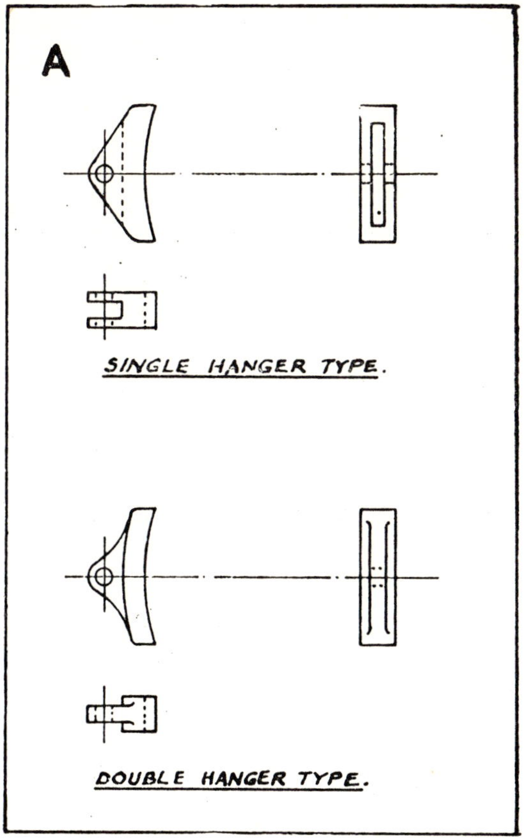

132 Single and double hanger brakes

133 Making brake hangers

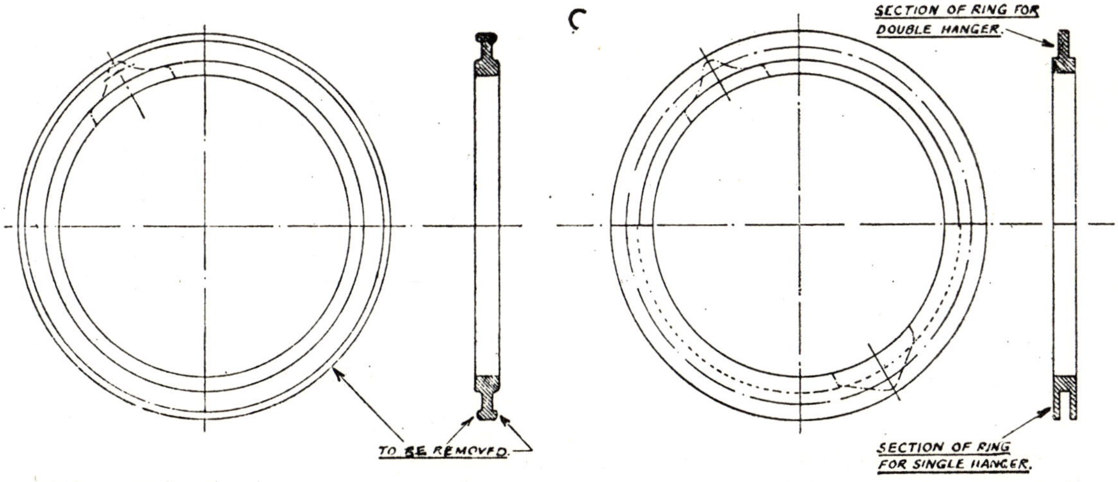

135

A

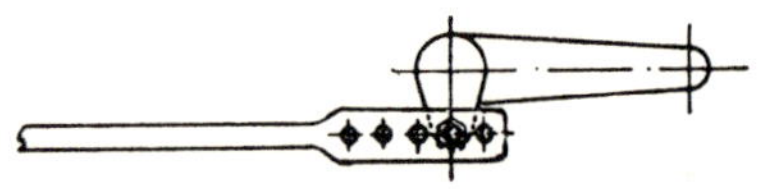

REAR PULL-ROD ADJUSTMENT.

B

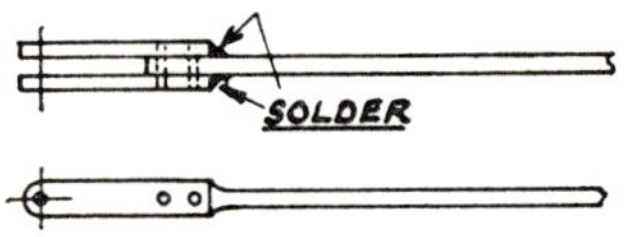

1. FORK BUILT UP. PINNED & SOLDERED.

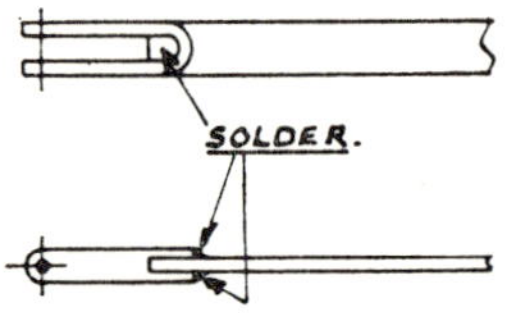

2. FORK BENT UP FROM STRIP. ROD LET INTO SAW-CUT IN END OF FORK. THE WHOLE WELL SOLDERED.

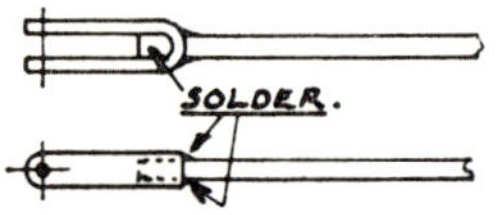

3. AS FOR 2, BUT ROD IS OF PIN WIRE LET INTO HOLE IN END OF FORK.

METHODS OF BUILDING UP FORKS OF PULL RODS. AFTER ASSY., CLEAN UP TO SHAPE WITH FILE.

C

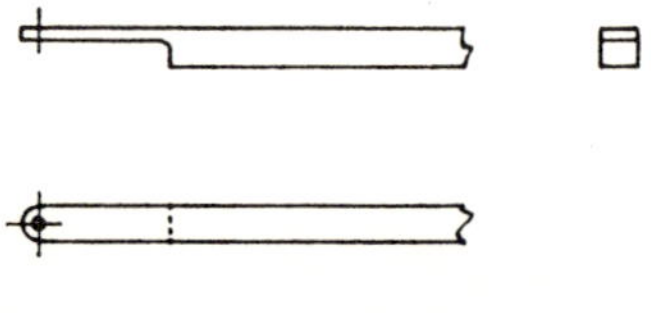

SIMPLE PULL ROD OF SQ. MATERIAL.

136

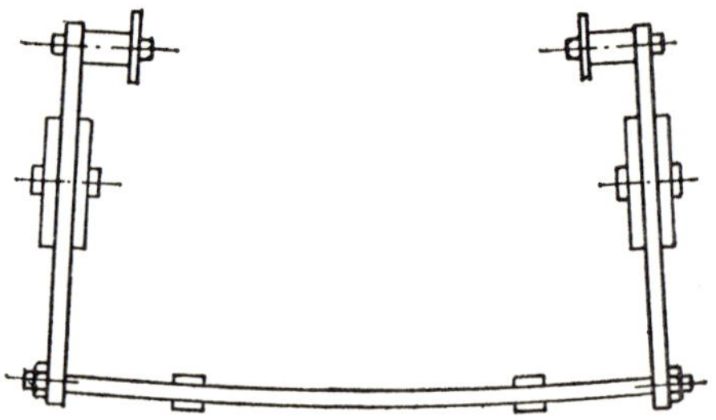

BEFORE ASSY.

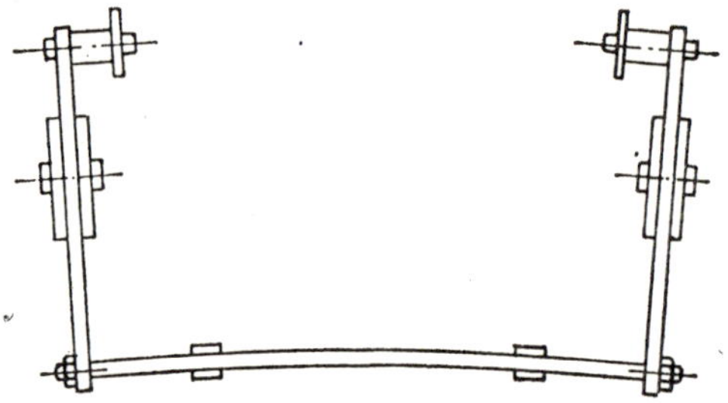

DURING ASSY.

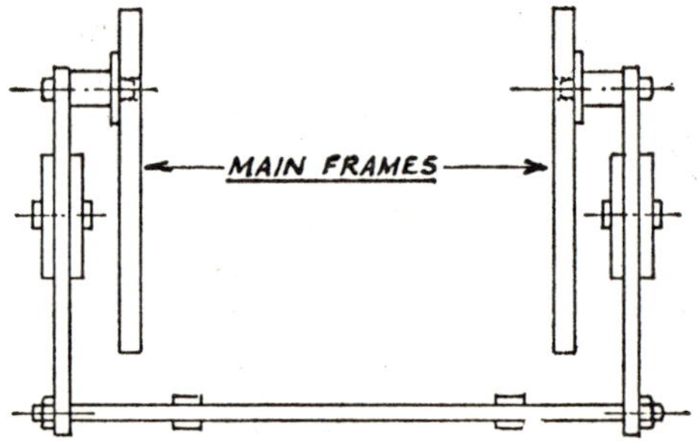

ASSEMBLED.

"SPRING-ON" METHOD OF ATTACHING BRAKE GEAR.

the former as there is always the danger that the insulation may get rubbed off.

The transverse beams used with inside rigging should be dealt with in the same way as the hangers. The ends should first be filed square and then radiused with a file, or they may of course be turned. In O gauge they should be threaded No. 14BA but in 4 mm. scale left plain and soldered to the hanger. The finished beam is shown at C of fig. 132, and when marking out do not forget the holes for the pins which secure the pull rods. Use the same gauge of material as for the hangers, and if brass or nickel silver is employed it should be of the half hard variety. The transverse rods used with outside rigging should be of a suitable gauge of pin wire—16 SWG or $\frac{1}{16}$ in. is about right for gauge O; their ends should be reduced and threaded as for the beams, and remember that the ends must be left long enough for a distance collar of appropriate length to be inserted between the hanger and the eye of the pull rod so that the latter may stand clear of the face of the wheel tyre after allowing for any end play that the axle may have. This is shown at D in fig. 132, and it may be noted in passing that the ends of the beams or rods need only be threaded for a sufficient distance for the nut to be tightened.

We now come to the rigging itself. Outside pull rods present no particular difficulty, for they will be made from suitable strip material filed to drawing. We shall deal with marking out and drilling the holes later. The rear pull rod which connects to the short arm of the brake shaft probably has an enlarged end with a series of holes in it as shown in A of fig. 135, so that its effective length can be adjusted as the brake blocks wear. If the brake shaft is fitted to the model, the rear pull rod can be connected to its short arm with a small hexagon headed screw—No. 14BA in O gauge—or it can be pinned and soldered; in the latter event, the brake shaft must be removeable from the frames so that the whole brake gear may be demountable as a unit. In many cases the brake shaft will be concealed behind the rear footstep; it may then be omitted if so desired and the rear pull rod attached to the frame by one of the methods shown at A of fig. 132 for brake hangers.

Reference to figs. 126-9 will show that the reproduction of the prototype layout of inside rigging not only presents a much more formidable problem than outside rigging, but in many cases is rendered impossible by the unavoidable presence of some part of the mechanism or the collector gear, two-railers are not, of course, affected by this latter factor nor should the stud-contact fraternity, since the shoe is below the level of the brake rigging. If the modeller finds the inclusion of inside rigging practicable and decides to have a go, he will probably find that the slotting of the forked ends of the pull rods—particularly the longer ends that pass over the transverse beams and extend to couple to the equalising levers—his main difficulty unless he is fortunate enough to possess a power driven slitting saw, so at B of fig. 135 we show some suggestions for getting round this problem. The pull rod which connects the rigging to the short arm of the brake shaft is generally circular in section and incorporates an adjusting warwick (see figs. 126-9 again). A method of modelling this form of pull rod is given in fig. 135, B3.

Inside brake rigging is, however, so inconspicuous that few modellers will probably feel the urge to reproduce it in detail even when this is practicable, and in fact a quite adequate effect can be obtained by making the pull rods of square wire without reducing the section between the forks, and treating the ends as shown in C of fig. 135. The equalising levers may be put in or omitted according to taste and the same applies to the brake shaft, the final pull rod to the brake shaft can be simplified on the same lines as the others. As with this construction we have somewhat reduced the strength of the joints by omitting half the fork, all these joints should be soldered up after the brake gear has been finally adjusted, except of course the connection between the final pull rod and the brake shaft or frame, which must be removeable as in the case of outside rigging. Some modellers may prefer a still simpler construction using pin wire instead of beams and the same material for the pull rods with plain soldered connections; this method is probably the only one generally practicable for models as small as 4 mm. scale, but the stronger construction outlined above is far preferable for the larger scales.

The pull rods should be riveted to the beams with small pins, and the forked ends will have to be marked out and drilled accordingly, the marking out being done from the holes already drilled in the beams. Lightly secure each brake block to its wheel with binding wire so that the beams cannot flop about, drill one hole in each pull rod and mark out the other from the beam. Finish the eyes of the pull rods after drilling and then assemble them to the beams, securing them with little rivets as mentioned. Now remove the binding wire from the brake blocks and slacken them back so that the wheels run quite freely; nothing looks so bad as some brake blocks nearly touching their wheels and others several scale inches away and the above procedure will do much to prevent this happening as it takes care of any little inaccuracies which are almost certain to have crept into the work. All that now remains is to connect the end pull rod to brake shaft or frame. Finally, to strengthen up the whole structure, run a fillet of solder at the joints between pull rods and beams. The above assembly procedure applies also to outside rigging.

Another method of securing brake rigging to the loco frame is worth a mention as it has been successfully applied in O gauge. In this method, which is illustrated in fig. 136, the hangers are permanently secured to the hanger brackets, and the latter are provided each with a small peg or spigot at the back which fits into a plain hole drilled in the frame, the spigots being slightly tapered. Use is made of the fact that half-hard brass has a certain amount of natural spring and the whole assembly is held in position on the engine frames by the springiness of the beams. Before assembly, the beams are given a slight set so that the hangers cant towards one another at their upper ends; to assemble the brake gear to the frames, the beams are bent the opposite way to the set, which has the effect of spreading the upper ends of the hangers apart and enabling the spigots on the hanger brackets to be sprung into their holes. The top view in fig. 136 shows the beam and hangers before assembly, the centre sketch during assembly, and the bottom sketch after assembly; it is advisable to clip a small piece of shim brass over the frame when the brake gear is being assembled or removed to prevent the spigots on the hanger brackets damaging the paint. The great advantage of this method is that only one screwed connection between brake gear and frame is necessary—that at the end of the final pull rod—and it thus avoids the fiddle of having to disconnect each hanger from its bracket; it also obviates the use of what is probably an oversize nut or unsightly screw to secure the hanger to the bracket. If phosphor bronze strip is available, use it in preference to brass for the transverse beams as it possesses a higher degree of springiness.

The Westinghouse Brake Air Pump

Although not part of the brake gear itself, there is one item of brake equipment which it is appropriate to deal with here and that is the air pump of locos fitted with Westinghouse brake. Before the Grouping, many railways, and particularly the Scottish lines, used this brake, and the throb of the air pump was also a familiar sound to those who used the Brighton, North Eastern and Great Eastern. Fig. 137 shows the pump, in diagrammatic form; the steam cylinder is on top and the compressor cylinder below, the pistons being upon a common rod. The action is automatically controlled by the pump governor which admits steam to the pump when the air pressure falls to a certain predetermined value, and shuts it off when the pressure has risen to the working figure. We do not think that the making of the pump calls for much comment; basically it is a straightforward lathe job, and the pipes will, of course, be brass or copper wire of suitable gauge preferably screwed into tapped holes in the cylinder bodies, otherwise soldered into plain holes. The amount of detail that is put into the pump is a matter for the skill and inclination of the indidivual, but in any case it is advisable to try and obtain a close-up photo of the pump of the class of loco you are modelling as the run of the pipes is liable to vary and so also may the details of the pump itself. The pump was generally fitted on the side of the firebox, but other positions were often adopted as drawings and photos of individual engines will show. The problem of fixing the pump to the model may present some difficulty and in fig. 138 we have outlined some suggestions for dealing with this. A shows a fixing suitable for firebox or cab side (e.g., CR and LBSCR locos). A stud of suitable size—say No. 8 or 10 BA for O gauge—is screwed into a hole drilled and tapped from the back of each cylinder. A distance tube of such a length that the pump will stand vertically in its correct position is placed over the protruding end of each stud; the firebox, cab side, etc. is marked out and drilled to receive the studs and the pump is secured by nuts on the inside. When the pump is fixed by this method to a curved surface like a firebox side, washers will have to be soldered at the back of the holes, and their back faces dressed up square forming true bolting faces for the nuts to tighten against, and the ends of the distance tubes must be so shaped that they fit snugly both against the pump cylinders and the firebox side. At B is shown an alternative fixing suitable where nuts cannot be fitted from inside, e.g., a smokebox side. In this case the pump cylinders are drilled right through clearing size and the holes are lightly countersunk on the fronts of the cylinders. Distance tubes are used as in A and the smokebox side is marked out, drilled and tapped to receive countersunk headed screws which secure the cylinders from the front. After fixing, the heads of the screws are carefully cleaned off to the curvature of the cylinders with a fine file. If the metal of the smokebox or other part is not

137 Westinghouse brake air pump (drawn approximately double size for 7mm scale)

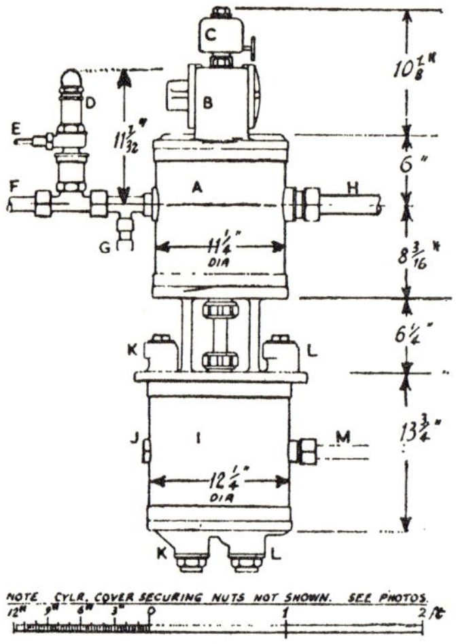

A. Steam Cylinder.
B. Steam Chest.
C. Lubricator.
D. Pump Governor.
E. Air from Main Reservoir.
F. Steam Supply.
G. Auto Drain Valve.
H. Steam Exhaust.
I. Air Pump.
J. Air Inlet.
K. Suction Valves.
L. Delivery valves.
M. Air to Main Reservoir.

138 Westinghouse brake air pump fitting to firebox and boilers

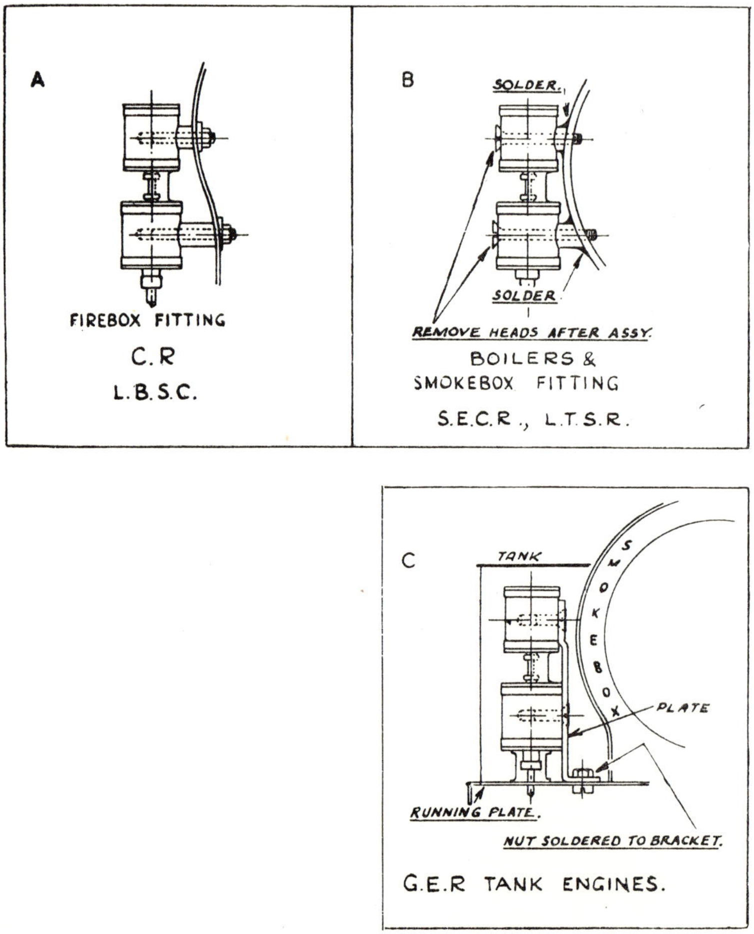

thick enough to take a thread, proceed as above but tap the distance tubes and solder them to the loco; they should be screwed to the smokebox, or whatever part of the pump is being attached to, during the soldering operation to ensure that they are correctly and squarely positioned. The distance tubes now act as fixed nuts and the pump is fixed as before. C shows a method that can be used to secure the pump to the running plate by means of a bracket screwed to both cylinders at the back. The sketch is self-explanatory and the only points to watch are that the cylinders should be slightly flattened at the back to give a reasonable seating for the bracket and that, as the steam cylinder is of smaller diameter than the air pump, either the bracket must be bent as shown or a packing piece inserted between it and the steam cylinder. Those who are satisfied with a simpler fixing, may of course secure the pump by means of a screw from the underside of the running plate direct into the air pump with a suitable packing piece between to position the pump at the correct height, but this a rather lazy way of doing the job, and the result will not be very pleasing in the larger scales, but it would be all right for OO gauge, as the pipes to the pump give a certain amount of support in themselves.

Preparing for the Superstructure

We have now practically completed the loco chassis except for the drawhook by which we attach the engine to the train via the tender. A sprung drawhook should always be fitted and this will be dealt with when we come to tender construction. At the moment all we need is a bar of fairly heavy gauge metal with a hole in each end.

One end is attached to the drag plate or casting under the cab at the rear of the loco and the other end protrudes through the slotted back buffing plate of the engine. This slot should be as long as possible between the two buffing plates upon which the tender bears. The distance the hole in the bar should be from the buffing plate is a matter for experiment on your own layout. A test should be made on a reverse curve as this represents the most extreme condition you are likely to meet.

Owing the under scale curves on the average layout the tender has to be more than scale distance from the engine and no hard and fast rule can be laid down as to the correct distance required. Many factors enter into this such as the type of engine, radius of the curves and overhang of the rear of the loco etc.

The next item to be dealt with is the superstructure or sheet metal work as the larger scale brethren call it. This to most of us is perhaps the part of greatest interest, but before commencing it is worth while to study carefully the preceding articles and work to a definite system. It need hardly be said that a soldering iron is essential together with a tin of Flux and some Grade A tinman's solder, or resin cored solder which combines both Flux and solder, although a tin of Flux paste will still be required to clean the soldering iron.

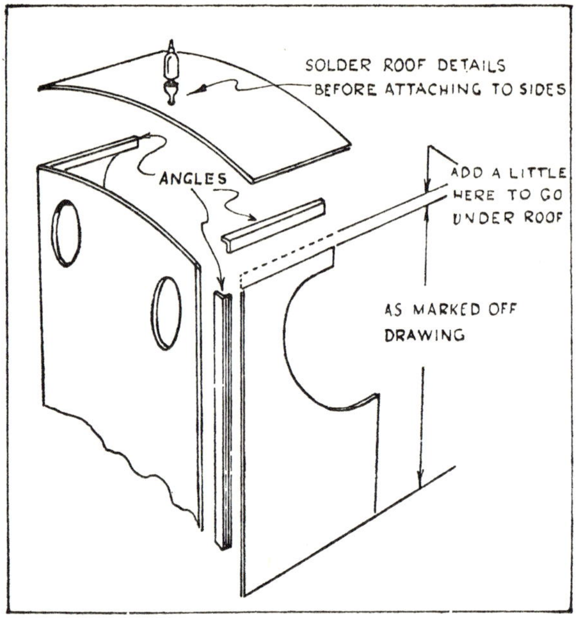

139 Erecting cab front and sides

Soldering

So much has been written on the subject of soldering that it is not proposed to reiterate at any length here, except to repeat that *cleanliness* is absolutely essential both in the metal to be soldered and in the soldering iron itself. If in these days of costly non-ferrous metals such as brass and nickel silver, the modeller is lucky enough to acquire some old brass or copper these must be cleaned either chemically or with emery paper before fashioning into parts to be soldered.

If the model is being made of tinplate be careful not to remove the tin during the cleaning process as it will very quickly rust, especially if the model is taking a long time to build or if an acid type of Flux has been used in its construction. It is always better to use "Fluxite" when working with tinplate as the natural greasy consistency of this compound helps to keep away the rust bogey.

For cleaning the soldering iron use an old coarse file or a wire cleaning brush such as used for cleaning files. If our iron is of the gas type, illustrated earlier in these articles, merely give it enough gas to keep it warm when not in immediate use. An electric iron will always keep itself warm, but one can always save current by switching it off when not required for a period. Never use an acid flux with an electric iron as it will eat away the iron and with gas heated irons look out for a green flame coming off the iron. If this is seen turn down the gas at once and clean the iron immediately. Never attempt to solder with it in this condition as the iron has been burned and must be filed clean again and tinned by dipping in melted solder.

The shape of the soldering iron is again, a matter depending on the size of the model. For all practical purposes a chisel shaped head will be found to have the most general use. The authors generally use a piece of $\frac{3}{8}$ in. diameter copper rod filed to this shape. Some electric irons are obtainable in this size.

A word about the solder itself. This must contain antimony to prevent contraction on cooling. Grade A solder mentioned earlier contains 66 per cent tin, 33 per cent lead and 1 per cent antimony. Its melting point is 180 deg. C. or 340 deg. Fahr. Do not use Plumbers' solder, as this contains more lead than tin, and is only used for joining lead pipes. Resin cored solder contains 50 per cent lead and 50 per cent tin, and is generally used for electrical work. Fine tinman's solder contains three parts of lead to two of tin, and is the next best to use if grade A is unobtainable. Needless to say the melting point of the solder must be below that of the metal to be joined. We know that white metal axle guards disappear sometimes and it is a good idea to use a solder of lower melting point than white metal. For the benefit of those who want to solder these fittings, a table is given showing the various solders and their melting points. It will be seen that pewterer's solder will meet this white metal axleguard condition.

Grade A	1 lead	2 tin	340° Fahr.
Coarse Plumber's	3 lead	1 tin	480° Fahr.
Ordinary Plumber's	2 lead	1 tin	440° Fahr.
Fine Tinman's	2 lead	3 tin	335° Fahr.
Ordinary Tinman's	1 lead	1 tin	370° Fahr.
Pewterer's	1 part bismuth, 1 lead, 1 tin, 201° Fahr. (bismuth added to reduce melting point)		

So much for soft soldering as it is known in the engineering profession. Most treatises on model making contain very little reference to hard soldering, more commonly known as silver soldering.

The authors are very keen on this latter method when making a small model both because of its permanency, and chiefly because of its adaptability to fabricating small parts, such as forked joints in brake rigging. If these are fabricated by soft soldering they will not last the proverbial five minutes, if the model does much work, and such fittings as lamp brackets and other excrescences will last much longer if they are silver soldered.

Silver solder can be obtained in sufficient quantity by using the cases of old watches, brooches and other bric-a-brac usually lying in the domestic jewellery box or odds and ends drawer. Do not use silver coins as apart from the legal aspect of the case, these contain a certain amount of nickel. Silver solder can be obtained from most jewellers' suppliers in the Clerkenwell district of London.

For silver soldering you will need a supply of borax to use as flux and a couple of ordinary house bricks, or one brick broken in half. Commercial silver contains 36-38 per cent copper, 18-20 per cent zinc and 42-44 per cent silver.

The parts to be joined should be wired together with a piece of fine iron binding wire and the joint liberally coated with borax. Place the whole on top of the two bricks, or alternatively use one brick as a table and another at the back to deflect the flame on to the joint.

A blow pipe will be required and for model making the mouth blowpipe is preferable to any other type of blowlamp. With a mouth blowpipe a local heat can be obtained and it is not necessary to heat up the whole of the work.

Now cut up the silver solder into small strips proportionate to the parts being operated upon and lay the strips on to the joints together with the borax. Heat up the work to red heat when the borax will flow, taking with it the silver solder into the joint. It may seem awkward at first, but it is really quite simple once the knack is obtained. Experiment on some odd pieces first

On cooling, the borax will be found to have a glass-like surface which must be chipped off and the joint filed carefully to shape. Do this filing on a separate piece of paper so as to preserve the silver filings which can be used next time by mixing them with the borax.

In all soldering jobs, never be in a hurry. Take time, care and above all be clean. Do not use a soldering iron like a wood saw, and saw along the joint—WAIT until the metal around the joint has heated up sufficiently to allow the solder to run. Cold metal will not solder, neither will a good soldered joint be made in a draught, or in the open air. Keep your workshop door closed in windy weather, and as a final matter of interest, a soldering iron is only made of copper because it is cheap and normally convenient. Any metal which is a good conductor of heat and has a good capacity for heat can be used. Silver, platinum and gold will all make good soldering bits, far superior to copper. Silver because it is a better conductor of heat, and gold and platinum because they do not oxidise. Oxidisation is the great enemy of all metals and is caused by contact with the atmosphere. This is why we use flux in all kinds of soldering to counteract the effects of oxidisation. Perhaps there is an Indian Prince with a gold soldering iron !

Before we get on with the actual job of erecting our locomotive, we will now require a dead flat piece of wood about 12 in. by 6 in., or if the loco is larger than this an old drawing board will be ideal. It should be preferably old and well seasoned wood, and fairly thick—about 1 in. Do not use plywood as this will warp with heat. If there is any tendency to warp, the piece of wood should be screwed to the bench, but the authors prefer that the wood should be removable in order to survey the model during erection and study its appearance from time to time to see that all is square. An old furniture panel of oak or elm would be an ideal base, but any polish should be scraped or planed off, in case it catches fire during soldering, or bubbles up and oxidises the joint being operated on. When we have obtained this flat piece of wood we can commence on the parts of our superstructure.

Any parts that are duplicated, such as cab sides, splasher sides, tank sides, step backplates, etc., should always be filed up together. It is not proposed to go into the relative methods of fretsawing, or cutting the parts, as the authors use both methods. Some modellers cannot get on with fretsaws and use shears instead, or the drilling and filing method. Each has its devotees and to lay down any rules would serve no useful purpose. The real accuracy comes in the marking out—avoid freehand curves in cab sides, always use the compasses. Most of the radii are given on the drawing. When the part is marked out, cut or fret roughly to the marked lines and solder the parts together along the straight edge. In the case of a cab side this would be along the front edge, or a tank side along the bottom edge. Insert two vice clamps of soft metal in the vice to protect the work from being marked by the vice jaws and file to shape all round, leaving the soldered edge until last. When this edge is filed up to the marked line, the parts will fall apart, and so avoid the necessity of having to melt them apart. In making splashers it is only necessary to mark one out. Place this on top of the other three or five as the case may be, according to whether the engine is six or four coupled. Roughly cut the remainder, and as before solder them along the bottom edge; file them all up together.

The authors usually turn up splashers of the beaded edge type (such as GWR) in the lathe as the correct moulded edge can be obtained this way. Some earlier singles also had this moulded edge around the splasher. It was found that a complete circle will usually make three splashers when sawn across the cord of the circle with a fine saw, and a complete circle will make the two for a single. It is also possible to turn the tops as well, but a lot of metal is wasted this way and it is easier to make the tops separately from sheet.

The sketch shows how to erect the cab front and sides to avoid the gap that usually occurs when the side is made to the drawing, and the front or spectacle plate is also made to the drawing. This occurs because in a drawing the edge of the overhanging cab roof is usually taken as the top of the side. This is not so, as the side goes up under the roof. Care must be taken here, and the sketch explains itself. It will avoid that "cab seems to low" look. When erecting such things as cab sides, tank fronts, tender backs, etc., a piece of angle should always be soldered in the corners. Never rely on a butt soldered joint to be permanent, least of all if the tender is expected to hold water or spirit. Another golden rule in erecting a locomotive is always to solder inside as far as possible; this will avoid excessive scraping and cleaning and consequent falling to pieces.

When it is necessary to solder outside the model, as in the case of steps etc., a small scraper should be made from an old square swiss file. Never use a file to clean up soldered joints. Apart from the fact that it clogs the file, one cannot avoid filing the model as well, and these file marks show under the paint. Having now made the cab sides, and possibly the front plate, we come now to the footplate.

The usual method is to make this all in one piece, cut out spaces for the mechanism, wheels, etc., but one thing never seems to be done and that is to chamfer, or file the edge to a scale equivalent of the original. Most models footplates are much too thick owing to the fact that a scale equivalent of the original footplate would be far too thin. However the footplate, whatever method is going to be used to make it, should be cut the full width of the engine, and the correct length. If a curved footplate such as LNER, allowances must be made for the bends, but in the case of other railways only cut the straight part the correct length—the drops should be made separately. As there is always a little overhang at the break of the drops, only commercial toys are made in one piece. This is convenient from a press tool point of view. To ensure that the drops are exactly the same width as the remainder, the whole footplate should be made in one piece, filed and chamfered. Make it a little longer than necessary, and when the drops are cut off and bent round a round bar of metal approximately the same diameter as the curved portion of the drop they will fit perfectly when the time comes to erect them. The buffer beams by the way should be on the chassis, but if they are not, these should be made at this stage.

Appendices

A Criticism by Col. G. G. Templer

The serial article entitled "Modelling Locomotives," by Mr. Roche contains much good advice, many useful wrinkles, some extremely artistic sketches, and a number of excellent drawings. Having distributed these few bouquets, I regret that I am now about to heave some major brick-bats.

To come straight to the point, I disagree profoundly with the general method of constructing steam-outline, electrically-driven model locomotives in gauges up to No. 1 advocated by Mr. Roche. I will come to my reasons in a moment, but first let me very briefly recapitulate. The articles advise general adherence to prototype practice in building the frames etc., and, in order to obtain access to the power unit, various parts of the super-structure, e.g. boiler unit, cab, running-plates, etc., are made severally demountable to the extent that any particular design may demand. Alternatively, the motion must be taken down, the springs disconnected, and the driving wheels with motor dropped.

It is my firm opinion—an opinion which is based on many years of experience and experiment, and which is supported by many other experienced model locomotive builders, both amateur and professional—that the whole of the super-structure of such models as we are discussing, from and including running-plate and buffer beams, should be built as one unit, and the chassis as a separate unit. I will proceed to develop this somewhat sweeping statement as an argument.

In the first place, everyone, including, I am sure, Mr. Roche, will admit that it is impossible in these small scales to reproduce to scale every item of the prototype, and no one but a lunatic would attempt such a task. I think we generally accept as a successful scale model one in which the external lines and details of the prototype are faithfully reproduced, and which performs satisfactorily in service; to get the right adhesion factor, we fill the boiler with lead ballast, instead of tubes, and the motor occupies the space which ought to contain the brick arch, thermic syphons and so on. Now, I submit that as we have got to take poetic licence in large doses anyway, there is no possible point in complicating the chassis by fitting elaborate stretchers, drag-boxes, etc. presumably assembled with a multitude of small rivets and a lot of new words. None of this detail—except in very exceptional cases—can be seen when the model is running and few, if any, model locomotive builders have the time to spare to put in this invisible detail. How many of us are fortunate enough to expect to be able to complete our planned model railway, assuming a reasonable expectation of life?

But there is a much more vital objection to this method than the mere time factor, and that is that it spoils the scale appearance of the front end view—and the plan for that matter—by taking the frames above the running-plate. I wish to emphasise that in these small models, where the frames have to be appreciably narrower than scale, no part of the chassis should rise above the running-plate. Earlier, Mr. Roche argues correctly that we have no choice but to accept narrower-than-scale frames, but he pooh-poohs it and this is where he is so wrong. Evidently, he is a stickler for scale, as he says we must reduce our frame width by 4 in. equivalent to 2.3 mm., which he says is "rather a lot, but not noticeable." Only an 8 per cent error! And confined to one important dimension which makes it stand out. Mr.

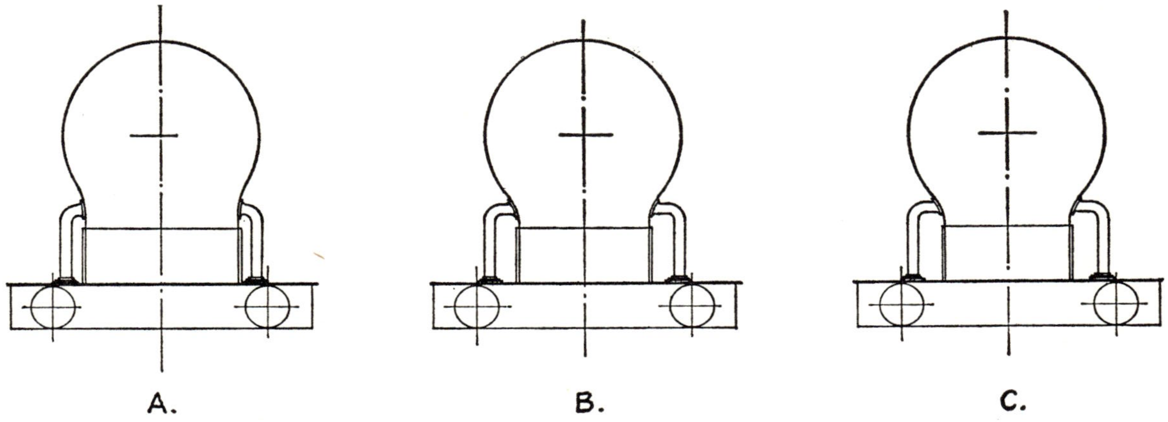

140 Frame widths

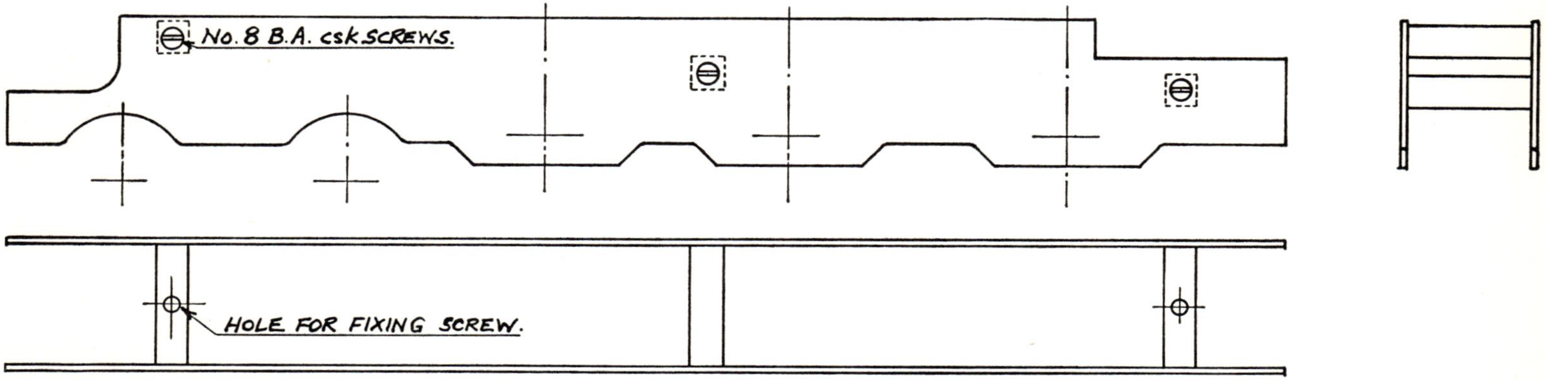

141 Simple chassis design

Roche goes on to say that generally speaking this width will be too great and advises 26 mm. I personally maintain that for ordinary everyday practice where multi-coupled locos in gauge O are required to negotiate curves down to 5 ft. 0 in. radius, 26 mm. is the minimum safe over-frame width to afford adequate end-play on coupled axles, and sufficient clearance between backs of wheels and frames. Let us see where this takes us. If we accept 30 mm. as being the scale equivalent of the across-frames dimension, we lose 4 mm. in fine scale by reducing it to 26 mm. and 5.5 mm. if META standard wheels are used. Now if the frames are carried above the running-plate, the whole proportion of the front profile will be hopelessly upset, and to bring this point home I show in fig. 140A the front view of the GER Claud Hamilton reproduced from Mr. Roche's own drawing, and in figs. 140B and C the same front end with the frames squeezed in to suit fine scale and META wheels respectively. If this does not convince you, take any prototype you like and make similar front views yourself. Observe, by the way, that the addition of lamp irons and vacuum pipe is going to accentuate the discrepancy from scale. In parenthesis, I must mention that fig. 140A is drawn to scale for gauge O to the dimensions given on Mr. Roche's drawing, but to what extent these are correct I do not know; but I am afraid that several dimensions on that drawing do not tally with the drawing itself, and there is no doubt that several of the dimensions themselves are incorrect, as a brief examination of the drawing will show. But to revert to the main argument, it is in my opinion hopelessly inconsistent to take the utmost pains to get the side view of your model correct to scale and then to sacrifice the scale appearance of the front end on the altar of a slavish adherence to prototype practice.

Before leaving the frames, I must comment on material. I see that Mr. Roche suggests that we can get nearly down to scale thickness by using thin steel plate I entirely disagree with the use of steel for frames; it rusts like nobody's business, it is a nuisance to solder, and plate of that thickness is too thin to take screw threads. Now I know Mr. Roche says we musn't solder things to frames, and we musn't use tapped holes only plain holes; well, take my advice and ignore this, for it is very useful to be able to solder to the frames if you want to, and there are many items such as brake hanger brackets and sandboxes which are conveniently and quite justifiably fixed to the frames with screws. Frames should be of *brass* and 18 SWG is about the right thickness. Another disadvantage in the use of steel for frames is that, according to some authorities, no ferrous metal of any appreciable mass should be in proximity to the permanent magnet of the mator.

To come now to something constructive, the chassis of a model locomotive should be of the simplest possible design maintaining the correct profile along the bottom edge where it can be seen. There is no doubt that the best design is the one which has been used by most experienced model locomotive builders for many years, and in fig. 141 I give a sketch of it as applied to a typical modern British 4–6–0; note that it is secured to the superstructure by two fixing screws only, one through each of the end stretchers which are of square brass fixed to the frames by countersunk screws. A third stretcher is shown, but is only required in the case of the longer locos., since the insulating blocks which carry the pick-ups will generally afford sufficient extra stability to the structure. To expose the power unit for periodic maintenance, all that is necessary is to remove the two fixing screws and lift off the superstructure—literally the work of a few seconds; re-assembly is almost as quick. I need hardly emphasise that cylinders should be attached to the frames and not the superstructure, for it is an unmitigated nuisance to have to strip down the motion every time the motor needs maintenance. Here, I believe I am at one with Mr. Roche. There are cases of course, particularly among the older designs, where the cylinders are actually part of the smokebox, e.g. the NLR 4–4–0Ts, GNR 8 ft. Singles, LNWR Webb 4-cyl Compounds, etc., but even here by a little ingenuity the back cylinder cover can be made separate and to come away with the chassis.

My final point of disagreement with Mr. Roche's method of construction is that, when the motor requires maintenance, it appears to entail breaking one or more joints between painted surfaces which is a quite fatal error because before long the paint is going to suffer badly. It is simply idle to argue that a properly built model ought not to have to be taken to pieces so often that serious damage can occur to the paint; this is sheer nonsense, for remember that *your tiny power unit is just as much in need of proper and regular maintenance as* any other machine, and there is not the slightest doubt human nature being what it is, that unless the exposure of the mechanism for periodic maintenance is a very easy and quick operation, it just will not get done. During the last two or three years I have seen several cases of motor units which have been allowed to get into the most appalling state simply because it was too much bother to attend to their maintenance. I sometimes wonder where the advice on the subject of building small-scale locos which one reads here and there is sufficiently tempered with experience of actual running conditions; it is one thing to build a glass-case model for exhibition purposes, and quite another to build one which is going to give satisfactory service, week in week out, and look as good. When I say that experience in running models is an essential background to successful design I am stating an unquestionable fact which I have proved personally.

In conclusion, let me say that I am no die-hard conservative in my outlook towards this most fascinating hobby of model locomotive building, for I am as ardent an enthusiast as any one in seeking ways and means for improvement, and perhaps in a limited way some of the work I have done in the past has not been without some small value in this direction; and it is because I feel that Mr. Roche's method of construction represents a retrograde step for the reasons I have explained that I disagree with it so fundamentally, and consider it to be the wrong advise to give the beginner and likely to start him on the wrong road. Moreover, I hold the opinion that constructional methods should be adaptable to either fine or META standards, and that they should be applicable to the models built not only by the man who is so fortunately placed that he can use scale curves on his system, but also by his less fortunate but far more numerous brethren who have to get their O gauge locos round 4 ft. radius curves, or give it up.

Although the above has been written from the O gauge 7 mm. scale point of view in particular, as no doubt will have been realised, I have no doubt that the main burden of the argument is applicable to all the smaller scales and gauges.

Replies from F. J. Roche

I must thank Colonel Templer, O.B.E., and Michael Longridge, for so ably augmenting my own notes and while agreeing with most of their remarks, I must take them to task upon some items.

Firstly, Colonel Templer. Once more we have crossed swords on the matter of frame widths. Whilst not considering myself an expert model maker, what is the poor amateur and beginner to do when such as we disagree? Taking a broad view of Col. Templer's article, he is advocating a return to the can with a chassis attached, a method which has seen the test of time no doubt, and is still largely used by the trade in model locomotive construction. I agree it is the ideal method on OO gauge 16.5 mm. scale (there is no alternative as the gauge is too narrow), but I was under the impression that O gauge enthusiasts were getting engineering conscious, and were building their models strictly to prototype, putting inside motion in prototypes, etc., where it shows, such as in old type 4–4–0s. Hence I gave hints on where to put motion plates, etc., and this cannot be done when the frames are one width apart on top of the footplate, and another below. To quote the Colonel's own remarks: "one has to sacrifice scale somewhere!"

If we construct our frames as suggested, and make dummy frame pieces at the front end the correct distance apart, this is all fine and dandy, but what about below the footplate where the wheels are still too close together due to the gauge being under-scale? In the case of the Claud Hamilton where the guard irons are bolted to the buffer beam, this will upset all attempts to make a nice scale front end anyway. The only way this can be done is to have a gauge of one's own, viz. 33 mm. in O gauge and 19 mm. in OO gauge, and then the model will not run on anyone else's layout.

Regarding the frame drawing in fig. 2, the Colonel has anticipated me. I had already drawn out a similar simpler form of frame assembly for those who prefer to build their locos this way. I do not necessarily advocate my method of construction in my articles but give several ways of doing the same job, and I advise readers to take Col. Templer's drawing when constructing frames of the simpler type. This frame would suit the LNER B1 4–6–0, but I would prefer to see them made of nickel silver, not brass. Bronze bushes should be put into the axle holes if the model is not to be sprung, such as a 4 mm. scale loco, and in O gauge if the mechanism has not bronze bushes, in the motor frames. Nickel silver takes paint better, especially when the main frames are painted any other colour than black, as in the older locos.

This brings me to the Colonel's final point, viz, painting. My method of describing models to come to pieces is for this very reason. Imagine trying to paint an old time loco frame with the wheels, motion, etc., all in situ, when the frames were claret colour, the wheels yellow, or blue, or green and sometimes the frames were lined out even behind the wheels! In a modern loco this does not enter into it, just spray the lot black and call it a day. Judging by the standard of cleanliness today, it would at least be true to type! I am sure the Colonel will agree, in the light of his own experience, that it is much easier to paint a model, piece by piece, and assemble it afterwards than to dodge all over the place with a mouthful of brushes of different colours touching out unwanted colours. Let him try a LBSC loco in Stroudley colours sometime, with the frame all assembled, with yellow wheels, and a claret colour main frame behind them. This is really not too bad as we only have a coupling rod in the way, but what about a Highland Jones 4–6–0 in the old colours?

Finally, I too am no conservative in the matter of building models, there is always room for improvement, and the skill of model makers of today is far greater than that of 20 years ago. They are more technically-minded, and many readers take a pride in machining as much as possible, and assembling items in an engineering-like manner by screwing or rivetting. The old-fashioned soldering iron admittedly is still used, but not to the extent that it was, and even now some model makers fight shy of a soldering iron. I cannot see that my method is a retrograde step. I admire the beautiful models of a GWR Castle and the little tank No. 1 that the Colonel has constructed, and which I have seen both in India and in this Country, as exquisite little examples of the craft I am out to foster and encourage, as no doubt is also Col. Templer, but I must ask him not to anticipate me. I will give simpler methods of constuction all in good time, when dealing with the smaller gauges. One more point, the drawing of the Claud Hamilton front end was taken from my sketch book, by tracing, and is *not to scale*. The measurements are there instead, and a note was on the drawing not to scale it but to stick to the measurements. This did not come out in the block as it was probably outside the alloted space. The drawing reproduced in fig. 1a is quite all right as it is the *original* Claud Hamilton with small round-topped firebox boiler as shown in the *Engineer* when the engine was built.

Gauge O Locomotive Construction

by Col. G. G. Templer

I trust you will allow me to reply to the comments on my recent article on the above subject made by Mr. Roche, as it seems that some considerable misunderstanding exists.

In the first place, there is nothing to prevent inside motion being fitted to a model on the can and chassis principle, and Mr. Roche's inference that it cannot be done if frames are different widths above and below is misleading.

Next, his statement that the wheels of O gauge models being of necessity, closer together than scale, coupled with a curious GER design feature of fitting guard irons to the front of the buffer beam, "will upset all attempts to make a nice scale front end anyway" is a considerable exaggeration, and the second factor, being special to a limited number of prototypes, is irrelevant to the general consideration. We are left, therefore, with our old trouble of the wheels being too close together, and I cannot believe that Mr. Roche can honestly maintain that this factor justifies the departures from the scale profile of the front view which are inseparable from the method of construction he has described, nor can I believe that anybody else would support such a viewpoint.

It appears unfortunate that I selected the Claud Hamilton class to illustrate the importance of maintaining the correct scale proportions of the front view, for I soon discovered that Mr. Roche's drawing, as he now explains, is not to scale, and I made mine from official information. The discrepancy between this and Mr. Roche's drawing is somewhat marked, and I hope that he will accept my apology for having quite unintentionally drawn attention to it, and for any confusion that may have resulted therefrom.

Now on the subject of painting, Mr. Roche seems to have read into my notes something that I never dreamed of. My notes made it clear that I disfavoured a method of construction which entailed breaking down the *superstructure* into several component parts to get at the power unit because of the damage to paint at such times. (I assume that such breakdown is necessary because in one of his instalments Mr. Roche mentions power units contained in the barrel of the boiler, and if such breakdown is not necessary the reason for such complicated construction arrangements is obscure). No one, unless headed straight for the nearest mental institution would attempt to paint any model complete with "wheels, motion, etc. all in situ"; surely Mr. Roche is not suggesting that with the can and chassis method, once the wheels and motion are assembled they are fixed for all time and cannot be taken down? Yet is it difficult to read any other implication into his remarks. Nothing is, of course, further from the facts, for if the chassis is sensibly designed and put together with screws, as shown in my drawing, it can be stripped for painting the two plates can be laid to all intents and purposes flat, and the most spectacular colour scheme imaginable executed on them under almost ideal conditions.

The above should be sufficient to show that Mr. Roche has actually only been able to adduce one factor in support of his case—the matter of the between-tyre dimensions—the remainder of his argument being either irrelevant or based on false premise.

I note that Mr. Roche's intention is to describe the can and chassis method and that he does not necessarily advocate the method he has already described; it would however, have been difficult to draw either of these inferences from his articles, and I hope he will forgive me for suggesting that had he described the conventional can and chassis method first, pointed out what, in his view, were its disadvantages, and proceeded to describe the methods he had evolved to overcome them, much confusion and misunderstanding would have been avoided.

Finally, I should like to thank Mr. Roche for the very kind things he has said about my two recently completed GWR models. I should also like to assure him that I am absolutely at one with him in my desire to foster the hobby of model loco building, and I trust that our spirited debate may result in some advance; it is only by the interchange of ideas and experience and by frank discussion that we can hope for progress.

In Conclusion

Most of this article has been concerned with driving and coupled wheels, since many special problems arise in this connection. In most cases the carrying wheels may be force fitted on both ends of each axle but a less powerful fit, in the nature of .0005 in. to .001 in. interference, is quite sufficient. I should like to emphasise that all the foregoing remarks apply to O gauge *only* and may or may not be suitable, in whole or in part, when applied to models of other sizes.

Wheels and Axles by Michael Longridge

I must confess I was disappointed after reading Wheels and Axles of Mr. Roche's article. For me, and I believe for others, the making and fitting to axles of driving wheels is one of the more nasty operations encountered in loco building, so I was looking forward to gleaning some real tips. Instead, however, Mr. Roche tells us how to turn the back of a wheel and drill it, then merely remarks, "the wheel may then be reversed in the chuck and finished off"; surely there must be a little more to it than that! How, for example, does one turn the flange if this part is held in the chuck?

Then, no mention is made as to how to ensure correct quartering of driving wheels when they are pressed on the axles as suggested. Many experienced 7 mm. modellers still prefer the one wheel forced on, one wheel screwed on method, the latter being locked by a grub screw half in the axle half in the wheel. Practical results suggest to me that this method cannot be improved upon for the average unskilled worker.

Does Mr. Roche seriously suggest that the small dimples in the ends of O gauge driving axles, shown by the drawing, are suitable for mounting between centres in the lathe? They are present in the driving axles of the engine I am now building, but only for appearance purposes.

Finally, there is no mention of drilling the wheels for the crankpins, which presumably has to be done before the wheels are permanently fixed on the axles. A crank-pin drilling jig which is rather more satisfactory than the one shown can be turned from a piece of mild steel bar, the circular top allowing several holes for different throws to be incorporated; the top should be somewhat thicker than as shown in the drawing in order to provide better support for the drill.

Turning and Fitting Wheels and Axles in Gauge O

Many keen modellers in the smaller scales today realise the importance of adequate equipment and tools in the practice of their hobby, and so the possession of those two valuable machine tools, a lathe and a drilling machine, is no longer the rarity of 15 to 20 years back. Present day costs in the production of finished parts have also contributed to this trend, so I feel that a description of what was to me a closed book, until a short time ago, may

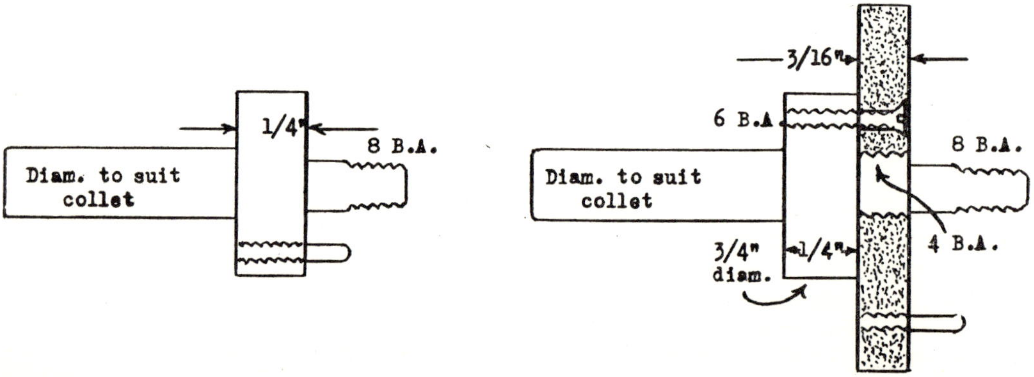

142 Wheelmaking jig

be of help to many who are building or about to build a complete O gauge engine, complete from the chassis upwards.

The wheels and axles are probably the most important feature of the whole job, since any deficiencies here will never allow the finished model to perform satisfactorily on the track. The following considerations are important:—

(1) the wheels must run true in every axis;
(2) they must be attached to the axles without any possibility of becoming loose:
(3) driving wheels must be correctly quartered or the coupling rods will bind.

Other considerations, such as correct back to back distance, are so well known that it is not necessary to cover old ground. Although the method I shall describe may not be the only method, it is a method which has been proved in the test of time by many experienced 7mm. enthusiasts; it is, moreover, a method which enabled me to obtain success as a newcomer to this kind of work. Several jigs will have to be made before the first wheel is finished but these can be used again and again for subsequent locomotives and I can only counsel patience to the eager modeller who is probably anxious to complete the job when confronted with the necessity for making jigs.

Turning Wheels—Facing the Back

The wheels will be cast in what is sometimes known as soft grey iron but which frequently produces an extremely hard wheel, particularly in the smaller sizes, owing to the rapid cooling of the casting. Such castings cannot be machined by normal means; the remedy consists in placing the castings in an ordinary domestic coal fire and leaving them there overnight while the fire gradually dies down. Unless this cooling is very gradual no amount of heating has any effect.

The casting is placed in the lathe chuck back outwards, i.e. the spokes face the chuck, and is held by the jaws of the chuck gripping the outside of the casting. Since castings are never round and no two are alike, a four-jaw independent chuck is preferable to a self-centering or scroll chuck, but the latter can be used. As the outside face of the wheel is inside the chuck there is a certain amount of luck in determining whether the inside rim of the wheel is truly centred; if it is off centre the efficiency of the wheel will not be affected but the finished appearance will suffer.

Turn the back of the casting flat, using a round-nosed tool with no top rake fed in from the outside towards the centre, first removing any stub at the centre of the casting if one is present. Do not lubricate at all when turning cast iron. The first cut for cast iron should always be not less than .015 in. to .020 in. to get under the skin of the casting, using the lowest speed provided by the backgear; after the first cut, remaining cuts may be taken at a higher speed, say about 60 to 100 rpm. Remember that .040 in. = 1 mm. (approximately). When sufficient material has been removed from the back of the casting, cuts of .005 in. should be taken, still with the round-nosed tool, backwards and forwards across the wheel between the centre boss and the rim in order to uncover the spokes. Continue this process

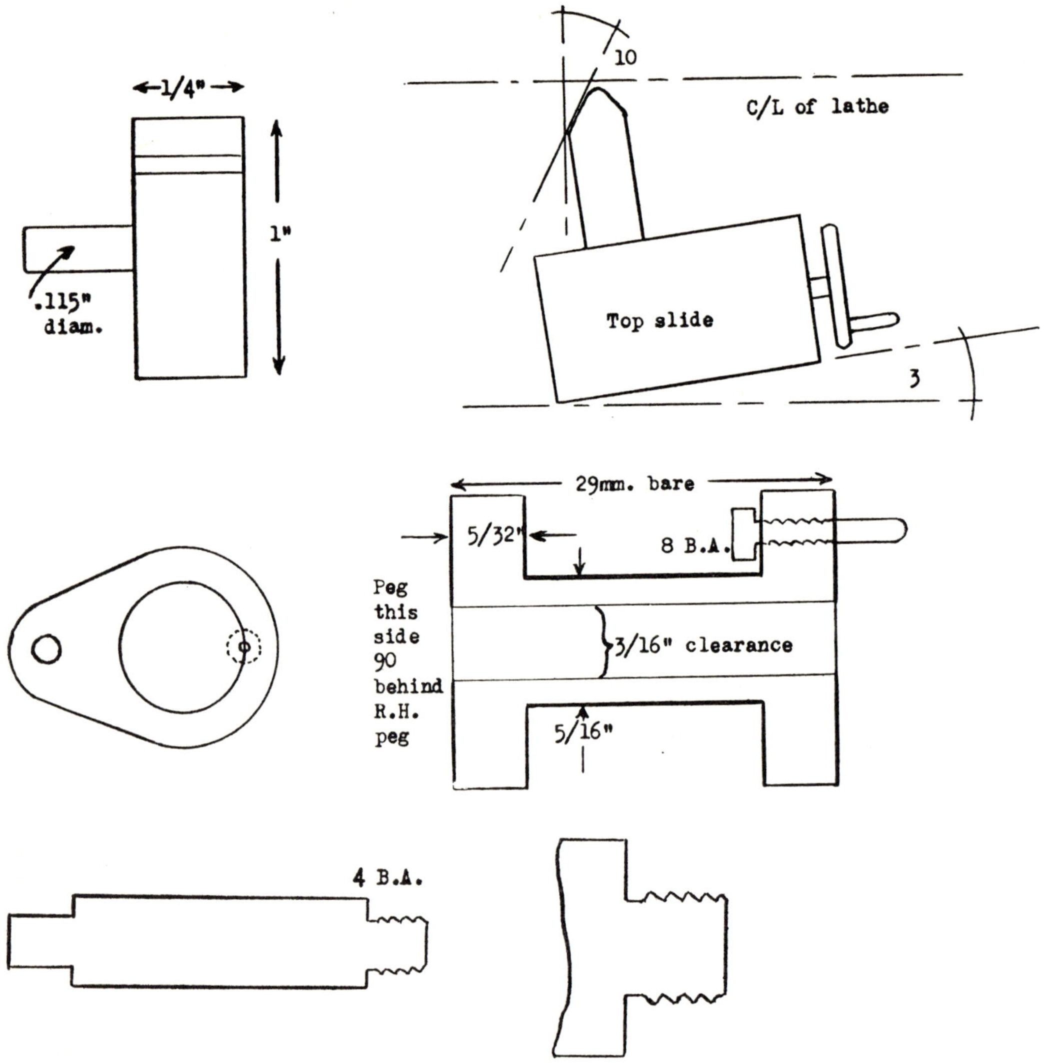

143 Wheel turning

as necessary, but remember that the spokes will have to be cleaned up by hand so do not continue turning the back of the wheel until the spokes are wafer thin.

The wheel is now drilled, using a small slocombe or centre drill in the tailstock to start the hole. Substitute the slocombe by a No. 44 drill and continue right through the wheel; next use a No. 34 and finally a No. 32. These numbers apply to driving and coupled wheels; bogie and tender wheels are frequently fitted to $\frac{5}{32}$ in. diam. axles and will then require an enlarged hole. All drilling should be done at about 200 rpm. The wheel may then be removed from the chuck. I expect I shall be criticised for not using reamers or boring tools in finishing the hole; all I can say is that what I am describing *works*. It is convenient to treat all the wheels for one engine thus before proceeding to the next stage.

Facing the Front

A jig is required for this operation as shown in fig. 142 left; it *must* be used in a collet, *not* a self-centering chuck (so called). It is turned from a piece of mild steel rod, the shank end being any convenient size to suit the collet used, the spigot end being finished to size *in the collet*. Diameter of the shoulder is about 5 mm. less than the finished diameter of the wheel's flange. For carrying wheels the whole jig may be in one piece but for driving wheels, in order to save unnecessary machining, a smaller shoulder may be used with a brass disc of the required size screwed to it as in fig. 142 right. A pin must be inserted in the face of the shoulder so that, when the wheel is mounted on the spigot, it fits between any two spokes of the wheel and thus provides a positive drive.

First operation is to face off the rim on the front of the wheel, using the round-nosed tool as before; the final cuts may be made with a knife tool, which will give a better finish. A groove should be turned in the inside of the rim to indicate the tyre of the prototype but if separate balance weights are to be fitted, in the case of driving wheels, this groove should not be turned until after the balance weights have been fitted. A round-nosed tool is then ground to the radius required between tread and flange (BRMSB dimension .029 in.) and set in the top slide of the lathe as shown in fig. 143 top right; the top slide should previously have been set round 3 degrees so that when the tool is fed in from the *front* of the wheel by the top slide the correct coning will be formed on the tread of the wheel and the correct taper of the front of the flange will likewise be obtained (BRMSB figure 10 degrees). When the required tread diameter has nearly been reached the flange may be reduced in diameter and roughly rounded off with a smooth file, the wheel being rotated at not less than 200 rpm.

It must be appreciated that by the use of this jig in a collet, the spigot on which the wheel is mounted will always run true, thus a wheel may be removed at any time and subsequently replaced in complete confidence that there will be no loss of accuracy. The centre of the wheel naturally cannot be turned for the time being since the nut on the spigot will be in the way.

Other Operations

Drilling and tapping for crankpins, etc.

In the case of coupled wheels, this will be the next operation. A jig is turned from a piece of mild steel rod to the dimensions shown in fig. 143 top left, mounted on the vertical drill table and the hole drilled at the correct distance from the centre for the required throw; with this type of jig several holes may be drilled to suit different throws according to the type of engine being modelled. In use, the wheel is placed face upwards on the drill table and the shank of the jig fitted into the wheel centre; the jig *must* be securely clamped down to the drill table before the hole for the crankpin is drilled with a No. 51 drill right through the wheel. N.B.—No centre popping is required when using this jig.

Half the number of driving and coupled wheels should now be tapped 4BA in their centre holes, using the tap in the drill chuck, each wheel meantime being firmly clamped to the drill table; the drill is, of course, rotated by hand for this operation.

Driving axles

These are turned from $\frac{3}{16}$ in. mild steel rod held in a collet and finished as shown in fig. 143 bottom left. It is *absolutely essential* that the end of the threaded portion be cut back as shown in the enlarged sketch, bottom right. Hold the finished axle in the collet, screw on a wheel as tightly as possible and run the lathe; it may be found that the wheel is out of true to the extent of .003 in. or .004 in. but this is easily rectified by making several light finishing cuts.

Treat all driving axles thus, finishing off the ends of each axle flush with the face of the driving wheel at the same time.

Retaining screws

A centre punch mark is made at the junction of the wheel and the axle (centre left fig.) and a No. 51 hole drilled half in the axle, half in the wheel, but should not pass right through the wheel, it is tapped 8BA. This is an operation which requires care, but lubrication will be found to help. The operator may prefer to use a No. 50 drill and make an oversize grub screw, which should be a steel and not a brass one. The grub screws need not be fitted until the final assembly of the running gear takes place.

Quartering and force fitting driving wheels

I am indebted to Mr. W. S. Norris for the subject of fig. 143 centre right; this simply-made universal jig is extremely useful. Unless dozens of locomotives are to be built a brass jig with steel pegs will prove adequate. Alternative positions may be arranged for the pegs, so that varying crank throws may be accommodated on the same jig.

We now return to the driving wheels, which are to be forced on to the plain ends of the axles; up till now only the backs of these wheels have been turned, but the holes for the axles and crankpins have been drilled. The diameter of the shouldered end of the axle should be, if possible, between .001 in. and .0015 in. greater than that of the hole drilled in the wheel: remember that 'miking' the No. 32 drill may not necessarily indicate the precise size of the hole it has made in the wheel and it may be wise to experiment first on a waste piece of metal rather than on a precious casting. When you are satisfied that the axle's shoulder is the proper diameter, the end of the axle should be slightly tapered, to the extent of about .001 in. after which the process of assembly may take place.

Adjust the two pegs in the quartering jig so that they project the maximum distance, screw all the tapped wheels on to their axles (making sure that each is fully home) insert wheel and axle in the jig so that the former is located by the protruding peg. Slightly bevel the centre hole in the back of the wheel, using a countersink rotated between the fingers, then place the wheel which is to be forced on together with the other items in the vice and gently tighten up.

It may be of advantage to place a piece of steel plate between each wheel and each face of the vice, largely depending on the type of jaws fitted. If is *of the utmost importance* to make quite sure that the screwed on wheel is dead flat against the jaw of the vice so that the axle is truly perpendicular thereto, likewise that the crankpin hole of the forced on wheel is properly located on its peg. When, and only when, you are satisfied on these points you may proceed to wind the vice steadily but firmly until the wheel is right home; the pair of wheels may then be taken out of the jig by unscrewing the screwed on wheel.

Finishing operations

Each axle with its forced on wheel is now returned to the lathe, being held in a collet as before, in order that the wheels may be completed, facing off rim and centre and forming tread and flange. All driving and coupled wheels may now have their crankpin holes tapped 8BA, using the vertical drill for this purpose as mentioned previously. Only the grub screws (steel, not brass) remain to be fitted, and the operation is complete.

Newly machined cast iron is apt to rust quickly, so it is beneficial to wipe over the finished wheels with oil and if they can be left in this state for a time so much the better, as a kind of skin forms eventually which is not so rust prone.

Balance weights

Some driving wheels require special balance weights, which may be attached by drilling and screwing 10BA. In the case of forced on wheels, this operation can only be done after the wheel is on the axle and has been faced off, but the screwed on wheels may be dealt with either before their centres are tapped 4BA or after, but in the latter case the balance weights must be attached before the forcing on process commences.

Reply to Mr. Longridge

Now for Mr. Longridge, and his wheel turning article. He also has anticipated me up to a point. His article is very instructive when dealing with one kind of wheel casting, but there are others ! However, for the moment we will deal with the type he has in mind, i.e., those with the spokes backed by a cast iron filling, and a spigot on the back.

All modellers are not alike, and apparently Mr. Longridge likes making jigs. I suggest in all humility that this is entirely unnecessary; and to quote his own remarks, "we like to get on with the job and not mess about making jigs," when we have only one engine in hand at a time ! His method of putting the wheel in the chuck back outwards, and apparently, if I read his article aright, turning off the spigot when exposing the spokes, makes the spigot unnecessary and the manufacturers may as well leave it out altogether !

To turn these wheels, all that is necessary is a 2 in. mike, or a caliper gauge, and a crank pin jig already described. I have turned hundreds of these wheels, and very rarely have I found one out of round. If one is found thus the manufacturers will replace it. As for finding no two alike, I entirely disagree. There is such a large range of these wheels, and that Mr. Longridge must have had a casting for a 6 ft. $8\frac{1}{2}$ in. wheel, and a casting for a 6 ft. 9 in. wheel sent him as a pair by mistake. To cut a long story short, all I do with these wheels is to mount them in an ordinary three-jaw chuck of the self centering type, the ordinary model maker does not want to spend half an hour juggling with a four jaw chuck to turn a round casting ! These chucks are meant for turning irregular masses such as a cylinder casting.

Hold the wheel by the spigot in the chuck, and rough turn the tread, taking enough off to merely get it truly circular—there is plenty of metal. Now reverse in the chuck and turn the spigot, again taking just a little off to get under the skin, and to make the spigot round and parallel. We now have a spigot that is true with the tread. Reverse in the chuck again, and hold by the spigot, and finish turning the front, tyre, and flange. Correct profile of the tread is essential, and care must be taken to turn the flange to suit the wheel, whether it is leading coupled, centre driver and/or rear coupled. Dimensions of all these were given in an earlier article on a multi-coupled loco. The centre wheels have thinner flanges than the carrying wheels for curving. Try not to turn off the middle flange unless your curves are unduly sharp. Having now reached the stage when the front of your wheel is finished, carefully centre and drill the axle hole, using a slocombe as Mr. Longridge suggests to start the hole, but *please* use a reamer. The method Mr. Longridge suggests might work in his case, but we are not all alike—and it is better to be safe than sorry ! By all means make a profile tool, if the operator prefers, but *do not* use it to turn the flange and tread, but *only* to finish it. It should only have to take off a mere shaving in order to get bogie and trailing wheels all alike; driving wheel flanges are *not* alike; as previously stated

Having got thus far, reverse wheel in the chuck, and face off the back and the spigot until the spokes are exposed. Be very careful when the spokes are beginning to show as if too deep a cut is taken at this stage, you will tear out the spokes and the wheel will be ruined.

All that is necessary to do now is to finish the top of the flange to META depth according to whatever scale the modeller is using, round it off with a fine file, and the wheel is finished. That's all there is to it. They will all be the same diameter if your calliper or mike has been set correctly, and they will all be true because the hole was drilled at the same time that the tread was turned. To my mind wheel turning is the simplest job in the whole loco. I'd much rather turn a set of wheels than make a complete Walschaert's gear ! To turn wheels that have the spigot on the front, the same procedure applies. Get the spigot and the tread true with one another, before commencing turning. Face off the back first and drill the axle hole and deal with as much of the tread and flange as can be got at without catching the tool in the chuck jaws. Remove from chuck and force on a spare axle kept for the purpose, or screw it on. Replace in chuck and finish turning the front, but *do not* touch the tread and flange. Admittedly it is awkward with this type of wheel, and as a rule they are only found in the larger gauges, where wheels are always forced on, and the whole finished off between centres with a lathe steady. Wheels that have no spigot at all should be turned on a faceplate. Again these are only found in the large steam models.

Wheel turning in OO gauge is seldom indulged in as they are bought ready turned, and Mr. Longridge's jig would be ideal for this purpose when the tread and flange require trimming to a better profile than that supplied in the zinc alloy type of wheel.

Before leaving the subject of wheel turning, it is *essential not* to touch the turned parts of the wheel with your fingers unless they are very oily. The human hand has a certain amount of chemical composition in the sweat which has the effect of depositing a hard surface on a freshly turned cast iron surface, and the tool will soon be dulled. Do not use oil to turn the casting as Mr. Longridge rightly tells us, but keep your hands oily, or wear greasy gloves.

The jig shown in the article for quartering the driving wheels, is ideal for the purpose, and should be made if the operator is not sure that he can do it by eye, or the workshop method of Vee block and scriber. It is essential to get all the wheels alike. If you have slipped up and forced on your first pair of wheels at 93 degrees, then force them all on at this angle. Do *not* correct your mistake, otherwise the rods will bind. We are only dealing with an electrically-driven model of course. I do not agree with the vice method of forcing on wheels. A much more accurate method is to use the lathe, and back centre, giving a direct *push* through the centre of the axle. The vice method very often results in a split wheel, or at the very least, wobbly wheels, because any but a machine vice is not truly parallel. Again I recommend readers reading the earlier part of this book. Many will not agree with Mr. Longridge's method of screwing one side and forcing the other, neither will they agree with mine of forcing both the wheels on the axle, because of the servicing problem of electric motors, but both methods are far superior to lock-nuts, and with the screwing method at least one wheel can be removed if necessary. But, and here is the rub: the next time the wheel goes on it will tighten up *past* the 90 degree angle, and each time it is removed it will get worse, *ad infinitum*. Don't ask me why, it is just one of those things that happen with screwed fittings. However, other methods will be described for locking wheels in my next instalments. I thank Mr. Longridge for his contribution, and many will undoubtedly prefer his jig method of turning wheels, especially if more than one engine is being worked on at a time.

Readers now have alternative methods of doing the same job which is all to the good.